Sins of Christendom

Sins of Christendom

Anti-Mormonism and the Making of Evangelicalism

NATHANIEL WIEWORA

UNIVERSITY OF ILLINOIS PRESS
Urbana, Chicago, and Springfield

1 2 3 4 5 C P 5 4 3 2 1
∞ This book is printed on acid-free paper.

Library of Congress Cataloging-in-Publication Data

Names: Wiewora, Nathaniel, 1981– author.
Title: Sins of Christendom : anti-Mormonism and the making of evangelicalism / Nathaniel Wiewora.
Description: Urbana : University of Illinois Press, [2024] | Includes index.
Identifiers: LCCN 2023030772 (print) | LCCN 2023030773 (ebook) | ISBN 9780252045677 (cloth) | ISBN 9780252087783 (paperback) | ISBN 9780252055393 (ebook)
Subjects: LCSH: Evangelicalism—Relations—Latter Day Saint churches—History—19th century. | Latter Day Saint churches—Relations—Evangelicalism—History—19th century. | Anti-Mormonism—History—19th century.
Classification: LCC BR1641.M67 W54 2024 (print) | LCC BR1641.M67 (ebook) | DDC 289.3/32—dc23/eng/20231116
LC record available at https://lccn.loc.gov/2023030772
LC ebook record available at https://lccn.loc.gov/2023030773

Contents

Acknowledgments

I owe a debt a gratitude to so many people, places, and institutions for making this book possible. Christine Heyrman is a model mentor, gracious and incisive. She has supported, inspired, and cheered me on at every step in this process. Anne Boylan and Rebecca Davis read this project in an earlier stage and helped me see new connections and think about the project in the broadest possible fashion. Leigh Schmidt provided a valuable reading of the draft, asking significant questions.

I am deeply appreciative to my colleagues and friends who read all or portions of this book. Thank you to Philip Barlow, Christopher Blythe, Todd Brenneman, Christy Croxall, Allen Diles, JR Duke, Josh Fleer, Janiece Johnson, Josh Probert, and Ryan Smith.

Numerous archivists and librarians facilitated this research. Thank you to the staff at Church History Library in Salt Lake City, L. Tom Perry Special Collections and Harold B. Lee Library at Brigham Young University, Harding University Special Collections, New York Public Library Special Collections, and the University of Delaware Library and Special Collections.

Multiple institutions provided fellowships or funding that made the research and writing of this book possible. Thank you to all my colleagues at Harding University; they are remarkable colleagues and teachers. The Charles Redd Fellowship in Western American History gave my several days at the L. Tom Perry Special Collections. A short-term research grant at the Neil A. Maxwell Institute for Religious Scholarship was a scholar's dream. My time spent researching and writing, and in conversation with their community of scholars, moved this project to completion. Thank you to Spencer Fluhman and the staff there. Faculty Development Grants from the College of Arts and Humanities at Harding University provided me with the resources to present research from this project.

I have benefited from the expertise and graciousness of the staff at the University of Illinois Press. Alison Syring is a dream to work with. She has guided this process with care and interest.

Finally, I am thankful to my family. My parents, Ron and Jane Wiewora, instilled a love of the past in me from a small child. I am grateful for their love and continued support. Writing this book began before the birth of my daughters, Ruth and Rose. I love them more than they will ever know. My largest debt is to my wife, Kristen. She blesses my life every day. My dearest thanks go to her.

Introduction

When Ezra Booth converted to Mormonism, he "conscientiously believed it to be of God." This new religious movement made him experience "deep and powerful" feelings "to a degree to which . . . [he] had been a stranger." Having joined Mormonism just a few years after its emergence in western New York, Booth described the attraction of this new religious movement as a spectral presence. He said, "[I]t haunted me by night and by day, until I was mysteriously hurried, as it were, by a king of necessity, into the vortex of delusion." Mormonism delighted and stimulated his soul, but after leaving the church several months later, he concluded that he was in the thrall of "mental derangement." Booth found that "*prophecy* and *vision* had failed, or rather had proved false." These failures made Booth suspect that "things were not right" with Mormonism, and he prepared his mind "to review the whole subject." He concluded that there was nothing more to Mormonism than "a deeply laid plan of craft and deception." Booth worried that that his time away from "the light of truth" had made him a "devoted slave" to "delusion" and "falsehood. "Thanks be to God," Booth wrote to a friend, that "the spell is dissipated" and that God allowed him to see the "hidden things of darkness."[1]

Booth spent much of his young life searching for the voice of God. He joined the Methodist Church at a young age, and then became a circuit rider, traveling the western frontier preaching to any willing audience at any available location. Once he married and had children, he ended his itinerancy. While ministering to a Methodist church in Mantua, Ohio, Booth continued his hunt for spiritual truth. His religious journey led him to convert to Mormonism. The leaders of Mormonism, he explained to a friend, offered the "restoration of the apostolic church with all the gifts and graces with which the primitive saints were endowed." Mormon teachers further proclaimed "repentance and baptism for the remission of sins," according to Booth. Booth ultimately concluded that Mormonism was false, misguided, and dangerous, but ironically much of what he had found persuasive about Mormonism comprised the core of Booth's earlier evangelical Methodist faith.[2]

Alike, but different. These simultaneous perceptions of difference and sameness about Mormonism have continued within evangelicalism up to the present day. When asked in a recent poll to describe Mormonism, white evangelical Protestants conjured up a seemingly contradictory set of terms. They associated Mormonism with cults and plural marriage, but thought of Mormons themselves as good people and model citizens. White evangelical Protestants saw Mormonism in the most negative terms, with almost half defining Mormonism as something other than orthodox Christianity. The other half, however, considered Mormonism no different from their own evangelical faith.[3]

Evangelicals in the nineteenth century responded to Mormonism with predictable religious animus, but anti-Mormonism had wide-ranging consequences in antebellum America. Heresy hunting shaped evangelical beliefs and practices. In their earliest years of encounter, evangelicals developed a vibrant anti-Mormonism and simultaneously disagreed with their coreligionists over the same complaints they leveled against Mormonism. The sense that Mormonism was too similar to their own faith displayed and deepened divisions within the evangelical movement. They accused each other of being like the followers of Joseph Smith in order to define orthodox evangelical beliefs and practices.[4]

The rise of an anti-Mormon impulse within evangelicalism suggests something unexplained in the stories of anti-Mormonism, Mormon studies, antebellum evangelicalism, and religious intolerance. Writers have studied the animus directed toward Mormonism since the movement first appeared on the religious landscape in the 1830s. Whether Mormon or non-Mormon, critic or apologist, nearly all these writers have described Mormonism as a very different kind of faith from evangelicalism. Apologists of Mormonism have primarily seen the intensity of the evangelical opposition as a marker of their own movement's veracity and resilience. Even scholarly and nuanced students of Mormonism and anti-Mormonism have reinforced this distinction. David Brion Davis viewed attacks on Mormonism as part of a broader paranoia about internal subversion within nineteenth-century America. Anti-Mormonism became popular because of nativist fears that secret cabals had undermined the economic and political future of the United States. Religious intolerance functioned as a way to promote unity, clarify national values, and establish the legitimacy and authority of American institutions, according to Davis. Despite these rich and well-researched histories, both views have taken for granted that antebellum evangelicals rejected Mormonism because they saw it as completely foreign.[5]

Recent scholars have continued this examination of the cultural consequences of religious prejudice, but these authors have made few connections between evangelical anti-Mormon rhetoric and internal evangelical debates. The creation of an invented Mormonism propelled evangelicals to question the direction of their own movement, and they used anti-Mormonism to make compromises and to settle differences within their own ranks. Terryl Givens stressed how religious prejudice directed toward Mormonism was not about economic, political, or social factors. He believed faith fashioned intolerance in nineteenth-century America. Givens argued that what motivated anti-Mormonism was the way Joseph Smith made Mormonism a historically present faith, revealing contradictions within nineteenth-century Protestant Christianity. Spencer Fluhman likewise demonstrated an irredeemable tension between Mormonism and Protestantism. In his analysis of how Protestants saw Mormonism as an imposter religion, a deluded faith, and a fanatical belief system, Fluhman argued Mormonism allowed Protestants to define what was and what was not a religion. Since Mormonism was not a legitimate faith, Fluhman argued American Protestants could deny the followers of Joseph Smith the privileges of religious tolerance.[6]

Studying the close association between evangelicalism and Mormonism brings into relief the chaotic and contentious rise of antebellum evangelicalism. Most studies of the evangelical relationship with Mormonism have placed the former's religious animus in the context of the evangelical ascent to cultural and political dominance. The robustness of evangelical intolerance, in this view, arose from their dominance of American society. Considering the ways antebellum evangelicals used anti-Mormonism to settle scores within their own ranks complicates a progressive story of the success of antebellum evangelical culture and ideas. Religious prejudice toward Mormonism played a significant and unexpected role in the shaping of evangelical Christianity in antebellum America. As a product of human culture and historical context, antebellum evangelicalism never had an essential or monolithic identity. Evangelicals never believed or practiced the same faith as their coreligionists. Evangelicalism only had the meaning that its adherents gave to it, and they sought to define it in a way that fulfilled their own religious agenda.[7]

Antebellum evangelicals came to understand who they were by what they did not want to become. Anti-Mormonism served as a proxy for other issues within evangelicalism itself. Most of these matters concerned the revivals of the Second Great Awakening, where more eastern, educated, and urbane evangelicals concluded that many of their western coreligionists had gone beyond the bounds of appropriate religiosity. They feared their revivalist coreligionists had abetted the rise of Mormonism itself, and they compared them to the followers of Joseph Smith to denounce and excommunicate them. Looking more closely at the uses of anti-Mormonism then demonstrates a religious house of cards, where the creation of an evangelical empire brought with it a perverse tendency toward infighting and an impulse to exclude those who did not agree with them.[8]

Understanding the various ways antebellum evangelicals invoked Mormonism in their internal debates about the beliefs and practices of evangelicalism depends on understanding what evangelicals themselves said about Mormonism. Interactions with their leaders and converts created a mental image of Mormonism for evangelicals. What evangelicals assumed and said about Mormonism was very rarely true. Rather than adjudicating the veracity of anti-Mormon charges, reading this religious intolerance in dialogue with the history of antebellum evangelicalism demonstrates how evangelicals used anti-Mormonism for their own religious purposes. Authors of evangelical books, newspaper articles, and pamphlets explicitly compared their coreligionists to Mormons. Studying anti-Mormonism as a cultural movement shows the power and uses of religious animus, as well as the dialogue that existed in the stories of antebellum evangelicalism and Mormonism.

This story begins in western New York in the late 1820s. Large numbers of people in that region gave their lives to Jesus within traditional Protestantism and sizable numbers flocked to religious innovators, such as Joseph Smith. As Mormonism began to attract adherents within their own religious redoubt, evangelicals responded with increasing aggression. Between late 1829 and about 1831, evangelicals developed a formulaic set of criticisms about Mormonism as the Latter-day Saints moved out of their western New York home. Chapter 1 explores these earliest charges, as well as the ways these instances of religious intolerance reflected ongoing debates within the evangelical movement over belief and practice. Evangelicals lumped Mormonism with followers of faiths based on rival revelations, like Muslims. They also characterized Mormonism as an overly enthusiastic religious movement, sharing similarities with the Shakers. Since several of the founders of Mormonism participated in treasure hunting, antebellum evangelicals charged Mormonism with dabbling in occult practices. Evangelicals finally compared Mormonism to discredited civic groups, like the Freemasons. Through the deployment of these earliest criticisms of Mormonism, as well as personal attacks on the character and family of Joseph Smith, evangelicals constructed an imagined Mormonism. They made the followers of Joseph Smith out to be too emotional, too tied to their religious scriptures, and too focused on defrauding their followers.

A wholesale rejection of the Mormon prophet at this earliest stage would suggest an unbridgeable chasm between the two groups, but something more than just paranoia lay behind the evangelical reaction to Mormonism. Some of the first evangelical criticisms of Mormonism attacked the followers of Joseph Smith for creating a new religious faith, using the Book of Mormon in a selective fashion, and muddling religious truth. Evangelicals had within their own ranks coreligionists who seemingly manipulated the Bible to suit their own personal or theological agenda. Evangelicals additionally feared the emotional displays of Mormonism because they believed the worship services of Latter-day Saints were overly emotional and fanatical. The malevolent descriptions of early Mormon worship services mirrored critical depictions of evangelical revivals sweeping across antebellum America. At the same time they developed these early critiques of Mormon religious practices, some evangelicals worried that revivalism had succeeded in encouraging turbulent emotions, endangering the social order, and unmooring converts. These evangelicals concerned about revivalism would later conclude that their coreligionists had enabled the rise of Mormonism.

The evangelical group that felt most under siege by Mormonism in these earliest years of encounter was the Stone-Campbell movement. Building on the earliest criticisms described in chapter 1, chapter 2 explores the relationship between these two religious groups. Leaders of the Stone-Campbell movement made some of the earliest uses of anti-Mormonism to modify their beliefs and practices. Both movements shared a dedication to restoring Christianity to its earliest forms and impulses. Rival claims of restoration, along with attacks from other evangelicals that members of the Stone-Campbell movement were actually Mormons, led the leaders of the Stone-Campbell movement to distance themselves from Mormonism. Contrasting themselves with Mormonism was not the only reason for this systematic and vigorous antagonism. The leaders of the Stone-Campbell movement deployed anti-Mormonism to further an internecine religious agenda. For Alexander Campbell, one of the leaders of the Stone-Campbell movement, this meant ridding his movement of elements that supported radical spiritism.

After these early years of interactions, antebellum evangelicals broadened their criticisms of Mormonism to include charges of immoral economic practices, creation of a spurious new religious scripture, and participation in a variety of fanaticisms. On socioeconomic terms, antebellum evangelicals attacked Mormonism for mixing God and mammon. Chapter 3 examines how antebellum evangelicals understood Mormonism's economic practices. They depicted Joseph Smith as poor and lazy, but also as someone who used personal charisma to enrich himself and turn religion into big business. Smith had not just committed a temporal sin, according to these evangelicals, but he had transgressed against the will of God through his establishment of a communitarian economic system. The charges against Mormonism's economic practices coalesced toward the end of the 1830s when Smith unsuccessfully established a bank, convincing many evangelicals that the leaders of Mormonism had a mercenary desire for wealth.

Many of the concerns about dishonest behavior within the evangelical movement resembled the charges leveled against Mormonism. A group of evangelicals had become anxious that some of their coreligionists used faith as a device for profit, while others argued that evangelicalism had enabled individuals and businesses to go beyond the limits of a moral economic system. Evangelicals also became concerned about a growing obsession with wealth, a rise in celebrity within their own movement, and the institutionalization of religion through the Benevolent Empire. Apprehension about these economic developments led evangelicals opposed to the new-found corporate nature of evangelicalism to use religious animus against Mormonism to blame their coreligionists' pursuit of wealth for the rise of Mormonism itself.

Concomitant with these economic criticisms, evangelicals built on older concerns and voiced new opposition to Mormonism's scriptural practices. Chapter 4 uncovers the evangelical relationship to Mormonism's scriptural practices in light of their own complicated history of understanding the Bible. They continued to contend the Book of Mormon was crude and contrary to the Bible, and they also elaborated a set of contentions that Joseph Smith deliberately plagiarized the Bible for his holy writ. What was novel about evangelical charges concerning Mormonism's scriptural practices in the 1830s and 1840s was an obsession with finding out the actual author of the Book of Mormon.

These accusations about the inaccurate and inauthentic nature of the Book of Mormon mirrored evangelical concerns and creeping doubt about their own Bible. Growing numbers of evangelicals had begun to see the Bible as a historical document. An increasing awareness that the Bible was a product of the past, in combination with the belief that any person could read and interpret the Bible for themselves, led some evangelicals to place the blame for this development on the theological creativity of the Second Great Awakening. Seeing these same developments within Mormonism, these critics sought evangelical peace by limiting the variety of translations and by placing constraints upon theological creativity through the use of anti-Mormonism.

Much of the evangelical criticisms of Mormonism coalesced around the founding of the Mormons' Nauvoo in the 1840s. Chapter 5 looks at how evangelicals identified a spiritist, martial, and sectarian fanaticism at Nauvoo. They continued to see Mormons participating in popular supernaturalism with the consequence of fostering a blind and dangerous belief. Evangelicals also charged the Mormon community at Nauvoo with acting aggressively through their military displays. Nauvoo finally revealed to evangelicals a sectarian fanaticism, one that encouraged Mormons to see themselves in exclusive terms. A growing group of evangelicals critical of revivalism concluded that evangelicalism itself suffered from the same variety of fanaticisms. These antirevivalists charged that the excesses of their own movement had directly caused the rise and shape of Mormonism. These evangelical critics of revivalism saw camp meetings replete with popular spiritism and enthusiastic extremes. Revivals, according to these evangelicals, had a militaristic character that led to an aggressive arrogance and inauthentic conversions. Evangelicals critical of revivalism finally came to conclude that some of their more radical coreligionists shared with Mormonism a common sectarian fanaticism.

By the 1840s, evangelicals fully expected that their constant assaults would have relegated the Latter-day Saints to a historical footnote, but doubt had already begun to creep in anti-Mormon polemics. At Nauvoo, some evangelicals critical of revivalism concluded their own movement needed to respond to Mormonism in a new fashion. They believed evangelicalism itself needed to change or else Mormonism would triumph. Their ideal for what to become was, unexpectedly, the religiously devoted Mormons. Evangelicals became anxious that Mormonism had figured out the secret to acquiring religious converts. While Mormonism would never pose a serious threat to evangelicalism, this fear of loss of followers to the Mormons drove antirevival evangelicals to focus increasingly on institutional solutions to the spread of Mormonism.

Evangelical calls for more missionaries, more religious education, and more religious infrastructure ironically came at the very moment of evangelical domination of antebellum American culture. The specific remedies—outlined in chapter 6—to respond to Mormonism suggests that some evangelicals had become concerned about the very methods that had brought evangelicalism success. Evangelicals critical of revivalism concluded that many of their coreligionists had no fixed convictions or practices. Using anti-Mormonism to portray their coreligionists as heretics fashioned a more respectable faith, but in doing so evangelicals also fostered a revanchist faith that valued opposition and retaliation.

CHAPTER 1

"The Greatest Fraud of Our Time in the Field of Religion"

What Antebellum Evangelicals First Thought about Mormonism

John Sherer rushed to stop Emily Coburn from making a grave mistake. Coburn had left home in the summer of 1830 to join a new religious community. Her family feared this decision would endanger her eternal salvation, so they sent Sherer to Colesville, New York, to bring her back home. In a melodramatic account, narrated for the consumption of his fellow evangelicals, Sherer, a Presbyterian minister, said he located Coburn at the home of Newell Knight, Emily's brother-in-law. Evidently arriving at exactly the right moment, Sherer claimed Coburn was mere moments away from renouncing her orthodox Christian faith. He tried to convince her to come with him, but she refused. Sherer next tried deception, telling Coburn that her family had traveled with him and were waiting nearby. Recognizing his deceit, she tried to flee. He grabbed her, but Coburn's sister appeared "and the two women being one too many for him . . . he was obliged to sneak off without accomplishing his errand."[1]

Sherer did not give up easily. He obtained a power of attorney from Coburn's family to force Emily to return to her parents. Once home, this young woman's heavenly status became the talk of the community. Clergymen from various denominations visited her, prayed with her, instructed her, and plied her with religious publications in hopes she would recognize the potential peril of her near conversion. They failed. Coburn's sister visited her several weeks later, and Coburn used this opportunity to follow through on her initial attempts. Coburn renounced her Presbyterian faith and joined what became known as the Church of Jesus Christ of Latter-day Saints.[2]

Coburn's decision baffled Sherer. Writing Absalom Peters, the secretary of the American Home Missionary Society (AHMS) in October 1830, he wondered about Coburn's backsliding. Sherer told Peters that a sense of enchantment had drawn Coburn to this new faith. Mormonism, he said, had a sacred text that was "calculated to suit the marvelous, and unthinking," and "no man in his right mind . . . [could] think the Book or the doctrines it contains, worthy of the least notice." This new church also had unusual religious practices, according to Sherer, members pretending to "work miracles, such as casting out devils, and many other things." Sherer concluded his letter by lamenting that he could not understand why Coburn would join a religious group that had hypocritical, false teachers who only sought temporal riches.[3]

Although he thought Mormonism unlikely to endure, Sherer's letter to his AHMS supervisor was filled with anxiety about its appearance on the religious scene. Sherer referred to the followers of Mormonism as blasphemers, hypocrites, fanatics, and infidels. If he did not think Mormonism would amount to much, Sherer's response was curious. Even stranger, because the total number of converts to Mormonism by 1830 numbered fewer than one hundred disciples, so it posed no real threat to Sherer's churches.

Yet Sherer's reaction to the emergence of Mormonism was far from unique among his evangelical coreligionists in western New York. Many expressed similar feelings. Between 1829 and 1831, evangelicals in western New York and Ohio attacked Mormonism largely through analogy. Antebellum evangelicals compared Mormonism to despised religious groups, enthusiastic religious movements, dabblers in occult practices, and discredited civic organizations. In addition to attacks on the character of Joseph Smith and his family, this exhaustive set of charges against early Mormonism coalesced into a set of anti-Mormon themes evangelicals would carry with them for several decades. The crux of these charges—that the followers of Joseph Smith used religious texts improperly and worshipped with too much emotion—resembled debates within evangelicalism over what constituted orthodox belief and practice. Anti-Mormon themes would give antebellum evangelicals a powerful tool to define and shape evangelical beliefs and worship.

Background for the Evangelical-Mormon Encounter

The world in which evangelicals first encountered Mormonism teemed with energy and excitement. While relatively unsettled until after the

American Revolution, western New York and eastern Ohio saw their populations explode in the first decades of the nineteenth century. Landless farmers from the east escaping a prolonged economic downturn saw limitless possibilities in a region filled with cheap, abundant, and fertile land. The most important influence on the region's changing fortune was the opening of the Erie Canal in 1825. Even earlier, construction of the canal stimulated a boom in the economies of the towns along the canal route. The building of the canal brought tens of thousands of laborers, many of them immigrants, to the region.[4]

An influx of newcomers and money, in conjunction with the opening of the canal, changed the fabric of life in western New York. Merchants no longer had to take the costly and onerous wagon roads to get their goods to market. Finished goods and raw materials now moved quickly from east to west and back again. Shops offered the latest goods from faraway places like New York City and Europe. Along with stores carrying luxury items, new businesses opened in the canal zone to service the new canal boats, and hotels and public houses to accommodate the passengers and crews. Building of the canal created new tourism possibilities in western New York, like Niagara Falls.[5]

The Erie Canal made this new world possible, but its construction also interacted with broader changes taking place throughout western New York and the entire nation during the antebellum period. As the nation transitioned from mercantilism to capitalism, a system of commerce developed based upon mechanized factory work, the rise of urban centers, and a revolution in transportation. These nationwide economic changes placed the market at the center of the lives of western New Yorkers. Society had new economic and social possibilities. People could consume an ever-expanding number of goods. A farmer in western New York could now hope to become a middle-class artisan, lawyer, or doctor. Young people could now hope to lift their families out of poverty by working in one of the numerous textile factories. These economic changes came at a cost. Material success no longer rested solely in an individual's own hands. Success or failure increasingly depended on economic factors in distant markets. Working conditions varied widely based on the whims of plutocratic factory bosses. This economic transition caused anxiety and pain, leaving many more behind than it pushed ahead.[6]

The disruptive nature of these economic and social transformations provided a context for the sizable number of people in western New York who sought help from a higher power and joined evangelical churches. Thousands experiencing social and psychological turmoil experimented with various forms of religious expression in antebellum America, but evangelicalism came to dominate the region. Emerging at the beginning of the nineteenth century, evangelicals believed humanity was deeply sinful and could only be saved by the grace of Jesus Christ. This evangelical strain permeated numerous denominations. While Baptists, Methodists, and Presbyterians dominated the movement, the evangelical style of religiosity also appeared in Congregationalist and Episcopalian churches. Evangelicals' own experience of God's grace convinced them of the authenticity of God's word. They believed the Bible was the unique revelation of God and that most American churches were spiritually bankrupt. Traveling preachers and expositors of the Bible railed against the lack of emotion and conviction in established congregations. They used camp meetings and a declamatory preaching style to call people to repentance. Evangelical ministers wanted to awaken Americans to a conversion experience, an emotional and individual recognition of the helplessness of humanity in the face of sin and the palpable need for God's mercy.[7]

Evangelical religious ferment was particularly strong in western New York because of the work of Charles Finney. His successes in converting large numbers of individuals led western New York to become known as the Burned-over District. In a region split by divisions of class, culture, politics, and economics, the Second Great Awakening called for the fires of a moral order that would cleanse towns of their perceived bacchanalian character and provide self-discipline for the workers of this new market economy. Finney, a self-taught, blunt former lawyer, drew on the practices of the frontier revivals of the Second Great Awakening, reworking these techniques for more urban settings. He held protracted worship services filled with groaning and crying, prayed for sinners by name, harangued possible disciples, and injected emotion into the conversion process. Finney used these techniques in an organized and systematic fashion. Part of his favorable results stemmed from his fusion of a scientific-like confidence in the ability to bring about a change of heart with a strong belief in the power of human potential. Finney and other evangelicals believed in the possibility of the total transformation of human character and the power of the United States to establish a heavenly paradise on earth. This optimistic and aspirational Gospel appealed to those living in the Burned-over District. While self-interest certainly played a role in the efflorescence of evangelical religion, all participants in the Second Great

Awakening wanted eternal security. Attempting to provide answers to the fundamental questions about life and the human capacity to avoid sin, evangelicals worked to reform their own lives and to create a more righteous society. Only a revival of faith, many evangelicals believed, could prevent the nation from descending into chaos.[8]

The earliest evangelical critics of Mormonism emerged from this tempestuous religious subculture, and they came from a variety of backgrounds. Some of these initial critics had theological training or experience in ministry. John Sherer attended the evangelically inclined Andover Seminary prior to joining the American Home Missionary Society. Diedrich Willers attended theological schools in Europe prior to emigrating to America as a minister for the Dutch Reformed Church. Alexander Campbell received a rigorous education at the University of Glasgow. However, not all of these early evangelical critics of Mormonism had this kind of in-depth theological training. Primitive Baptists, who lost a number of members to the Mormon Church during the first few months of the latter's existence, saw theological training as anathema to a pure understanding of the Bible and effective evangelization.

The residents of the region, with their neighbors and family converting to Mormonism, had firsthand, albeit biased, experience with many of the key figures of early Mormonism. Writing in local newspapers or drafting letters to friends and other interested parties, they drew upon their experiences with Joseph Smith to try to discredit Mormonism.[9]

Antebellum evangelicals aired their earliest views about Mormonism in a variety of venues. Sherer, Willers, and other clerics who discussed the emergence of Mormonism wrote letters to denominational organizations, home congregations, or other evangelicals having their own first encounter with Mormonism. Most evangelical criticisms of Mormonism appeared in published, printed material. Evangelical periodicals contained religious news, appeals for financial support, devotional literature, missionary accounts, and ethnographies of new religious groups, like Mormons. Nearly two hundred of these evangelical periodicals existed by the 1830s, with more appearing daily in the western part of the United States, the hearth of Mormonism. Religious periodicals based in the vicinity of early Mormonism offered firsthand accounts and descriptions of the players in the evangelical-Mormon encounter. Many of these evangelical newspapers reprinted anti-Mormon polemics from secular newspapers, demonstrating how evangelicals reused any available sources to further their own religious agenda.[10]

Early anti-Mormon polemics comprised part of a larger antebellum evangelical community of print. Churning out Bibles, pamphlets, religious novels, memoirs of godly persons, tracts, hymns, and other religious works, antebellum evangelical publishers told their readers what to believe, how to live, and techniques for winning the world for Jesus. Evangelical editors also defined for their readers whom they should view as sinners. This print culture gave evangelicals a significant amount of cultural power in shaping religious meaning and gave evangelicals themselves a sense that they comprised a global community of believers.[11]

Antebellum evangelical publishers tried to shape religious public opinion through the creation and sharing of anti-Mormon texts. Authors and editors added to, subtracted from, and altered anti-Mormon texts. This created a brood of anti-Mormon texts in dialogue with one another. As part of a larger evangelical print community, the creators and transmitters of these religious polemics first wanted to reinforce orthodox Christian beliefs through the denigration of another religious group. By causing doubts about the validity of Mormonism, these evangelical publishers hoped to prove that they were the only true believers. These evangelical editors further invoked anti-Mormonism to promote their own universalist vision of Christendom, settling scores and disagreements with their coreligionists.[12]

Anti-Mormon Beginnings

The first recorded criticisms of Mormonism appeared in the local newspapers of western New York. Most of these newspapers had a common layout, similar to other early American newspapers. They contained evergreen articles relating to manners, nature, and a wide array of other subjects. Periodicals also contained classified advertisements for goods, as well as information related to shipping on the Erie Canal. International, national, and local news typically made up a smaller portion of the newspaper. The editors of these local newspapers lit upon the arrival of Mormonism in the summer of 1829. After one local newspaper, the *Wayne Sentinel*, announced the Book of Mormon's forthcoming publication, newspapers throughout Palmyra and Rochester reported on these events as well. They wasted no time referring to it as "the greatest piece of superstition that has ever come within our knowledge," according to the editors of the *Rochester Daily Advertiser and Telegraph*. These earliest reports in local newspapers became a template for the more comprehensive attacks on Mormonism that evangelicals would launch in the first few months after the sect's emergence.[13]

The *Palmyra Reflector* dominated much of this breaking coverage throughout 1829, the immediate months surrounding the beginnings of Mormonism. The Freethinker Abner Cole, editing under the pseudonym Obadiah Dogberry, published this newspaper to promote free inquiry and rationalism. The newspaper masthead carried an epigram from Alexander Pope: "Know then thyself, presume not god to scan! The proper study of Mankind is MAN." Cole's newspaper derided organized religion of all kinds, but he saved his venom for enthusiastic faiths, which he characterized as enslaving people through "unnecessary and uncommanded rites and practices." Cole found in Mormonism a quintessential example of irrational exuberance. With its mysterious origin story and the particular demands placed upon its followers, he believed it represented the worst of religious fanaticism.[14]

A series of fortunate circumstances gave Cole access to the Book of Mormon before its publication. Cole printed his newspaper at the publishing house of Egbert Grandin, the publisher of the *Wayne Sentinel*. Joseph Smith had contracted with Grandin in 1829 to print the Book of Mormon. Cole's time spent at Grandin's publishing house printing his own newspaper evidently gave him an advance look at the Book of Mormon. Cole used this preview to publish long passages from Smith's religious writ in his *Palmyra Reflector*. He mocked the Book of Mormon mercilessly, sarcastically describing its appearance as a "great and marvellous thing." Cole placed Smith in a long line of false messiahs who pretended to have a direct connection with God.

Saving particular vitriol for Smith's account of the golden plates, Cole compared his own difficulty in translating foreign news to Smith's translation of the plates themselves. He said Joseph Smith "never had half the trouble that we experience in deciphering the unseemly scrolls" because Cole lacked Joseph Smith's "editorial spectacles." Cole also charged that Smith deceived people into believing his false religion. Zealous followers would leave their jobs and homes on the command of Joseph Smith. Cole claimed to know one "honest Attourney" preparing to abandon "his lucrative profession, and enter upon the preaching of the 'Gospel according to'—Jo Smith."[15]

As part of his history of the publication of the Book of Mormon, Cole composed a scatological parody to demonstrate the strangeness and perniciousness of Joseph Smith's revelation. He titled his effort the "Book of Pukei," meaning a sickly person. Cole's satire placed Joseph

Smith alongside a locally known religious eccentric named Luman Walters. Composed in pseudobiblical language, the piece highlighted the ridiculous nature of Mormonism origin story. The story began, "and it came to pass in the latter day" that the "idle and slothful" said to one another, "let us send for Walters the Magician, who has strange books, and deals with familiar spirit." These lazy people wanted Walters to tell them where the treasures of the Nephites could be found. Walters acquired a large following, and his disciples begged him to translate a book that would enable them to find untold riches. Leading them to Manchester, Walters performed a ceremony used by many treasure hunters throughout the Early Republic to break the enchantments that guarded the treasure. He drew a circle around the location of the treasure with a sword, and then Walters sacrificed a chicken "for the purpose of propiciating [*sic*] the prince of spirits." His followers began to dig for treasure, and when they did not find any riches, they concluded Walters must have lied to them. Cole determined Walters's mantle next "fell upon the prophet Jo. Smith Jun." Cole ended his satire by noting that all of these events would be faithfully recorded in the "Book of Pukei."[16]

Cole also published attacks against any kind of organized religion, whether Mormonism or evangelicalism. He attacked Sabbatarians, the Sunday mail movement, and any other Christian organizations that fused politics and religion. After leaving the Palmyra area, Cole began printing a newspaper in the 1830s solely dedicated to refuting the activities of Charles Finney. Despite this animus toward evangelicals, Cole's writings in the *Palmyra Reflector* ironically played a significant role in framing early evangelical opinions about Mormonism. Evangelicals reprinted many of his articles. By reading, absorbing, and deploying some of Cole's descriptions, evangelicals accepted Cole's characterizations of Joseph Smith's dalliance with dark magic, the bizarre nature of Mormonism's origin story, the tendency for disciples of Mormonism to become deluded followers, and the human origins of the Book of Mormon. Antebellum evangelicals would extend the criticisms of this freethinking polemicist in a more systematic fashion and then deploy them for their own religious purposes.[17]

At the same time Cole began to publish his articles in the *Palmyra Reflector*, newspapers in Rochester, located a mere sixteen miles from Palmyra, also took notice of the origins of Mormonism. These papers propagated many of the same anti-Mormon themes as the *Reflector*.

The *Rochester Republican*, a publication devoted largely to mercantile matters, reprinted the Book of Mormon's title page and advertisement from the June 1829 edition of the *Wayne Sentinel*. Under the headline, "A New Way of Raising the Wind," the publishers of the newspaper reminded their readers to be cautious of "any scheme" that will find "dupes."[18]

Edward Scrantom became one of the first evangelicals to take public notice of the rise of Mormonism in his newspaper, the *Rochester Gem*, in early 1830. Under the headline "Imposition and Blasphemy!!—Money Diggers, &c.," he printed a lengthy riposte about what he saw as the bizarre origins of Mormonism. Scrantom sarcastically reviled the "ignoramous near Palmyra" who pretended to find some "Gold Plates." This unnamed imposter (whom everyone would have recognized as Joseph Smith) said the plates had "engraved characters of marvellous and misunderstandable import, which he, nor no other mortal could divine." These plates, Scrantom caustically remarked, contained an "unrevealed Bible!" Referring to Martin Harris, the acquaintance of Smith's who paid for the first printing of the Book of Mormon, Scrantom wrote that someone either "more credulous or more cunning" than the pretender who found the plates "ordered the translation thereof, mortgaged his farm, sold all he had, and appropriated it to the printing and binding of several thousand copies of this pearl . . . of *great price*!" Another example of the unbelievable nature of the Book of Mormon, according to Scrantom, was that it contained the accounts of several witnesses who claimed to have seen and touched the plates, even though God had commanded Joseph Smith "not to show the plates, on pain of instant death." These factors led Scrantom to doubt the existence of the plates, foreshadowing later evangelical demands that Mormons produce the plates. He passed along a rumor that even if the plates lay in the middle of the street "beneath the broad glare of a meridian sun," no one could see them, except for "he who was commanded."[19]

The discussion of the golden plates led Scrantom to attack the character of Joseph Smith and his family because of a recent occurrence that had "played off upon the inhabitants of Rochester and its vicinity." His character assassination of Smith's family centered on their participation in money digging. Scrantom's story began when the Smith family's "wonderful son, of about 18 years, discovered a round stone of the size of a man's fist." Followers of this young boy wanted him to use this seer stone to locate the fabled treasure of Captain Kidd. This child "oracle" placed the stone in a hat, looked into it for a period of time, and then proclaimed treasure was nearby. His disciples immediately began to dig for the treasure, and according to Scrantom, after digging for a short time, they heard "the scream of demons,—the chattering of spirits—and hissing of serpents rent the air, and the treasure moved!" They consulted the boy seer, who informed them that the treasure had moved to a "Deep Hollow." Scrantom concluded his account by discussing how a magistrate compelled the Smiths to leave Rochester because of all the individuals they had duped in this scheme.[20]

Antebellum evangelicals in nearby areas added details like the angelic visitations to Joseph Smith to these descriptions of the origins of Mormonism. The evangelical editors of the *New-York Enquirer* focused on Smith's claim that an angel named Moroni visited him and told him about a set of golden plates, buried in a nearby hill, that told the story of the former inhabitants of North America. Smith claimed he found the plates the next day, but was unable to take possession of them due to his own covetousness, according to these eastern evangelicals. The account continued that Smith returned to the hill again and again for four years before he could obtain the plates. During this time, according to these evangelical editors, Smith had to atone for his sins and demonstrate his faithfulness. He finally retrieved the plates in 1827, and Smith spent the following three years translating what became the Book of Mormon. Upon completing his translation efforts and prior to the publication of the Book of Mormon, according to these evangelical accounts, Smith allowed several witnesses to view the plates in order to confirm their existence.[21]

Evangelicals referred to these earliest accounts of the golden plates as religious delusion, a template that other evangelical editors would build upon in future years. The publishers of the *Geauga Gazette*, a Stone-Campbell periodical from the Western Reserve, provided one of the earliest descriptions of the golden plates just a few months after the formation of the Mormon Church. The editors of this evangelical periodical described how an angel appeared to an unnamed Joseph Smith. This heavenly being directed Smith to "open the earth at a place designated, where he would find the new revelation engraved on plates of metal." Smith did as he was told, according to these editors, and upon digging, the editors of the paper said that he "discovered an oblong stone box tightly closed with cement." He opened the box and found "a bundle of plates resembling gold, carefully united at one edge with three silver wires so that they opened like a book." The editors described the plates as seven inches by six inches with the thickness of tin, and they commented Smith could only translate the document by "looking through two semi-transparent stones." These Ohio evangelicals recounted that Smith used these tools to translate the text from the plates to a scribe. Smith needed an amanuensis, the evangelical editors derisively noted, because of his illiteracy. The editors concluded the golden plates no longer resided on earth. The revelation had "escaped . . . in a supernatural manner and are to be again revealed when the events of time shall require them."[22]

An efflorescence of information about this new religious sect quickly spread throughout the region following these initial accounts. The *Buffalo Patriot* reported "considerable curiosity, in some parts of the country" had arisen regarding Mormonism. Interested parties throughout the area sought information from any source to learn about the origins, beliefs, and practices of Joseph Smith and his followers. These initial discussions of Mormonism did not engage in critical thinking about the source or truthfulness of their information. Evangelicals reprinted material from any newspaper, secular or religious, as long as it contained some new item about Mormonism. Asserting much more in this early period of interaction than they could prove, evangelicals passed on rumors and hearsay about the character of Joseph Smith, the beliefs and practices of Mormonism, and the foundation myths of this new religion.[23]

The evangelicals who first encountered Mormonism characterized it as an "imposition and blasphemy" unworthy of their time. Like Newcomb's and Scrantom's papers, these other initial evangelical critics focused on a relatively narrow range of concerns about Joseph Smith and his followers. Several evangelical critics boasted about not having read the entirety of the Book of Mormon. John Sherer believed Mormonism's sacred text appealed only to the most naïve in society. Since he was not marked by unaffected simplicity, he did not feel the need to read the entire text. David Marks, a Freewill Baptist minister, likewise felt he only needed to skim about one-third of the Book of Mormon before he got the book's essence and "could feel no interest in a further perusal." The German Reformed minister Diedrich Willers, writing from a town nearby to Mormonism's epicenter, found only a cursory glance necessary to reveal the Book of Mormon as the "tempting work of man."[24]

Early Anti-Mormon Analogies

Attitudes shifted as Mormonism moved beyond its western New York hearth. As Mormonism attracted more adherents, the evangelical anti-Mormon chorus sang louder and more in unison. Whereas early descriptions of Mormonism were imperfectly formed, antebellum evangelicals drew on these early images to develop a more coherent and organized attack against this upstart faith. In the earliest years of their encounter, between late 1829 and 1831, antebellum evangelicals attacked Mormons by comparing them, variously, to the followers of faiths based on rival revelations, to the adherents of enthusiastic religious movements, to dabblers in occult practices, and to the members of discredited civic groups. Evangelicals also tarred the character of Joseph Smith and his family. This cornucopia of criticism—the analogies and the personal attacks—laid a foundation for evangelicals to draw from as they felt increasing anxiety about Mormonism, and as they began to use anti-Mormonism for their own religious purposes.

Antebellum evangelicals initially compared Mormonism to other religions that claimed divine inspiration. Noting the perceived similarities between Islam and Mormonism became a central plank in the evangelical assault on Mormonism by the middle of the nineteenth century. As evangelicals increasingly learned about the Mormon practice of polygamy and Mormonism's attempts to set up a theocracy in the western territories of the United States, it became difficult for evangelicals, and most Americans, not to see Mormonism as an American version of Islam. Writings defining themselves in contrast to these two faiths, which antebellum evangelicalism viewed as similar, picked up in number and volume throughout the nineteenth century.

The juxtaposition of Islam and Mormonism actually began right at the conception of Mormonism. Alexander Campbell, writing in early 1831, referred to Smith as a "Mahometan," and other evangelicals compared Martin Harris with Ali, one of Mohammad's closest confidantes. Harris, an early convert to Mormonism and a wealthy farmer in Palmyra, mortgaged his farm to pay for the publication of the Book of Mormon. The connection to Ali had to do with Smith's duplicity. These early evangelicals understood Joseph Smith as preying upon Harris's credulity, leading him to believe "without a reason and without a murmur."[25]

Antebellum evangelicals also made a direct connection between the Book of Mormon and the Koran. They believed both Islam's and

Mormonism's holy writs were false, copied from preexisting texts, and products of history, not eternal texts. These early evangelicals found many parallels between the two sacred texts. Alexander Campbell thought both scriptures used similar modes of argumentation to support their authenticity, each appealing to evidence within and outside the texts themselves. These early evangelicals latched on to how neither the prophets of the Koran nor the Book of Mormon translated the books themselves. Joseph Smith enlisted Martin Harris, his wife, and several others to transcribe his prophetic visions, and these evangelicals noted that Mohammad likewise needed an amanuensis. Both texts, according to early evangelical critics of Mormonism, represented pseudo-scriptures. As antebellum evangelicals learned more about Islam, they concluded Mohammad cobbled together a new religion out of preexisting cultural artifacts. Popular biographies of the founder of Islam described how Mohammad combined Christianity and Judaism, with a dash of excitement, to feed to an unsuspecting Arab populace. George Bush, a religion professor at New York University and editor of several evangelical dictionaries, insisted Islam was simply a Christian heresy. Depictions of the Book of Mormon followed the same pattern.[26]

Comparing Mormonism and Islam resonated because of Americans' growing interest in Islam and the Middle East. Numerous studies of Islam appeared in the same printed materials and newspapers that discussed the emergence of Mormonism. Evangelicals, and many other Americans, devoured these studies of Islamic theology, stories of captivity, and descriptions of the Middle East. Contemporary accounts of Islam and the Middle East shared the assumption that Mohammad had a quasi-evangelical mission to "restore" true religion and the "unity of God." Despite this promising beginning, he ultimately started a religion under false pretenses for the purpose of deceiving people. Evangelicals believed the same about Joseph Smith.[27]

While comparisons to Islam placed Mormonism in the category of both despised non-Western faiths and religions based on competing revelations, comparisons to the Shakers and the followers of Jemima Wilkinson allowed antebellum evangelicals to associate Mormonism with adherents of other enthusiastic and extreme religious movements. Similarities existed between the Shakers and Muslims, who both claimed revelations that superseded those in the Old and New Testaments. By comparing Mormonism to these three enthusiastic religious bodies, antebellum evangelicals understood that Mormonism would lead directly to delusion, confusion, violence, and social disorder.

These analogies then gave evangelicals a ready language to tar both their religious opponents and their coreligionists when it suited their religious agenda.

Early evangelical witnesses to Mormonism made explicit comparisons between Latter-day Saints and the Shakers. Comparisons to the Shakers allowed antebellum evangelicals to charge early Mormonism with embracing visionary tendencies. Infamous after the American Revolution, Ann Lee converted hundreds in New York and Massachusetts to a message of celibacy, abolition of private property, and perfectionism. She was a charismatic and visionary, who claimed sacred knowledge existed within herself as the Public Universal Friend. Alexander Campbell, in his seminal work on anti-Mormonism, wrote how he knew about the "elect Lady" of Shakerdom who "was the head of this party, and gave them [the Shakers] a new bible." Ann Lee, he said, spoke several languages, conversed with the dead, and "appointed the sacred dance and the fantastic song, and shivering, swooning and falling down acts of acceptable devotion."[28]

Highlighting the enthusiastic and visionary elements of Mormonism and Shakers became a way for antebellum evangelicals to emphasize how misguided religious belief could lead to unorthodox religious practices. Benton Pixley, writing in the Baptist-leaning *Christian Index*, underscored how Mormonism declares "there can be no true church where the gift of miracles, of tongues, of healing . . . are not exhibited and continued." He ironically noted that some Mormons died, but unfortunately for them, "none have been raised from the dead." The editors of the *Baptist Register* concurred, remarking Mormonism pretends "an ability, as in ancient times, to speak with tongues; and that Smith is able to hold [contact] with celestial spirits whenever he pleases." It was not just Joseph Smith who claimed to experience visions, according to these early evangelical witnesses to Mormonism. Many Mormon disciples experienced supernatural occurrences, including one follower who claimed to see the "New Jerusalem and passed through its apartments."[29]

Early antebellum evangelical witnesses to Mormonism also characterized Mormons as similar to the enthusiastic religious followers of Jemima Wilkinson. Edward Scrantom said Mormonism came from the same roots as "Jemima Wilkinson-ism." A member of the Stone-Campbell movement said Mormonism was like "Wilkinsonianism" because leaders of both groups had made substantive additions to the Bible. Abram Benton, a local Presbyterian, charged Joseph Smith "formed the blasphemous design of forging a new revelation . . . so that he might . . . [become] the founder of a new sect, which might rival, perhaps the Wilkinsonians." Wilkinson in many ways preached a relatively orthodox theological message, but she rejected the traditional Christian understanding of a physical resurrection. She concluded only souls would transcend to heaven. Placing Mormonism alongside the followers of Jemima Wilkinson, whom they widely understood as a false prophet, allowed antebellum evangelicals to see Joseph Smith as similarly disingenuous and overly enthusiastic.[30]

In addition to faiths based on rival revelations and other enthusiastic religious movements, early antebellum evangelical witnesses to Mormonism also compared the followers of Joseph Smith to practitioners of the occult. Antebellum evangelicals, in this vein, most often associated Mormonism with treasure hunting. This comparison allowed evangelicals to attack the veracity of Mormon teachings, cast aspersions on their religious practices, and undermine the character of Joseph Smith. Treasure hunters used seer stone, supernatural dreams, divining rods, and other techniques to locate buried riches. Mormonism emerged in a region local newspapermen described as full of treasure hunting. One local newspaper reported that treasure seekers became "so firm in the belief that it may be *dug up*, that they will traverse hill and dale, climb the loftiest mountain, and even work their way into the bowels of the earth in search of it." These same local newspapers circulated tales of immense treasures located in hills of upstate New York and Vermont, with one periodical recounting that some lucky residents discovered over fifty thousand dollars on the shores of Lake Champlain.[31]

Early Mormonism quickly acquired a reputation as a group of occult treasure-hunters with both evangelicals and non-evangelicals. James Gordon Bennett, a budding journalist in the early 1830, referred to Mormons as the "money diggers of Ontario county." In his 1834 affidavit about Joseph Smith's earliest years, Palmyra resident William Stafford told a widely circulated and widely held story about the Smith family and their associations with treasure hunting. Stafford claimed to have first met the Smith family in 1820 near Palmyra, where he claimed they had spent much of their time digging. Instead of engaging in honest labor, the family worked for hire, assisting others in finding treasure buried in the hills of western New York. Stafford said that on one occasion Joseph Smith's father asked Stafford for help because his son "had been looking through his glass and had seen 2 or 3 kegs of gold and silver under the surface of the earth." Stafford followed along, and in his account of the event described how Smith's father participated in an occult set of practices. Smith senior first made a circle twelve to fourteen feet in diameter and stuck a row of hazel sticks in the ground to ward off evil spirits. He made another circle inside the larger circle, according to Stafford, and then he walked around it three times, plunged a steel rod in the center, and commanded silence so as to not arouse the evil spirit. Stafford told a similar story where the Smith family came to him with what he believed was a plan to defraud him. The Smiths claimed Joseph Smith had located treasure. All they needed to acquire these riches was one of Stafford's black sheep as a sacrifice. They told Stafford of their plans to take the sheep to the location of the treasure, slit its throat, and lead it around in a circle while bleeding. According to Stafford, only the blood of a black sheep, they believed, would appease the wrath of the spirit guarding the treasure.[32]

Describing Mormonism as practitioners in the dark and occult arts allowed evangelicals to denigrate Mormonism and its founder as immoral, deceitful, treacherous, stupid, and uncivilized. The Presbyterian Benton said Smith had the "character of a glass-looker." Because of his immoral qualities, Smith, he believed, pretended to be able to discover lost goods, hidden treasures, and mines of gold and silver. Since Joseph Smith could not actually find treasure and did not want to go to jail for falsely claiming to be able to do so, Benton said he "lied for safety to the sanctuary of pretended religion" in order to "amuse his followers." Treasure seeking and the Book of Mormon comprised part of a scheme Joseph Smith hatched to make money and acquire disreputable fame, according to Benton.[33]

Joseph Smith's participation in the occult practice of money digging not only marked him as lacking in character; antebellum evangelicals also used this charge as evidence of his using a ruse to gain people's confidence. This charge would grow into a larger part of evangelical perceptions of Mormonism's economic practices in the following decades, but in these early years, it allowed evangelicals to define Joseph Smith as someone who engaged in financial fraud. The Presbyterian Jesse Townsend, who resided near Mormonism's early hearth, reminisced that Smith was the originator and leader of these expeditions. Townsend charged that Smith had a charismatic ability to excite and deceive "the imagination of his few auditors, and made them all anxious to lay hold of the bilk axe and the shovel." Smith was cunning, and he "pretended to look and see chests of money buried in the earth," according to this Presbyterian. Benton likewise charged Smith with taking advantage of a poor farmer named Josiah Stowell. Stowell spent large sums of money hunting for treasure on the advice of Smith, who "pretended he could see, and told him where to dig, but they never found their treasure." Benton lamented that the credulous Stowell received nothing for his efforts.[34]

Charges that Joseph Smith was a money digger represented not just attempts to tar his personal character. Antebellum evangelicals used these attacks of necromancy to paint him in opposition to the legacy of the American Revolution. They saw him as opposed to the republican values that they believed had proved important in America's founding. Eber Howe discussed how Smith's participation in this supernatural economy allowed him to dominate individuals and make them do what he wanted. This kind of magical control, evangelicals believed, led individuals into a state of dependency by making them lose the ability to choose for themselves.[35]

Smith's history of money digging also allowed antebellum evangelicals to smear Mormonism with having deceitful origins. Describing the Book of Mormon as "Something New," the Stone-Campbell editors of the *Evangelical Inquirer* explicitly connected Mormonism to a treasure-seeking milieu. They claimed to have heard, "especially among certain loose classes of society, that treasures of great amount were concealed near the surface of the earth." Part of this rumor, they passed along, was that Indians, the descendants of "the ten lost Israeltish tribes" had hidden the treasure. Followers of Joseph Smith, like other treasure hunters of the region, had sought out the riches, and these Stone-Campbell editors said "ignorance and superstition of these fanatics soon conjured up a ghost, who they said was often seen and to whom was committed the care of the precious deposit." The Mormons "did not succeed and as the money was not dug up, something must be dug up to make money," according to these editors. In these stories, Smith managed the conspiracy from "behind the curtain," but he wasn't the real mastermind because of his perceived limited intellect. These Stone-Campbell editors instead charged that a secretive group of other individuals chose Smith, a "suitable tool," to be a "great prophet of the Lord." Rather than a treasure of gold and silver, which they could not find, these Stone-Campbellites said this cabal had determined "the hidden golden treasure, is to be a golden bible and a new revelation."[36]

Charges of money-digging also allowed antebellum evangelicals to depict Joseph Smith as uncivilized. The treasure-hunting activities of the Smiths existed in an antebellum framework where a refined and middle-class evangelical population began to view treasure hunting as a symptom of cultural backwardness. Common people participated in money digging, according to respectable antebellum evangelicals, because they lacked ambition, had little work discipline, and remained attached to outdated folk beliefs. Antebellum evangelicals saw these kinds of people, unable to adapt to the changing economic landscape, in moralistic tones. This judgmental attitude was in flux as evangelicals slowly dissociated themselves from this kind of supernatural economy in the postrevolutionary period.[37]

In addition to despised religious groups, enthusiastic religious movements, and dabblers in occult practices, antebellum evangelicals finally compared early Mormonism to discredited civic groups, like the Freemasons. The evangelical editor Henry Newcomb in September 1831 made an extended comparison between Freemasonry and Mormonism. He hoped that by this point Mormonism would have gone extinct, but the "frailties" of human nature have allowed the followers of Joseph Smith to submit to a leader who claims to have "have infinite powers to work miracles, raise the dead, cleanse lepers." The Mormons practiced obscene and blasphemous religious practices, he said, rolling "naked on the floor, and [they] exhibit a variety of grotesque and unseemly forms, that humanity would blush to name." After recounting these ribald and scandalous activities, Newcomb said these activities of Mormonism made them "the most blind and deluded people we have upon record," like the Freemasons. Mormon disciples believed "their leader to be the real Jesus Christ, and that both he and themselves have infinite power to work miracles." The Masons similarly believed Masonry was divine, the "hand maid of religion," and a sure passport to the "Celestial Lodge above, where the Supreme Architect of the Universe presides." Both professed confidence in "foresaying things to come"—raising the dead on the "five points of fellowship, &c. &c." If evangelicals believed the "religious ceremonies of the lodge room representing Moses and the burning bush, and drinking wine out of a human skull" were blasphemous, then they should draw the same conclusions about Mormonism.[38]

The comparisons antebellum evangelicals used and did not use to describe the earliest years of Mormonism reveal the writers' frame of reference. Placing Mormonism alongside despised religious groups, enthusiastic religious movements, dabblers in occult practices, and discredited civic organizations served a number of purposes for antebellum evangelicals. It allowed them to characterize Joseph Smith as a false prophet, like Mohammad or Jemima Wilkinson. Mormonism also encouraged unchecked religious enthusiasm, according to antebellum evangelicals, like the Camisards or Ann Lee. They finally believed that Mormonism participated in strange religious practices, like occult treasure hunters or Masons. All of these comparisons, as well as the likening of Joseph Smith to a confidence man, resonated in a western New York milieu full of counterfeiting and fortune-seeking. Antebellum evangelicals would develop these analogies in greater depth and more complexity over the next two decades of interaction. These comparisons gave evangelicals a way to discredit Mormonism, but religious intolerance also became a tool to prove that evangelicals practiced the only correct form of religion.

Early evangelical witnesses to Mormonism seemingly compared the followers of Joseph Smith to every despised religious group, but they did not make some obvious comparisons. The earliest evangelical polemics about Mormonism did not make direct comparisons between Mormonism and Roman Catholicism or Native American spiritualism. Roman Catholicism had begun to attract growing numbers of converts in the Ohio Valley by the 1830s. Many evangelicals feared Catholicism's next target would be evangelicals. With Islam on the other side of the earth and with Masons, Camisards, or Shakers already disappeared or discredited, antebellum evangelicals may have found it less anxiety-inducing to compare Mormonism to groups that stood no chance of expanding in western New York and eastern Ohio. Time may have played a role as well. It may have also been easier for evangelicals to compare Mormonism to newer discredited religious movements, rather than the longer-lasting Roman Catholic Church.[39]

Character Attacks on Joseph Smith and His Family

In addition to identifying Mormonism with abhorrent religious groups, frenzied religious activities, occult practices, and discredited ideologues, evangelicals undertook a campaign of slandering Joseph Smith and his family to destroy confidence in his new religious movement. One of the most common charges leveled by evangelicals and non-evangelicals about Joseph Smith was that he was willfully unemployed. The editors of the *Broome County Courier* described him as a "careless, indolent, idle, and shiftless" person who spent most of the time at local taverns. James Gordon Bennett said Smith lacked "any positive defect" but had a "great dislike to labor" even though was a "stout able bodied fellow." Bennett believed Smith could have earned a living if he wanted, but Smith lacked the necessary fortitude and desire for physical labor. Orasmus Turner, an apprentice printer and future antiquarian, said Joseph Smith used to venture into Palmyra with "little jags of wood" from his home to sell, and would patronize the "village grocery too freely." Turner said he would "sometimes find an odd job to do," but he could never hold down regular employment.[40]

Antebellum evangelicals, during these earliest years, also thought Joseph Smith lacked intelligence. Recounting the origin story of Mormonism, where the angel Moroni appeared to Joseph Smith, the *Rochester Gem* and several other papers noted how "an angel appeared to a poor ignorant man residing in or near Palmyra in Ontario County." Alexander Campbell and the editors of the evangelical *Christian Herald* used the literary quality of the Book of Mormon to denigrate Smith "as impudent a knave as ever wrote a book." Henry Newcomb reported the Book was "discovered and decyphered by a very ignorant man . . . [who] can write nothing except it be dictated to him." Because of Smith's simplemindedness, the editors of the *Rochester Advertiser and Telegraph*, a local Presbyterian newspaper, argued that Smith, "who could neither read or write, was found able to translate them [the golden plates], and somebody else, equally ignorant, to transcribe them."[41]

Since Smith then lacked the education or the shrewdness to write the sacred text himself, evangelical observers sought the true author of the Book of Mormon. The editor of the *Broome County Courier* argued Sidney Rigdon had actually composed the Book of Mormon. Rigdon was a former Stone-Campbell preacher from Ohio and early convert to Mormonism. In this explanation of Rigdon as the real intellect behind Mormonism, Smith became a "money dreamer," while Rigdon was provided the spiritual explanation for the Smith's activity since Rigdon was "a preacher of various religions, and a teacher of almost all kinds of morals." The Smith family, then, according to these antebellum evangelicals, turned their pecuniary occult practices into more validly religious efforts by portraying Smith as "the chosen one of God to reveal this new ministry to the world." Rigdon actually first met Joseph Smith months after the publication of the Book of Mormon, but illogically for many antebellum evangelicals he became seen as the true author of Mormonism's holy writ.[42]

Alongside charges of Joseph Smith's idleness and ignorance, antebellum evangelicals charged him with being a moral reprobate and grifter. A local Presbyterian minister said his "impostures and low cunning gave him a reputation for being smart." This minister, Jesse Townsend, suggested Smith would steal and hide property that belonged to his neighbors, and then "for a price, he would look in his stone and tell where it was." Abram Benton, another local Presbyterian, accused Smith of being a "disorderly person" and brought him to court on that charge in 1830. Multiple accounts of this trial exist, but key details, like the verdict, differed in each of the trial reports. Whatever actually took place—whether a judge found Smith guilty of disorderly conduct and warned him out of town or Smith faced a series of trumped-up charges—matters less than the widespread perception among evangelicals that Smith was immoral and a crook.[43]

Joseph Smith's family and inner circle came in for the same kind of character assassination. As Mormonism grew larger, evangelical witnesses looked to Joseph Smith's family for an explanation of how he had created such an imposture. The editors of the *Salem Gazette* said the Smiths became known as a "people admirably suited to the promulgation of a new Bible and a new religion." They claimed the Smith brothers had a predisposition toward drunkenness, lying, and gambling. Manchester resident and fellow money digger David Stafford reported in a widely circulated evangelical publication that while they worked together digging a coal-pit, Joseph Smith Sr. often became intoxicated and quarrelsome. Lucy Smith, Joseph Smith's mother, did not fare much better, according to Orasmus Turner's memory. She singled out her son for notoriety because she believed "a Prophet was to spring from her humble household." Turner concluded that Lucy Smith raised her son to believe that he was going to be an instrument "in some great work of new revelation."[44]

The attacks on the character of Joseph Smith and his family, as well as the conflation of Mormonism with despised, scary, and secretive religious organizations allowed evangelicals to denigrate Mormonism in a geographically rooted and historically specific fashion. As Mormonism spread, evangelical charges against this new religious upstart grew more vigorous and coherent. Evangelicals came to believe that their fellow congregants from "all the denominations . . . left to join the "Mormontish converts." When recounting the Mormon emigration to Ohio, the editors of the *Brattleboro Messenger* encapsulated these fears and anxieties. They said proselytes flooded to Mormonism within just a few weeks, and that converts included "many intelligent and respectable individuals. The prospects of obtaining still greater numbers in this county, is daily increasing." Newspapers throughout the United States paid attention to these first conversions. For instance, the *Haverhill Gazette* told its readers that "Mormonism, a new Fanaticism, has recently gained a number of new proselytes in Bakersfield, Fairfax and Fairfield, Vt." Evangelicals could not fathom why people continued to join Mormonism. These "silly women, and still more silly men, whose minds are shrouded in a mist of ignorance" defied evangelical expectations. Members of the Stone-Campbell movement in Ohio reported that "hundreds of the rabble and a few intelligent citizens of the western part of New York and the eastern part of Ohio" converted "with the wildest enthusiasm" and "embraced a feigned revelation purporting to be literally new." Diedrich Willers believed evangelical Christianity could only survive if they understood and refuted the "greatest fraud of our time in the field of religion."[45]

Other groups attacked Mormonism in the late 1820s and 1830s for many of the same reasons as evangelicals. Freethinkers, Unitarians, Catholics, and nonreligious individuals also saw Mormonism as based on a false revelation, overly enthusiastic, participating in occult practices, and part of discredited civic organizations. Many of these other anti-Mormon polemicists even used religious intolerance to advance their own particular faith agendas in the antebellum period. While some of these other groups' criticisms of Mormonism overlapped with evangelicals, *Sins of Christendom* focuses on the evangelical component of anti-Mormonism for a few reasons. Antebellum evangelicals developed some of the most robust and systematic anti-Mormon critiques in the years leading up to the Civil War. As a study of the growing cultural power of evangelicalism, this book focuses more narrowly on the uses of anti-Mormonism by evangelicals themselves. The specific components and truthfulness of religious prejudice matter less than how certain evangelicals used them to further their own religious interests.[46]

This kitchen-sink-like approach to denigrating Mormonism would seemingly indicate that anti-Mormonism sprang from feelings of difference between the two faiths. Many non-evangelicals deployed the same criticisms as evangelicals did against Mormonism in these early years. But more than just wholesale rejection lay behind the evangelical response to Mormonism in these earliest years. Some of the first evangelical criticisms of Mormonism accused the followers of Joseph Smith of reading the Bible inappropriately and worshipping in an overly enthusiastic manner. Antebellum evangelicals were divided among themselves over the same set of issues. They attacked their coreligionists for changing the Bible to suit their own preferences and they feared overly exuberant worship services. The evangelical group that felt the most pressure from these two fears in these earliest years of the evangelical-Mormon encounter was the Stone-Campbell movement. Some of the leaders of the Stone-Campbell movement worked to distance themselves from Mormonism because of attacks coming from other evangelicals, as well as competition from Mormonism itself. Anti-Mormonism worked to distance the Stone-Campbell movement from Mormonism, but it meant much more to the leaders. Some of the leaders of this restorationist group used anti-Mormonism to define the beliefs and practices of their still nascent movement and thus further their own religious agendas.

CHAPTER 2

"Restoration of Body and Mind"

Anti-Mormonism and the Making of the Stone-Campbell Movement

David Burnet felt spiritually disturbed. As a Baptist minister in eastern Ohio during the late 1820s, he felt his denominational home had not gone far enough to restore Christianity to its New Testament origins. Burnet consequently adopted the restorationist ideas of Alexander Campbell, and Burnet encouraged the rest of his congregation to join him in this journey. He began to publish a newspaper in June 1830—the *Evangelical Inquirer*—to further this restorationist effort. Burnet and other sympathizers of the Stone-Campbell movement succeeded in the 1830s and 1840s in converting hundreds of thousands to their cause, but they faced difficulties before this exponential growth. Burnet described a series of struggles just as members of the Stone-Campbell movement had begun their evangelization efforts in eastern Ohio. In a March 1831 issue of the *Evangelical Inquirer*, he dedicated an entire issue to "a feigned revelation purporting to be literally new." Just six months after the publication of the Book of Mormon, Burnet saw Mormonism as enough of a religious rival that it required a comprehensive and dedicated response.[1]

Burnet was not alone in his feelings about Mormonism. In the earliest years of encounter, evangelicals of all stripes in western New York and eastern Ohio heaped scorn on their Mormon neighbors. Evangelicals drew on these earliest descriptions, and they compared Mormonism to despised religious groups, enthusiastic religious movements, dabblers in occult practices, and discredited organizations. Evangelicals also attacked the character of Joseph Smith and his family. By injuring Mormons through these attacks, evangelicals hoped to define this new faith and to blunt the spread of Mormonism. Some of these antebellum evangelicals also found among their Mormon antagonists a useful foil to determine the essential qualities of evangelical identity. They drew upon the early religious animus described in chapter 1 in order to define evangelical identity in their own image.

The volume and the uses of religious animus waged against Mormonism in these early years demands explanation because the total number of Mormon adherents was so small. Anti-Mormonism did not just stem from petty rivalry. Antebellum evangelicals certainly saw Mormonism as a threat, but numerical competition does not alone entirely explain the evangelicals' earliest responses or the uses of anti-Mormonism within internal evangelical politics. Disenchanted evangelicals decamped to Mormonism from many denominations, not just the ones directly affected by the growth of Mormonism. The Freewill Baptist preacher David Marks hinted at this broader appeal when he noted that there are always "people who are fond of new things." Another Ohio observer noted that "among the Mormonitish converts are found person from among all the denominations, Presbyterians, Methodists."[2]

Much of the initial anti-Mormon fusillade emanated from members of the Stone-Campbell movement, a group on the margins and at odds with the larger body of evangelical Christianity. Members of the Stone-Campbell movement in these earliest moments of encounter denigrated Mormons for their introduction of the Book of Mormon and their enthusiastic expressions of religiosity. The followers of Joseph Smith, they believed, had invented a new holy writ out of whole cloth and caused religious confusion through their convenient reading of scripture and blatant plagiarism of the Bible.

Authors and editors appropriated anti-Mormon texts for their own purposes. They used anti-Mormon texts to mark out the boundaries of an imagined evangelical community that usually revealed much more about the author of the text than the evangelical community itself or Mormonism. Publishers from the Stone-Campbell movement used arguments for religious intolerance in a conservative fashion to constrain what they saw as unorthodox religiosity, and to promote their own restorationist vision of Christendom. When members of the Stone-Campbell movement first met Mormonism, the former was a movement still very much in flux. It had only recently merged with other restorationists, and this new religious family disagreed among themselves over how to read the Bible and worship God. Using anti-Mormonism to define the beliefs and practices of their movement, a tendency seen throughout the evangelical movement in the coming years, first expressed itself when some members of the Stone-Campbell movement sought to deploy religious animus to moderate their movement.

The Early Relationship between the Stone-Campbell Movement and Mormonism

The Stone-Campbell movement had a complicated and uneasy history with the wider antebellum evangelical movement. Members of the Stone-Campbell movement shared much in common with antebellum evangelicalism. Both groups accepted the need to have a conversion experience, the importance of Jesus' atoning death on the cross, the necessity of basing one's faith on the Bible, and the need to share the Gospel with others. Members of the Stone-Campbell movement spoke the "language of Canaan" that came from a conviction of their individual sinfulness, the ecstasy of conversion, and the assurance of God's grace entering their lives. They also wove together republican politics and commonsense moral reasoning. Although members of the Stone-Campbell movement shared this evangelical ethos, they also remained alienated and distant from the wider evangelical movement. They vehemently rejected creeds, obsessed over proper church order, and insisted on the necessity of baptism by immersion. Despite the sectarianism of many members, the Stone-Campbell movement fit in with the broader evangelical movement. The earliest moments of the Stone-Campbell movement relied on transatlantic evangelical culture, ideas, and missionary impulses. Campbell, one of the founders of the Stone-Campbell movement, came to defend the broad array of American Protestantism by the middle of the nineteenth century and considered other evangelicals as religious colleagues. He believed the unity of all Christians could only occur within the framework of the restoration of the ancient Gospel and order. Campbell willingly took up the broad mantle American Protestantism in public debates against Catholicism and skepticism. Other evangelicals, too, saw members of the Stone-Campbell movement as part of the broader evangelical movement in America. Robert Baird, the English evangelical observer of American religion, hesitated to name them as evangelicals in 1844, but he eventually did so "because their creed, taken as it stands in written terms, is not heterodox."[3]

In anti-Mormon charges about how Mormons used the Bible and expressed their religiosity, proximity, not just difference, drove antebellum evangelicals, and members of the Stone-Campbell movement in particular, to reject Mormonism. A belief that Mormonism and the Stone-Campbell movement were part of the same phenomena instilled a sense of fear within some members of the Stone-Campbell movement that people might confuse the two groups. Thomas Campbell worried the Stone-Campbell movement would become "liable to the charge of having originated the scheme" because of their common efforts at restoring the primitive Gospel. The editors of the *Evangelical Inquirer*, a journal closely associated with the Stone-Campbell movement, warned their readers in early 1831 that the "Baptist Chronicle of Kentucky and similar works" have "endeavored to fasten this imposition upon the current reformation." Some members of the Baptist Church in Kentucky had evidently made a series of "ungentlemanly insinuations" comparing the Stone-Campbell desire to restore the ancient order of things and Mormonism's restorationist impulses. They were not the only ones to compare the Stone-Campbell movement and Mormonism in these first years of encounter. Warren Isham, a newspaper editor in eastern Ohio, referred to Mormonism as "Campbellism Improved." One missionary belonging to the American Home Missionary Society lumped Mormonism and members of the Stone-Campbell movement together as instances of infidelity.[4]

This proximity to Mormonism—in accused, actual, or feared forms—led members of the Stone-Campbell movement, along with Unitarians, to become some of the most ferocious early critics of Mormonism. While the Stone-Campbell movement and Unitarians disagreed stridently with one another, both of these movements, in different ways, wanted to restore Christianity to its purest form. The Stone-Campbell movement wanted to restore the primitive Church, while Unitarians wanted to jettison all of the historical detritus that had built up around contemporary Christianity. Both made restorationist arguments, claiming to reason solely from the Bible. Just as the Stone-Campbell movement and Unitarianism had begun to acquire traction in American culture in the late 1820s and early 1830s, Mormonism arrived on the scene claiming to partake in the same project of renewing the Church to its purest form. The familiarity of the criticisms used by the Stone-Campbell movement would give them a powerful tool to organize an incoherent religious movement.[5]

The Familiarity of Stone-Campbell Criticisms of Mormonism

The earliest Stone-Campbell critics of Mormonism attacked the followers of Joseph Smith for creating a new religious revelation to meet their personal religious inclinations and for muddling religious truth. When the Stone-Campbell editors of the *Evangelical Inquirer* first described the Book of Mormon, they placed Smith and his revelation in the same category as the "thousands of religious teachers . . . [that] believed they were especially called (sometimes by miracles) to preach the gospels they proclaim." While writing those specific words about other Christian sects, members of the Stone-Campbell movement used the same language to describe Mormonism, preparing them to see the Book of Mormon as an example of another sectarian religious text. According to David Burnet, Joseph Smith had manipulated a religious text because "in the absence of intelligence, ingenuity is put to the torture for the discovery of other materials and the basest passions are enlisted in the furtherance of projects." Thomas Campbell, father of Alexander Campbell, charged that he would handle the Book of Mormon just as he had treated "every other ism that has been . . . since the commencement of the Christian era." These "isms" included Mormonism, Shakerism, and any group that denied the "sufficiency of the holy scriptures of the Old and New Testaments" by creating a new revelation.[6]

In these earliest years of encounter, many antebellum evangelicals believed Mormonism had manipulated the Book of Mormon to look like the Bible in order to confuse people about the truth of the Bible. The Baptist minister David Marks wrote that the Book of Mormon contained several lengthy extracts of scripture, like the whole of the Sermon on the Mount and significant portions of Isaiah. In addition to actual elements of the Bible, Alexander Campbell saw the Book of Mormon deliberately copying biblical doctrines, "all the great controversies—infant baptism . . . justification, the fall of man, the atonement, transubstantiation, fasting, penance, church government, religious experience." About Mormonism's holy writ, the editors of the Baptist *Christian Watchman* warned "the doctrine taught in it, is similar to that of the free-will Baptists." Beyond just being a pastiche of biblical texts and doctrine, antebellum evangelicals complained the Book of Mormon used pseudobiblical language and overtly evangelical doctrines to sound like the Bible. The editors of the *Christian Watch-*

man believed that because Joseph Smith was familiar enough with the Christian Bible, he could easily include large sections of it in his own religious product. Once Mormonism spread to eastern Ohio, a group of unidentified Palmyrans wrote a letter to the residents of Painesville, Ohio, in March 1831 warning them about the spread of Mormonism to their area. Laying out what to expect from this new religious movement and how to defend against its advances, these Palmyrans noted "the book [Book of Mormon] is chiefly garbled from the Old and New Testaments."[7]

Mormons made much of the affinities between the Bible and the Book of Mormon, much to the chagrin of evangelicals. In their earliest years, Mormons may have highlighted these similarities as a way to make themselves more acceptable to the broader evangelical milieu of the period. One of Mormonism's early chief spokesmen, Sidney Rigdon—himself a former member of the Stone-Campbell movement and veteran of evangelical revival meetings—claimed the Book of Mormon did not "enjoin a single virtue, prohibit an additional vice, or exhibit a new attribute to God." Rigdon not only claimed the Book of Mormon shared a common moral purpose with the Bible, but also wanted his listeners to see the Book of Mormon as a continuation of biblical revelation.[8]

The claims of early Mormonism selectively abusing religious texts and lifting passages from the Bible struck a nerve in evangelical circles because they suffered from similar tendencies. Members of the Stone-Campbell movement specifically positioned themselves as the Christians most dedicated to reading and understanding the Bible in a literal and straightforward fashion. Often within the same newspapers criticizing Mormonism, members of the Stone-Campbell movement worried about the presence of so many different translations of the Bible and kinds of creeds within the evangelical movement. The Stone-Campbell editors of the *Evangelical Inquirer* reprinted an article from the Presbyterian-inclined *New York Evangelist* about this worrisome development within Christendom, noting that all the "denominations of Christians" are all very jealous over their rights, or privileges; "they are very tenacious of creeds and their forms." Writing contemporaneously with the appearance of Mormonism, these evangelical editors condemned their own movement for allowing too much personal opinion in scriptural interpretation, asking rhetorically if it was "not the custom of the present age, to adopt a set of opinions, make little advancement in the knowledge of God." Reflecting a desire to do away with all denominational sects and inherited modes of scriptural interpretation, the editors of the *Evangelical Inquirer* extended this analysis to describe the consequences of so many man-made religious texts and creeds. The addition of writs created a cacophony like the "sounds emitted by the six hundred mouths" of a "great monster." If evangelicals continued to follow this "gospel of sectarianism," these Stone-Campbell editors thought it would inevitably lead to Christians acting like "the ancient Gallic and modern African tribes," who lived "by pillaging one another."[9]

Evangelical charges against the ways early Mormons used and misused the Bible also struck a nerve because of what it revealed about the place of the Bible in antebellum evangelical circles. The Bible was central to the spiritual life of evangelicals, and they treated the Bible as inspired revelation. It provided essential explanations and motives for daily living. Since the Bible was the only source of religious authority, its primacy in the religious imagination of evangelicals meant they could use it as a litmus test to determine the orthodoxy of other Christians. One Stone-Campbell author charged that the "gospel of each sect . . . [was] found in its approved writings or records." A different minister commented, "[W]e now have Calvinian and Arminian gospels, indeed a gospel for every sect; that is, the peculiar opinions of these several societies."[10]

All evangelicals continued to accept the Christian Bible as authoritative, but different translations raised the challenge of accuracy. An unintended consequence of the Bible publishing boom was that these new translations challenged the notion of a common version of the Bible. While antebellum evangelicals developed this argument in greater depth in the coming years, as shown in chapter 4, some evangelicals already recognized in these earliest moments of encounter with Mormonism that simply putting a Bible in the hands of every American had failed to end faction and party feeling. Commenting on this pervasive tension, a Stone-Campbell editor said some evangelicals called into question even the most innocent scriptural changes. He asked if even those who read the Bible in the original Greek or Hebrew "are severely reprehended and accused of reading and making new bibles, what shall be said of those who substitute their own notions, expositions and isms, for the sacred text?"[11]

In addition to the ways early Mormonism misused religious texts, antebellum evangelicals also attacked the first followers of Joseph Smith for an enthusiastic style of worship. Their earliest descriptions of Mormonism's worship services focused on how they were divorced from reality, how they embraced a radical spiritist quality, and how the leaders of Mormonism manipulated their management. Antebellum evangelicalism used exaggerated rhetoric to describe Mormonism's religious practices as dangerous, but also alluring. Evangelicals originally converted in the heat of revivals and camp meetings joined Mormonism in ever increasing numbers in the early 1830s, and evangelicals attributed these conversions to the overheated religiosity of Mormonism. The reality of early Mormon worship services was very different. Early Latter-day Saint church meetings included many of the same elements as evangelical services, including singing, preaching, praying, and reading from the Bible.[12]

Evangelicals charged early Mormon worship practices with being "wild to the very farthest bounds of imagination" and "singularly successful in carrying into effect their solemn fooleries." The editors of the Presbyterian periodical *Western Luminary* told a story of one Mormon leader who "jumped twenty five feet down a wash bank into a tree top without injury. He sometimes fancies he can fly." These same Kentucky Presbyterian editors wrote that another "man of color, a chief man . . . is sometimes seized with strong vagaries and odd conceits." The editors of the *Western Luminary* claimed that almost all of the followers of Joseph Smith profess to "receive sensible demonstrations of . . . the Deity." The editors of the Methodist Episcopal *Christian Advocate and Journal and Zion's Herald* told a similar story about a young Mormon prepared "to receive a message from heaven." They believed he attracted a coterie of other Mormons who "repaired to the spot designated, and there as they solemnly assert a letter descended from the skies and fell into the hands of the young man." The letter served to strengthen the young man's faith and inform him "that he would soon be called to the ministry," according to these Methodist Episcopal editors. The followers of Joseph Smith believed the letter itself was of a strange quality, as "the style of writing was the round Italian, and the letters of gold." The "favored youth" immediately attempted to copy the communication, but as fast as he wrote, "the letters of the original disappeared until it entirely vanished," and these New York evangelicals concluded incredulously that Mormons believed "this letter was written in heaven by the finger of God."[13]

Antebellum evangelicals saw early Mormon worship services engaging in radical spiritism and popular supernaturalism. Evangelicals reported how the earliest followers of Joseph Smith spoke in tongues, believed in the supernatural, and experienced the indwelling of the Holy

and thinking in worship was Charles Buck's *Theological Dictionary*. Published first in 1802, this religious text went through many editions during the antebellum period. Presbyterian, Baptist, Methodist, and Stone-Campbell churches and ministers in both the United States and England recommended Buck's dictionary as a religious text that would promote religious growth without embracing the rising dominance of fanatical enthusiasm in the evangelical movement. These ideas would prove influential among evangelicals who grew increasingly concerned about revivalism, some of whom blamed their coreligionists for causing the rise of Mormonism.[18]

In the face of the charismatic revivals sweeping the nation, Buck chose a moderate path between enthusiasm and reason in order to determine the appropriate levels of religious enthusiasm and religious experience. As a representative for a moderate variety of Calvinist evangelicalism, Buck looked askance at the magnetic appeal and charm of religion, but he did not reject enthusiasm wholesale. He rather told his readers that enthusiasm was simply "that noble ardour of mind which leads us to imagine any thing sublime, grand, or surprising." Religious enthusiasm became dangerous, according to Buck, when it "signifies any impression on the fancy, or agitation of the passions, of which a man can give no rational account." Arguing this term derived from "the wild gestures and speeches of ancient religionists, pretending to more than ordinary and more than true communications with the gods," Buck defined religious enthusiasm as an "impulse of the mind which leads a man to suppose he has some remarkable intercourse with the Deity, while at the same time it is nothing more than the effects of a heated imagination." If antebellum evangelicals would no longer fall prey to the lure of enthusiasm, they would learn mankind should "expect no new revelations, no extraordinary gifts, as in the apostles' times."[19]

Buck believed fanatical enthusiasm could lead to false experience. He thought "a system believed, or a mind merely informed will produce little good, except the heart be affected." Under false experience, people can be "alarmed, have changed the ground of their confidence, have had their imaginations heated and delighted by impressions and visionary representations." These misguided individuals would see and hear "such wonderful things, they think they must doubt no more of their adoption into the family of God." While Buck thought Christians needed to worry about counterfeit emotional experiences, they also needed to avoid the other extreme. He thought some of these same misguided people heard "all experience profanely ridiculed as enthusiasm."

This stance of labeling all enthusiasm as bad had led evangelicals to "embolden" some to "despise every caution as the result of enmity in internal religion, and to act as if there were no delusive or counterfeit experience."[20]

Buck laid out four ways for Christians to determine if religious experience was genuine or counterfeit as a way to assist his evangelical readers. He believed experience should accord with "the revelation of God's mind and will, or what he has revealed in his word." Buck also remarked experience should not increase one's confidence; experience should "promote humility" and teach man about his "own weakness." Experience should excite people "to be ardent" in their devotions and sincere in their "regard to God," but it could also be abused. Buck finally thought it an "abuse of experience, when introduced at improper times, and before improper persons."[21]

Heretical, prideful, and abusive forms of religious emotion were exactly what antebellum evangelicals saw in both Mormonism and in increasingly extreme forms of revivalism. Early Mormon worship services even looked a lot like revivals. Mormonism's fits of "jabbering," "speaking foreign languages by divine inspiration," and "apish" actions invariably reminded evangelicals of any of the myriad revivals associated with the Second Great Awakening. Many of the earliest Mormon converts also came from visionary-inclined evangelicals or those most influenced by camp meetings and revivalism. With their own tensions over religious enthusiasm, many antebellum evangelicals critical of revivalism saw the enthusiastic religious expressions of Mormonism as the logical extension of the excesses of evangelical enthusiasm. In the later 1830s and 1840s, these evangelicals concerned about revivalism would charge that their fellow evangelicals had aided and abetted the rise of Mormonism.[22]

When Mormonism first came into contact with the Stone-Campbell movement, the Stone-Campbell restorationists focused on the ways the followers of Joseph Smith read holy texts, challenged the Stone-Campbell movement, threatened the social order, ignored rational beliefs, embraced anti-intellectualism, and went beyond the bounds of appropriate religiosity by embracing a popular spiritism. Matthew Clapp, the Stone-Campbell editor of the *Evangelical Inquirer*, relayed an account of one of the initial meetings of the two sects when four Mormon missionaries appeared at a Stone-Campbell meeting and rejoiced "at finding a people walking according to the scriptures of truth, and acknowledging no other guide." Clapp wrote that when these Mormon missionaries were "called upon for testimony, they appealed (like Mahomet) to the internal evidences of the book." When pressed, however, he described them as stumbling, eventually asking for a miracle because they were unable to prove the veracity of the Book of Mormon.[23]

Although Clapp successfully fended off the advances of the Mormon missionaries, he believed the followers of Joseph Smith posed a threat to the Stone-Campbell movement through the conversion of Sidney Rigdon. In the months prior to the arrival of the Mormon missionaries, Rigdon had broken with the Stone-Campbell movement, but many of his followers remained deeply committed to the restorationist vision. Clapp saw the conversion of Rigdon as dangerous because Rigdon brought with him over a hundred converts previously associated with the Stone-Campbell movement and because of the nature of Mormonism itself.[24]

Clapp investigated the conversion of Rigdon, and he concluded Rigdon converted to Mormonism because of the prophetic character of Joseph Smith, the supernatural claims of Mormonism, and the similarities of the Book of Mormon with the Bible. He described a scene where several of Rigdon's friends confronted Rigdon in Kirtland over his conversion to Mormonism. Rigdon "commenced a long detail of his researches after the character of Joseph Smith." Trusting in the character of Joseph Smith, Rigdon rejected accusations that Smith had faced legal trouble for violating the peace. Smith, Rigdon also believed, had supernatural gifts, like an ability to translate scripture from any language and "could lay his finger on every interpolation in the sacred writings."[25]

In addition to the supernatural evidences of belief, Clapp said Rigdon believed in the actual teachings of Mormonism and the Book of Mormon. According to Clapp, Rigdon believed the Book of Mormon did not include anything that contradicted the Bible. The Book of Mormon existed, Rigdon claimed, for the formation and government of the "millennial church," while the "old revelation was never calculated for that, nor could it accomplish that object; and without receiving the Book of Mormon, there is no salvation for any one into whose hands it shall come." It was an "ancient gospel," according to Rigdon.[26]

Even after the missionaries left, editors within the Stone-Campbell movement believed Mormonism left social disorder in their wake. Clapp described how a "scene of the wildest enthusiasm was exhibited, chiefly . . . among the young people." These people, according to Clapp, would "fall, roll upon the floor, and so mad were they, that even the females were seen in a cold winter day, lying under the bare canopy of heaven, with no couch or pillow but the fleecy snow." The young men, Clapp said, would get up on tree stumps and preach to imagined congregations, baptizing ghosts.[27]

Alexander Campbell and *Delusions*

The early evangelical themes of Mormonism's misuse of the Bible and enthusiastic religious practices both reflected internal anxieties within the Stone-Campbell movement, and this intolerance became a tool for Alexander Campbell to further his own religious agenda. Educated at the University of Glasgow, Campbell was steeped in the Scottish Enlightenment and Lockean liberalism, two modes of analysis he drew on to undermine Mormonism. Campbell immigrated to the United States in 1809, and he quickly established independent churches in the western part of the United States. Campbell and the movement associated with him rejected religious beliefs not directly sanctioned by the Bible, advocated a congregational form of church polity, practiced a simple and informal worship style, and called for a populist hermeneutic premised on the inalienable right of every person to understand the Bible for themselves.[28]

Alexander Campbell published the first long-form systematic critique of the Book of Mormon and Mormonism early 1832. He intended to expose Mormonism as a false belief. Titled *Delusions: An Analysis of the Book of Mormon with an Examination of Its Internal and External Evidences, and a Refutation of Its Pretences to Divine Authority*, Campbell's anti-Mormon text proved influential for future evangelical objections to Mormonism. Antebellum evangelicals would draw on both Campbell's work of comparative history and the critical framework he used to undermine Joseph Smith's claim of a new revelation. On numerous occasions, other evangelicals reprinted vast portions of *Delusions* within their own works of anti-Mormonism.[29]

Campbell attacked Mormonism and the Book of Mormon in *Delusions* by first placing Joseph Smith in a long line of false prophets, recounting the seemingly unbelievable plot of Mormonism's holy writ, demonstrating the internal inconsistencies found in the Book of Mormon, and debunking the external evidences Mormonism used to verify Smith's revelation. Campbell began by arguing that Mormonism was nothing new. "From the Egyptians to the Jews to the Christians," he wrote, every age had its delusions. Campbell counted nearly twenty-five false messiahs throughout history. Smith was just the most recent. What was common about all these false messiahs was "many were deceived, and myriads lost their lives through their impostures." Campbell argued Smith was like the religious fanatics "Munster and Story," imposters "since the time of the Reformation." Both examples of religious fanatics, Campbell claimed these false messiahs taught Christians they "should put their possessions into one common stock, and live together in that state of equality . . . and that polygamy was not incompatible with either the Old or New Testament." These same religious fanatics also experienced religious visions and revelations, according to Campbell. Using these examples of false messiahs, he defined Joseph Smith as a charismatic individual who deluded thousands of disciples and would eventually lead them astray to their physical and spiritual death. What made Smith the worst kind of individual, he thought, was that the Mormon prophet was a hypocrite, like the others who did not believe in their own message and lacked the courage of their convictions. These kinds of comparisons to historical false teachers gave evangelicals a ready understanding of Mormonism, giving their anti-Mormon charges the weight of past heresies.[30]

Campbell then summarized the plot of Mormonism's religious text for the purpose of showing its falsehood. He described it as the "religious adventure of one Lehi." Campbell saw the Book of Mormon within the historical "romance" genre, but he also thought this characterization was too innocent. Since so many people had already fallen victim to the Book of Mormon, he believed stronger language was needed. Campbell saw Mormonism's holy writ as a patently false religious revelation, but he also spilled considerable ink criticizing the plot, language, theology, and coherence of the text. He may have reacted in this way because of the hundreds of followers flocking to Mormonism, its claims to be restoring the true church through a new revelation, and the seriousness with which Smith and his followers viewed their holy writ. Paralleling earlier language about sectarian bibles in the *Evangelical Inquirer*, Campbell referred to the Book of Mormon as the "bible of the Mormonites."[31]

Campbell spent the bulk of his text attempting to undermine the Book of Mormon by pointing out perceived inconsistencies. Campbell called into question the Book of Mormon's authenticity because of internal and external evidences, echoing a popular technique antebellum evangelicals deployed to demonstrate the veracity of the Bible. Antebellum evangelicals used internal arguments to prove the Christian Bible was a unique divine revelation because it was internally consistent, as well as in accord with reason, the deepest desires of the heart, morality, the needs of human nature, and the prerequisites for social order and justice. Campbell indicted the Book of Mormon for lacking all these elements. He wrote that the Book of Mormon lacked internal coherence, placing elements of Christian doctrine and history hundreds of years before the Christian era. Mormonism's holy writ, according to Campbell, "uttered all the events of the christian era, and developed the records of Matthew, Luke, and John, six hundred years before John the baptist was born." The Nephites believed in the "doctrines of the Calvinists and Methodists, and preaching baptism and other christian usages hundreds of years before Jesus Christ was born!" Campbell wrote sarcastically. He found it especially unlikely the Nephites took "upon them the name of Christ" over a century before the birth of Jesus Christ.[32]

The Book of Mormon also failed the internal test, according to Campbell, because it lacked a consistent narrative and contradicted itself. He said the Book of Mormon went against the dictates of the Levitical priesthood. In the Old Testament, according to Campbell, God killed non-Levites who approached the altar, but Smith made Lehi a member of the household of Joseph, and in the Book of Mormon, "God is represented as instituting, approbating and blessing a new priesthood from the tribe of Joseph." Campbell wrote the Book of Mormon likewise allowed temple worship in a place other than Jerusalem, against what the Bible commanded. He further wondered why the Nephites, one of the lost tribes of Israel, lacked any outrage over their expulsion from the Promised Land, while the Bible clearly said the Israelites of the Old Testament could not sing "the Lord's song in a strange land." These embellishments and inconsistencies led Campbell to remark that "Smith seems to have embraced the adage that the more marvellous the tale, the more credible the tale."[33]

Campbell finally saw the Book of Mormon failing the internal test because it privileged local knowledge over biblical history, spoke too much about contemporary concerns, and lacked uniformity. The Book of Mormon revealed to Campbell that Joseph Smith knew little about the geography or history of Judea. He wrote that the Book of Mormon made several obvious errors, like placing Jesus' birth in Jerusalem, rather than Bethlehem. Too much of Mormonism's religious writ, he believed, was about "every error and almost every truth discussed in N. York for the last ten years" instead of lasting spiritual truths about morality and justice. He also saw the Book of Mormon lacking an appropriate style. While Mormonism's holy writ "professed "to be written at intervals and by different persons during the long period of 1020 years . . . yet for uniformity of style, [he said] there never was a book more evidently written by one set of fingers." Campbell claimed the Book of Mormon contained a number of "Smithisms," so he had no doubt that Smith was the "sole author and proprietor" of the Book of Mormon.[34]

External evidence also called into question the truthfulness of the Book of Mormon for Campbell. Antebellum evangelicals used external arguments to reinforce the authenticity of the Christian Bible. By appealing to works of the Holy Spirit, including the seemingly miraculous expansion of early Christianity, antebellum evangelicals had an answer to newer forms of biblical criticism that questioned whether or not the authors whose names were on New Testament books had actually written them. They believed prophecy and miracles confirmed the veracity of the Bible, something Campbell saw lacking in the Book of Mormon. Regarding the three witnesses whose testimony confirmed the existence of the golden plates, Campbell doubted their story. He suggested they believed in the existence of the plates first, and then they "asked God if it was true." When commenting about Mormonism's claims that their true believers had spiritual gifts, Campbell asked for proof, wondering if they "can . . . show any spiritual gift?" Concluding with a snide comment, he said Mormonism's real spiritual gifts consisted of muttering "Indian" and trafficking in "new Bibles."[35]

Campbell had strong personal reasons to issue this powerful denunciation of Mormonism, the Book of Mormon, and Joseph Smith. He wrote he had "never felt myself so fully authorized to address mortal man in the style in which Paul addressed Elymas the sorcerer as I feel towards this Atheist Smith." Mormon missionaries to the Western Reserve had evidently misrepresented Campbell and his restorationist colleague Walter Scott as believers in the Book of Mormon. In addition to challenging the claims of some Kentucky Baptists who wanted to connect the Stone-Campbell movement with Mormonism, Campbell believed he had to issue this forceful denunciation in order to avoid confusion with this "impudent" delusion. Rigdon's conversion to Mormonism also deeply distressed Campbell. Rigdon had played a significant role in the early years of Campbell's restoration, along with other Mormon converts, like Oliver Cowdery, Orson Pratt, and Parley Pratt. Campbell attempted to explain Rigdon's conversion differently than Clapp, who looked at the reasons why Mormonism might have appealed to Rigdon. Campbell claimed Rigdon was mentally unstable. He pointed to Rigdon's embrace of the full manifestations of the Holy Spirit, like signs, speaking in tongues, visions from angels, and other bodily exercises as evidence for Rigdon's disordered state of mind.[36]

The religious movements led by Campbell and Smith shared important characteristics, while differing in key areas. Both the Stone-Campbell movement and Mormonism saw the United States as a chosen nation, placed importance on the restoration of the first-century church, and practiced baptism by immersion. Despite the similar impulses behind each of their religious projects, their disagreements over belief and practice led Campbell to see Mormonism as a heretical faith because of Smith's claims about his own prophetic authority and the Book of Mormon. Their visions of restoration also came into conflict, as Smith claimed to have restored apostolic and priesthood offices found in the Bible, a literal Promised Land for believers located in America, and continuing revelations from God.[37]

Alexander Campbell's Uses of Anti-Mormonism

The overlap between Mormonism and the Stone-Campbell movement gave Campbell a preexisting set of anti-Mormon charges to further his own religious agenda. His encounter with Mormonism came at a propitious time. Campbell's movement had recently merged with a group of committed restorationists. Many within Campbell's restorationist movement still believed in the reality of speaking in tongues, prophecies, visions, and spiritual dreams. He wanted to excise those beliefs from his religious project. At the end of the historical comparisons he made to Mormonism, Campbell placed Mormonism in the same category as "the Barkers, Jumpers, and Mutterers of the present age." He meant the participants in revivalism, and Campbell saw them as gluttonous participants in the "evils of sectarianism." Campbell's placement of revivalists alongside Mormonism aimed to use anti-Mormonism in order to win an argument with his coreligionists over appropriate religious beliefs and practices.[38]

Campbell shared a desire to restore the primitive Christian Church with many other individuals in the antebellum period. His restorationist movement joined with Barton Stone's Christian movement in 1832, creating the Stone-Campbell movement. Their merger launched one of the fastest growing evangelical groups in the antebellum period.

Stone and his followers, in general, practiced a much more ecstatic and emotional-based faith. Stone himself had participated in the Cane Ridge Revival in August 1801. This great revival in Kentucky saw intense manifestations of the Holy Spirit, like barking, jerking, and rolling. Stone took these practices back to his home congregation. He preached them widely, as part of his effort to bring about the unity of all Christendom.[39]

The movements spearheaded by Campbell and Stone had a contentious relationship from their initial unification. While both leaders wanted to restore the beliefs and practices of the first-century church, they differed over the practices and theology necessary to accomplish this goal. One of their major points of disagreement concerned the purposes of Jesus' death on the cross. Campbell believed in a traditional understanding of the atonement, that the divine Christ died in place of fallen humanity. Stone found that interpretation theologically embarrassing. He preached Jesus' death on the cross changed humans, not God, drawing people to accept God's free gift of salvation. Campbell and Stone also came to opposing interpretations of the Trinity. While Campbell accepted the orthodox understanding of God, Jesus, and the Holy Spirit as one being with different manifestations, Stone believed in one eternal God, that the Holy Spirit was not a separate person in the Godhead, and that Jesus possessed the fullness of the Godhead only after he came to earth. Stone's conclusions about the Trinity led Campbell to call Stone a Unitarian.[40]

The most intense confrontation between Campbell and Stone took place in 1830 and 1831, at the same time as their initial encounter with Mormonism. It happened as a unification movement among some of Campbell and Stone's churches in Kentucky had already begun. Stone initially opposed the merger of the two movements because of differences in naming conventions and admission requirements. Campbell's churches claimed the name Disciples of Christ as the only acceptable name for their churches, something Stone saw as unnecessarily narrow. Stone also opposed that Campbell's churches practiced closed communion, only allowing immersed believers to become full members of the church. In a series of sharply worded rebukes, Campbell accused Stone of sectarianism. Campbell did not believe the differences between the two groups so great that they could not work together to restore the ancient Gospel and order. When several of the two types of churches did unify in early 1832, Campbell gave tacit approval because he believed these unified churches would teach his version of restoration theology.[41]

Just a few months after the unification of Campbell and Stone's movements, while he wrote and published *Delusions*, Campbell began to accuse many of these unified churches of betraying the restorationist vision. Campbell wanted the unity of these two movements to rest on a set of core beliefs, not on a loose confederation with no clear standards. He thought some of these unified congregations held on to improper understandings of the Holy Spirit. The churches from Stone's movement had more exuberance and believed in a more active role for the Holy Spirit. These latent religious elements threatened Campbell's specific vision of unity. Campbell lashed out at some of these unified churches for embracing aspects of revivalism, like mourning benches, camp meetings, and emotional preaching.[42]

Campbell, along with his long-time colleague Walter Scott, positioned themselves against the more enthusiastic and charismatic elements of revivalism embraced by Stone and his followers. Campbell called this more emotional form of religion "idealess," "headless," and "heartless." Emotion dominated Stone's movement, according to Campbell. He believed that while these camp meetings had success in filling churches, the results were not worth it. Campbell thought revivalism produced converts who had no spiritual roots and "no clear perception of . . . the gospel." Campbell and Scott believed Stone and most of the broader evangelical movement misunderstood the correct role of the Holy Spirit in the life of believers and the Church. Campbell and Scott understood the workings of the Holy Spirit in a narrower fashion than Stone. They believed deliverance from sin depended on the Bible. They taught the Holy Spirit comforted Christians and convinced the world of the power of Jesus.[43]

Stone and many of the individuals he brought with him into the Stone-Campbell movement remained open to the power of the Holy Spirit and the use of revivals well after the union of the two movements. Stone believed the Holy Spirit played a central role in his own conversion experience. He described how he struggled with his own salvation for a lengthy period of time until the Holy Spirit spoke to him "aloud in the silent night, in the echoing grove around." He recounted that he confessed his sins and "saw that a poor sinner was as much authorized to believe in Jesus as first at last—that now was the accepted time, and day of salvation." Stone continued to speak warmly about all of the ecstatic exercises that characterized the Cane Ridge revival throughout his ministry, including the jerking, running, barking, and dancing. Stone insisted that Christians should be open to the power of the Holy Spirit.

Just after his union with Campbell in 1832, Stone wrote that "God has formerly communicated his Holy Spirit to obedient believers, and we have scriptural reasons for believing he yet does, and will to the end of time." Stone expressed regret for some of the more outlandish manifestations of emotion at Cane Ridge, but he thought "the good so far exceeded the evil." He even became distressed by the increasingly orthodox position that the gifts of the Holy Spirit had ceased with the death of the apostles. Stone quarreled with Campbell and Scott over the assertion that missionaries capable of confirming their testimony with perceptible expressions of the Holy Spirit was no longer possible. Writing to Walter Scott in 1836, Stone argued "Christians might have well worked miracles through the power of the Spirit in his own day and age were it not for disbelief."[44]

As Campbell's followers and Stone's followers began to comingle and join forces, Campbell worried about the integration of Stone's disciples, who practiced this more ecstatic and emotion-based faith. By placing Mormonism and Stone's more eclectic disciples in the same category in *Delusions*, Campbell used the cultural power of anti-Mormonism to stake a claim about the nature of appropriate religious behavior. Defining acceptable emotional religiosity in this fashion forced a number of his new coreligionists to accept his elimination of the radical spiritism of revivalism or to leave for new religious pastures. Writing about the union in 1832, the Ohio preacher Matthew Gardner confirmed these efforts. He complained that the preachers in the Campbell tradition sought to reform churches of other denominations over to their views, rather than allowing a diversity of theological opinion. Recalling Stone's movement, he said that they "arose upon the liberal ground of each individual enjoying and exercising his own private opinion." Gardner lamented how Campbell had "obviated" those differences.[45]

Relentlessly patrolling and surveying the boundaries of appropriate religious identity was how Campbell attempted to root out radical spiritism and religious enthusiasm. While unrelated to the question of the role of the Holy Spirit, Stone himself expressed feelings that Campbell often acted like a "dictator." Stone had grown upset because Campbell unilaterally decided that their movement should not call themselves "Christians" because others, like the Unitarians, had already done so. Stone disliked Campbell's chosen term "Disciples of Christ" because it was not scriptural. He concluded by issuing a warning about the power Campbell had amassed, wondering if "the Mormons, or should a new sect spring up still more heretical, and assume the title Disciples of Christ, what could we do?"[46]

Through his systematic critique of Mormonism, Campbell had a number of goals. He hoped this new faith would disappear when people realized its obvious imposture. Campbell also wanted to differentiate his own movement from this religious upstart. He finally saw the power of using anti-Mormonism to accomplish his own religious agenda.

Campbell was wrong on at least one account. Mormonism did not disappear. Over the course of the next two decades, people continued to convert to Mormonism. As the numbers of Latter-day Saints increased, evangelicals unleashed more complex and vociferous polemics against Mormonism's economic practices, scriptural practices, and the various kinds of fanaticism practiced by the followers of Joseph Smith. As evangelicals looked disdainfully at Mormons, they ironically saw quite a bit of themselves. The charges evangelicals used against Mormonism in the coming years brought to light some of the central tensions evident in their own religious movement. Not liking their reflection, for particular evangelical groups Mormonism became a tool to cudgel one another over a range of intramural issues. This pattern, inaugurated with Campbell, acquired force and coherence throughout the 1830s and 1840s.

CHAPTER 3

"Peddling the Holy Scriptures"

Anti-Mormonism and the Evangelical Relationship to the Market

A new kind of paper money began changing hands on the Western Reserve in the spring of 1837 that appeared nearly identical to some of the most widely circulated bills of the period. They contained stock images seen on other currency, like a man shearing a sheep, a stagecoach, and a railroad. The bills had serial numbers, they identified the location of the issuing bank, and they contained the names of the bank's president and cashier. What made these bills suspicious was found in tiny print. The managers of the Kirtland Safety Society, a bank established by Joseph Smith and other leaders of Mormonism, added the word "anti-" before "bank" and the suffix "-ing" after it.[1]

Whether because of their questionable value or because of their associations with Mormonism, the Kirtland "anti-bank" sparked an immediate reaction near its eastern Ohio home, a response that quickly spread throughout the nation. Samuel Lane, an Akron-based social reformer, derided the bills as poor imitations of genuine money. Writing in his periodical, *The Buzzard*, Lane informed his reader that "if a gentleman is engaged in passing counterfeit money," and he comes across a man with a lot of "'Kirtland Safety Society' [notes] on hand with which he is trying to gull the people, he has found a 'kindred spirit.'"[2]

Skeptics of the bank and the anti-Mormon vitriol surrounding its rise and fall spread quickly throughout the nation. E. G. Lee nearly started a riot in Frankford, Pennsylvania, for denouncing the financial practices of Mormonism and the Kirtland bank. Lee had received an invitation to speak at a Mormon meeting, and he used the bank as evidence that Mormonism was "one of the grossest pieces of fraud in a mere pecuniary point of view." Waving around one of the ten-dollar Kirtland notes, he insulted the Kirtland bank as trash. Lee saw the whole banking operation as a fairy tale because the managers had not paid the engravers, printers, or paper makers who had created the bills. He charged the bank with swindling people by putting the bank into operation in "open violation of the laws of Ohio." Around this point in his speech, one of the Mormon elders interrupted Lee. While the crowd wanted Lee to continue, according to his own account, the Mormon leaders of the meeting refused to let him keep talking. "Violence and clamor" ended the meeting without Lee having the opportunity to respond to the charges against him.[3]

From the early 1830s to the middle of the 1840s, evangelicals codified attacks on Mormonism's spiritual economy, like the Kirtland bank, into a vibrant anti-Mormon theme. In the earliest moments of encounter, antebellum evangelicals had characterized Joseph Smith as a lazy swindler. In the following decades, they expanded on these initial criticisms about Mormonism's relationship with money. This religious economy of Mormonism had a hodgepodge of disparate, and sometimes contradictory elements, according to antebellum evangelicals. Evangelicals charged Mormonism with mixing God and mammon, and they attacked Joseph Smith as poor, lazy, and intemperate. Antebellum evangelicals portrayed him as a religious crook who used faith to defraud his followers and to profit from their earnest belief. Evangelicals believed Smith organized all of Mormonism's spiritual activities and ecclesiastical structures in a corporate fashion, so religion would work efficiently to enrich its leaders. Turning faith into a big business enriched Joseph Smith, but it left his followers destitute, according to antebellum evangelicals. Like their views of Mormon theology, religious practices, politics, and social structure, antebellum evangelicals considered that Mormonism's economic practices revealed Joseph Smith and his followers as religious extremists.

Antebellum evangelical attacks on Mormonism's spiritual economy and financial methods reveal much more than evangelical intolerance. Evangelicals determined to cast Joseph Smith and his followers as avaricious swindlers show a movement deeply divided about its own relationship to material wealth and its institutional manifestations. Evangelicals criticized Joseph Smith for his obsession with acquiring wealth and celebrity, while at the same time facing an evangelical movement growing in riches and popularity. Through these attacks, they staked claims about the business of evangelicalism. Charges against

Mormonism's economic practices then allowed evangelicals to resolve their own apprehensions about the growing obsession with the accumulation of wealth, the rise of celebrity preachers, and the burgeoning growth of the Benevolent Empire. Using anti-Mormonism to reappraise the evangelical relationship to the market provided a way for evangelicals both opposed and supportive of the reform efforts of antebellum evangelicalism to make a case for their vision of religious identity.

The evangelicals' use of the specter of Mormonism's religious economy to work out their own relationship to the market economy took place alongside significant shifts within the American economy itself. Capitalism underwent large changes during the antebellum period and the market became a larger part of Americans' lives. The early years of the Early National Period saw the emergence of a national market economy connecting Americans into one large market, knitting together the country through the building of canals and railroads, furthering emigration westward, and fostering a risk-taking spirit. In the midst of these tectonic cultural and societal shifts, anti-Mormonism helped evangelicals to locate God amid this economic transformation.[4]

Antebellum evangelicals engaged with the spiritual economy of Mormonism in myriad ways. They did not see it simply as an economic problem, but in the context of changes within capitalism itself. Mormonism's religious economy had social, labor, and economic aspects. While antebellum evangelicals understood Mormonism and mammon through a traditional economic framework, they also saw it through the lens of class, ethnicity, gender, and race. Combining these various fields gave antebellum evangelicals an analytical framework to comprehend and denigrate Mormonism, as well as work out their own views of capitalism.[5]

Criticisms of Joseph Smith's Economic Character

From its earliest appearance, antebellum evangelicals trained their economic criticisms of Mormonism on the character of Joseph Smith, the founder and prophet of the Latter-day Saints. This avalanche of criticisms centered on his lack of character, with antebellum evangelicals variously describing him as poor, lazy, and irresponsible. They saw Smith's low socioeconomic status as indicative of his moral failings. Antebellum evangelicals claimed he refused to honor contracts, did not pay his debts, borrowed vast sums of money, and used his neighbors to obtain money in a duplicitous fashion. Smith finally, according to antebellum evangelicals, depended on others to make a living and often engaged in immoral methods of making money.[6]

Criticisms about Smith's character and his techniques for making money allowed evangelicals to blame Smith's lack of moral principles for his poverty. Some of the earliest descriptions of Mormonism found in evangelical newspapers focused on Smith's lack of money. Other common descriptions of Joseph Smith described him as a "country pauper." Evangelicals chastised his poverty because they saw Smith as unable to obtain or hold on to gainful employment. Smith's idleness quickly became part of the backdrop of Mormonism's origins in the minds of many evangelicals. In 1832, Ancil Beach, a Methodist itinerant, wrote to some acquaintances in western New York seeking information about Mormonism and received a withering set of criticisms about the founder of this new faith from six evangelicals. They described Smith as a man who "has lived in and about Manchester for several years . . . an idle worthless fellow."[7]

The poverty and unwillingness to work placed Smith among the "loose classes of society" in the evangelical imagination. For many antebellum evangelicals, lower-class people shirked their debts and responsibilities. In Eber Howe's *Mormonism Unvailed*, an anti-Mormon text widely circulated among evangelicals, Joseph Capron, a neighbor of Smith's in western New York, testified that Smith's attempts to make money through as little exertion as possible ultimately left him destitute. His poor character meant he was unable and unwilling to meet the financial obligations incurred during his schemes to make money. Smith had hunted for treasure on Capron's land, and on one of these trips, Smith came to Capron with the fabulous news that he had located a chest of gold watches. Smith made numerous attempts to dig up the treasure, taking out multiple loans from Capron and other local residents to finance these endeavors. Capron told Howe that all of these attempts failed. Creditors repossessed Smith's property, and they ran him out of town.[8]

The charges that Joseph Smith was poor because of his base character entered and became heightened by shifting evangelical perceptions of poverty. Puritans believed heads of household should obtain a kind of comfortable economic freedom; they should be able to provide for their families without relying too heavily upon others. Smith's inability to find work, to pay his debts, or to own property marked a lack of competency. By the first decades of the nineteenth century, perceptions of poverty had shifted. Evangelicals of all stripes saw the poor as responsible for their own socioeconomic status. They rejected an older view that explained poverty as part of the natural order or as something external to the debt itself, like misfortune or vindictiveness. Antebellum evangelicals now assumed that the laziness, immorality, lack of education, and criminality of the poor caused their destitution.[9]

Reliance on others did not just make Smith lazy, it also rendered him impotent. His inability to provide for his family made him a failed patriarch, in the minds of antebellum evangelicals. This contingent position led evangelicals to see Smith as unable to exercise control over subordinates, experience freedom from social dependency, or to fulfill his masculine role of provisioning for those in his household. Antebellum evangelicals attacked Smith's manhood when it came to the courting of his wife, Emma. In *Mormonism Unvailed*, the compendium of anti-Mormon charges financed by evangelicals, Isaac Hale gave an affidavit to a "distinguished citizen and a Christian" of western New York. He called Smith "saucy and insolent," and because of the young man's lack of character, in a contest of manly will, Hale denied Smith's request to marry his daughter. Smith ignored this refusal, marrying Emma anyway. After attempting to retrieve his daughter from what he saw as an unwise marriage, Hale offered Smith a job. In his affidavit, Hale claimed Smith refused this offer of honest employment because of his ongoing efforts translating the Book of Mormon. Hale concluded these charges against Smith with a lament that Smith's laziness and delusions would only bring pain and poverty to his daughter.[10]

Antebellum evangelicals likely saw the disagreement between Hale and Smith as not just a battle for Emma's affections, but also as a contest between men. This competition reflected evangelicals' changing views on the market. Individuals like Smith, a wage earner, increasingly depended on wealthier merchants, like Hale, in antebellum America. The emergence of a national market economy and the industrialization of New England had profound consequences for the relationship between people like Hale and Smith. Smith, a poorer white head of household, had his domestic authority eroded. His independence came under threat. Where they once worked alongside one another, this new political economy led to a division between these merchants and wage earners. The criticisms of Smith as a failed wage earner then played into an evangelical movement increasingly identifying with merchant capitalists.[11]

This battle between Hale and Smith as wage earners also fit in with larger redefinition of white masculinity occurring along with the emergence of a new political economy during the antebellum period. Capitalist changes created a generational split, where younger antebellum American men sought to take more financial risks than their forebears. This "go-ahead spirit" was publicly energetic, ambitious, and vigorous. Younger workers saw themselves as full of a vitality that their forebearers lacked.[12]

In the same way that they saw Smith's poverty as a moral failing, antebellum evangelicals saw Smith's poor character encapsulated in his career as a money digger. Joseph Smith had a long history of searching for treasure in his New England home, something commonly accepted by many of his contemporaries in rural Revolutionary New England. Most Americans by the 1830s, however, had come to view treasure seeking and other economic practices based on supernaturalism as uncivilized, coarse, and vulgar. Money diggers used divination, incantations, and other materialistic techniques since the colonial period to seek riches below ground, and these attempts spiked in the decades following the American Revolution because of a widespread economic downturn. Mostly poorer, rural individuals, money diggers believed they could find the treasures of Captain Kidd, Spanish silver mines, lost payrolls from the American Revolution, or other treasures. Seekers usually dug for riches in summer evenings because the heat supposedly caused treasure to rise to the surface of the earth, and they likewise believed the phases of the moon affected their chances of success. Seekers deployed objects, like seer stones or divining rods, to help them locate treasure. Once they located the precise location of the buried treasure, the seeker would engage in a series of incantations and rituals for the purpose of defensive magic. Witnesses suggest that seekers rarely found the treasure they were seeking, but they had an absolute conviction of the reality of their supernatural efforts and experience. Lack of actual success, the growing institutionalization of evangelicalism, and fraudulent behavior all led to a decline in popular support for this supernatural economy and materialistic faith.[13]

The persistence of this magical economy and its centrality to the early history of Mormonism allowed antebellum evangelicals to further denigrate Joseph Smith's character by associating him with the lower classes of people, just as they had done by highlighting his lack of employment. The compiler of *Mormonism Unvailed*, Eber Howe, saw Smith's participation in treasure seeking as an encapsulation of his laziness, indolence, ignorance, and irrationality. Through the inclusion of affidavits and other firsthand accounts, Howe detailed all of the various ways Smith and his family tried to make money through supernatural means. They ran treasure gangs, performed incantations to ward off spirits guarding the buried money, committed ritual animal sacrifice, relied on astrology, and used augury. Hearing about these activities underscored to antebellum evangelicals both the unorthodox religious beliefs and the questionable economic practices of Joseph Smith. Smith and his family employed these practices because of their "miserable" poverty, according to Howe. Since they were "not much disposed to obtain an honest livelihood by labor," they directed the "energies of their minds . . . towards finding where these treasures were concealed, and . . . acquiring their possession."[14]

The criticism of Joseph Smith as a money digger became a common method for antebellum evangelicals to discuss Joseph Smith's character and the ways he defrauded people for the purpose of financial gain. The evangelical apologist Origen Bacheler included testimony from over thirty different Palmyra residents who lambasted the character of the Smith family for their participation in money digging. These residents considered the Smith family "destitute of that moral character, which ought to entitle them to the confidence of any community." What animated much of their feelings was that they had become famous for spending "much of their time in digging for money which they pretended was hid in the earth." The Methodist Minister Richard Livesey similarly described how Joseph Smith and his family were "fortune tellers and money diggers, and that they often had recourse to trick of juggling for the purpose of finding money." Bacheler included several other affidavits, reprinting them from Howe's *Mormonism Unvailed*.[15]

At the same time antebellum evangelicals charged Smith with participating in the unorthodox activity of money digging, they highlighted how he deceived wealthy individuals to support and establish all of his money-making attempts. Martin Harris most notably received this kind of attention, where antebellum evangelicals accused Joseph Smith of misrepresenting religious truth in order to convince Harris to mortgage his farm to pay for the first printing of the Book of Mormon in 1830. Knowing Harris had a propensity for religious eccentricity, several Canandaigua evangelicals, when writing to a Methodist minister in Ohio, claimed Smith had chosen the perfect mark. While a "farmer of respectable property," Harris was either "deluded" or "insane." These men thought that extreme forms of religiosity appealed to Harris, and that Smith used these religious proclivities to sell Harris on the idea of becoming "responsible for an edition of 5000 copies of the Book."[16]

While Harris received the majority of attention directed at Smith's early backers, evangelicals also paid attention to other figures that Smith had misled into providing funding for his money-making endeavors. In their letter to Ancil Beach, the six Canandaigua evangelicals described how Smith had taken advantage of a "Mr. Fish," an "illiterate man of some property." He had supported several of Smith's treasure hunts, but the Canandaigua men described how Smith ultimately left Fish with little to show for his investment. They believed the founder of Mormonism wanted to "consume" what Fish "had gathered by his [own] industry." Fish eventually saw through Smith's subterfuge and cut his financial ties with the whole treasure gang, but that did not hinder Smith's rapacious desire for money. He approached Fish with a final offer, telling him he had "found a box, in digging in the woods, containing some gold plates with Characters upon them which none but himself could decypher." If Fish would only support his translation efforts, then they both would become enormously wealthy.[17]

The deceitful and crooked actions of Smith that allowed antebellum evangelicals to claim that he was a trickster also allowed them to compare Smith to other religious con artists. Among the most common of these comparisons were the French Prophets and Joanna Southcott. What evangelicals found common about all of these swindlers was the placing of their own pecuniary desires over the eternal needs of their followers. In the early years of the evangelical-Mormon encounter, Thomas Skillman, the Presbyterian publisher of the *Western Luminary*, compared Mormonism to "a similar delusion which raged some ten years ago in the case of the 'Pilgrims,'" and their prophet, "Old Isaac . . . [who] came from Canada with a few, and encamped in Woodstock." Many deluded people gathered to him, and they took his proclamations "for divine revelation." Skillman believed these people should have known better, but since they did not, they joined "Old Isaac . . . under the empty promise of being led to the holy land." Under Isaac's influence, they gave all their possessions to their purported prophet, and they then followed him down the Ohio and Mississippi Rivers until they reached the mouth of the Arkansas River. After several weeks on their exodus without any sight of their Promised Land, the survivors of the journey began to grumble about the veracity of "the Prophet's promise." Isaac "led them a little farther and set his staff in the ground at evening." At last, he proclaimed, they had reached the Promised Land. If the people waited until morning, his staff would "put forth bud and blossom." When his disciples awoke the next morning, Skillman was not surprised that "the staff was dry and the Prophet had vanished with all their money." Skilling warned that "from the resemblances between the Pilgrims and the Mormonites in manners and pretensions, we should think Old Isaac had re-appeared in the person of Joe Smith."[18]

The antebellum period had many such confidence men and tricksters, and many of the same evangelical periodicals discussing the early years of Mormonism included detailed depictions of these swindlers. Within the evangelical imagination, the most notorious of these swindlers was Nathaniel "Priest" Wood. During the winter of 1800, many evangelicals may have read how Wood acquired a large following of destitute followers on the frontier of Vermont. These downtrodden individuals believed that he was a prophet because of his ability to uncover hidden riches with a divining rod. Wood claimed other powers too, like the ability to heal the sick, locate water, predict the future, uncover treasure, and designate the chosen people of God. Wood acquired the services of a local diviner to locate deposits of silver and gold that they would use to build a new spiritual home. The myriad and overlapping activities of Wood reinforced for evangelicals the growing interrelationship of religion and economic fraud. His deception threatened the underpinnings of capitalism through a decline in trust. Through accusations of deception and fraud in economic matters, antebellum evangelicals sought to exercise supervision of the border between truth and untruth. This moderation of correct economic practices took place against other faiths and within evangelicalism itself.[19]

Anti-Mormonism and Grift

Seeing Joseph Smith as one of these con artists convinced many evangelicals that profit through underhanded ingenuity was the ultimate aim of Joseph Smith's new faith. The Methodist minister La Roy Sunderland concluded that since a convert to Mormonism imagines "himself an agent of God . . . he may steal or commit any other crime, and fancy himself doing the will of God all the while." Citing congressional testimony concerning the 1838 conflict between Mormonism and Missouri settlers, Sunderland argued Mormonism taught and practiced theft. The religious peripatetic Joshua Himes summed up this evangelical belief that the "one grand design of Mormonism is, to fill the pockets of its advocates with money." In his exposé on what he considered the delusions and monstrosities of Mormonism, Himes explained how pecuniary deceit demonstrated Mormonism's obsession with wealth.

As proof of the nefarious designs of Mormonism, Himes included many examples of converts who gave all their property to the Mormon Church. As someone who sought to restore Christianity to its primitive state, Himes contrasted the profligacy of Smith and the leaders of Mormonism with the asceticism of the apostles of the New Testament Church. Himes reported that Smith had netted several hundred thousand dollars from his new religion, and that he loved to display his wealth conspicuously. A Presbyterian clergyman "from the neighborhood of Smith's residence" had even informed Himes that "the impostor walks with a golden-headed cane, and dresses in the finest style."[20]

Antebellum evangelicals acquired a cynical attitude toward any Mormon attempts to raise money because they viewed the entire purpose of Mormonism as lining the pockets of its leaders. Some eastern antebellum evangelicals noticed that Mormon fundraising efforts increased in the years following the Missouri War. James M'Chesney cynically believed the leaders of Mormonism took advantage of sympathetic feelings toward Mormonism to enrich themselves. While they currently sought to raise money for "the widows and orphans for those who fell in the conflict in Missouri," M'Chesney thought this a misguided endeavor. Soliciting for donations for Mormonism, according to this New York evangelical, would give them strength and power and control the minds of individuals lacking critical faculties.[21]

As Mormonism spread overseas, antebellum evangelicals believed Smith's plans to enrich himself traveled with it. The editors of the Presbyterian *Christian Observer* claimed Mormon missionaries in England had made it their job to persuade the lower classes to sell "their little all" for the sake of the Mormon Church. These evangelical editors worried about the ways the "Mormonite delusions" had "made its appearance among the rural population of that country . . . with considerable and melancholy success." Mormon missionaries had convinced thousands to give up all their possessions, these evangelical editors believed, and the missionaries told them "that you must leave this country and go to America, there to remain with Jesus Christ until this wicked part of the world is destroyed."[22]

Seeing Smith as someone who wanted to use religion to enrich himself by defrauding others, evangelicals believed he used his persuasion, celebrity, and charisma to make tithing a condition of religious salvation. Origen Bacheler and other antebellum evangelicals relayed a story that Joseph Smith believed he alone possessed the magnetic charm to make money from religion. Joshua Himes further argued that Smith used his spiritual power of prophecy to acquire wealth from his followers. He pointed to Smith's collection of prophecies, the *Doctrines and Covenants*, where Smith wrote that "it must needs be that ye save all the money that ye can, and that ye gain all ye can in righteousness." The supposed defrauding of Martin Harris was the exemplar. By mortgaging his home to pay for the initial printing of the Book of Mormon, Harris showed a willingness to give up everything he had to Mormonism because of Smith's powers of spiritual persuasion. Himes wrote that Smith used Harris to convince new converts also to be willing to donate all their possessions to the Mormon Church when they joined Smith's "family." Himes believed Smith also intended to make spiritual swindling a family affair by convincing his followers to provide perpetual financial support to his family. Smith made a prophecy in 1841 that the Latter-day Saints should build their leader a residence, and Himes found it convenient that this same revelation promised this opulent domicile to "Joseph and his seed after him . . . from generation to generation, forever and ever."[23]

The nature of Smith's charismatic leadership made it nearly impossible for his followers to deny him what he wanted, according to antebellum evangelicals. Evangelicals believed Smith used his personality to profit off religion. Ezra Booth, the first well-known Mormon apostate and former Methodist itinerant, claimed Smith's subversion of both religion and the market led him to create his own church. This ex-Mormon charged that Smith would use divine claims to guilt his followers into giving large amounts of money to the Mormon Church. Booth claimed he also used his influence to rule by fiat and act as the sole "voice of the Church." He wrote "the authority of a commandment will easily untie the purse strings of those whose consciences are under their control," and "they find it much easier, and better suited to their dispositions, to write commandments, than to gain a livelihood by the sweat of the brow." When Smith demanded several thousand dollars for an elegant house, for example, Booth thought that Mormon disciples had little choice other than to follow this mouthpiece of God.[24]

Going beyond a simple preoccupation with wealth and the use of personality to solicit donations, evangelicals went further and attacked the leaders of Mormonism for using the structures and subsidiaries of Mormonism to enrich themselves. They accused Smith of turning religion into a big business and using faith to create money-making corporations, just as Joshua Himes noted that when residents of western New York used to come across Smith and Martin Harris in the earliest years of Mormonism, they referred to them as the "Gold Bible Company."[25]

One of the main ways antebellum evangelicals viewed Joseph Smith's scheme to profit off religion was through a calculated process of marketing the Book of Mormon. In *Mormonism Unvailed*, Eber Howe believed that starting a religious publishing concern was always Smith's plan from the start. He wrote that Smith and Martin Harris had made many "profound calculations" about whether or not they would profit from sales of the Book of Mormon. Describing the same initial publication of the Book of Mormon, the Baptist missionary David Marks described Smith's plans in a similar fashion. He wrote derogatorily of Smith's claims that an angel told him exactly how many books to print and at what price to sell them. The angel set the price point of the book at "one dollar and eight cents per copy more than the cost." Marks believed the angel had conveniently dictated the price, so that Smith "*might have the temporal profit*, as well as the spiritual." Evangelicals tracked sales of the Book of Mormon, and David Burnett, a Baptist minister working in Ohio, expressed relief that "the book, an octavo of from 500 to 1000 pages . . . did not meet ready sale." The leaders of Mormonism responded to this lack of demand by sending several hundred copies of the Book of Mormon to eastern Ohio. They considered this area a "better market" for selling their holy book. Burnett saw this move as a good business decision because Mormonism's sacred text quickly became a bestseller in this new market. All of these attacks that Mormonism had turned religion into big business convinced many evangelicals that the leaders of Mormonism had found ways to take advantage of the market in order to enrich themselves. This struggle of how to incorporate religion into a burgeoning market economy was something evangelicals would debate among themselves.[26]

Attacks on Mormon Communitarianism

Antebellum evangelicals did not just criticize Mormonism's spiritual economy for using the market to its own advantage, but they also saw it as subverting the proper economic order through the embrace of the abusive, prejudicial, dangerous, and sinful economic ideology of communitarianism. The leaders of Mormonism experimented with communitarianism in Kirtland, Missouri, and Nauvoo. With a desire to restore Christianity to its primitive beginnings, the leaders of Mormonism followed the early church's practice of holding all property in common. Converts usually deeded all their property to the church, or they would sell everything they had and gave the proceeds to the church. Smith and the other leaders of Mormonism controlled this central fund, and they would dole out land, goods, and money as they saw fit. Mormon congregants in return would receive enough for their own needs and for them to be able to assist the poor. Mormonism's leaders also required many of their members to follow the law of consecration; they had to sacrifice their time, talents, and property for the building of the kingdom of God, like the temples at Kirtland and Nauvoo.[27]

Evangelicals saw these communitarian arrangements first as a gross exploitation of vulnerable populations. In his letters to the *Ohio Star*, Ezra Booth remarked that because of the harmful nature of communitarianism, the mass of Mormon converts could not be held liable for their poor socioeconomic status. The followers of Smith "are actually poor," he believed, because of Smith's pursuit and enactment of a "different course as it relates to economy and industry." Booth claimed that following this path imprisoned and embittered converts by taking away all their money and by making economic livelihood dependent upon the whims of the leaders of Mormonism. The various appendages of Mormonism reinforced the abusive and capricious nature of communitarianism. Booth saw nefarious purposes in the establishment of the "Lord's printing press" and the "Lord's store-house," designed to support the growing Mormon population in the West. Through "these two grand engines, they expect to make the wicked feel the weight of their tremendous power."[28]

Since communitarianism so detrimentally dispossessed Mormon converts of all their possessions, evangelicals largely focused their ire on the leaders of Mormonism. James Briggs, one of the Stone-Campbell sponsors of *Mormonism Unvailed*, described Mormonism's converts as "a poor deluded people who deserve our pity and not our contempt." Truman Coe, a Presbyterian minister, believed that "many of the common people are industrious," and they could earn a proper living, if only their leaders allowed them. He found that the establishment of communitarian economic systems had forced most of Smith's followers into a state of "extreme indigence." When he spent several days at the Mormon community of Kirtland, Coe lamented that he saw the followers of Smith living in a "grotesque assemblage of hovels and shanties."[29]

Antebellum evangelicals believed not only that the practice of sharing all things led to exploitation of the poor, but they also saw communitarianism creating harmful inequalities of wealth within Mormonism. The leaders grew richer, while the mass of converts grew poorer. Thomas Campbell, an evangelical clergyman from northern Ohio, saw this phenomenon manifested at the Mormon community of Kirtland. He explained that "the society . . . [has] every thing in common" because of "interested motives of temporal belief." In *Mormonism Unvailed*, Howe argued that this economic system gave the poor a false sense of hope. When Mormonism first gathered in Ohio, a land rush took place. Wealthier Mormons acquired the best plots, according to Howe, leaving the impoverished with nothing, but the poor continued to arrive hoping to receive their promised reward because they expected to enjoy "all things in common."[30]

The charges about Mormonism's economic practices entered an evangelical milieu that viewed communitarianism as heresy and socially disordering. History taught evangelicals to look askance at communitarian attempts. This explains why the Anabaptists of sixteenth-century Europe figured prominently in evangelical critiques of the Mormon spiritual economy. Communitarianism also had an immediate valence. Mormonism was just one of many experiments in communalism in antebellum America. These include Shakers, Harmonists, Fourierists, as well as the followers of Robert Owen, George Rapp, John Humphrey Noyes, and many others. Antebellum evangelicals viewed all these communities with unease or uncertainty because of their blending of the temporal and spiritual, as well as their challenges to the nascent market economy. Communitarianism also represented patriarchy gone wrong. As evangelicalism became increasingly dominated by women in the pews, women participating in and leading reform efforts, and a more feminine faith in general, evangelical calls for female submission increased. For a patriarchal culture with strict patterns of inheritance, the idea of a community of goods threatened to undermine a male-dominated evangelical society.[31]

Antebellum evangelicals most commonly compared Mormonism's shared economy to the religious community at Munster of the 1530s. Comparisons to these early Anabaptists was common because it provided a way for antebellum evangelicals to characterize Mormonism and many of their coreligionists as engaging in an irrational kind of religious mania. Led by charismatic prophets that reminded evangelicals of Joseph Smith, Anabaptist revolutionaries seized the town, and these religious radicals preceded to enact their version of a religious utopia by abolishing all private property and embracing the practice of polygamy. When Thomas Campbell and other evangelicals compared Mormonism to these radical reformers, they worried history might repeat itself. Like the Anabaptists, Mormonism taught "the distinctions occasioned by birth, rank, or wealth should be abolished, that all christians should put their possessions into one common stock" and "live together in that state of equality." Evangelicals also drew comparisons between Mormonism's economic commune and Shaker economic principles. In *Mormonism Unvailed*, Eber Howe highlighted the ways that both groups placed all their followers' property into a common account, and that both promised prosperity to their followers if they embraced this economic system.[32]

Antebellum evangelicals finally believed the practice of Mormon communitarianism posed a socioeconomic threat. It hurt those most at the bottom of society—widows and orphans. Writing in the early 1830s, Joshua Himes reported that when two "defenceless females" converted to Mormonism, they turned over all their property to the church after having "have been led away by these false doctrines." They gave a combined $2,300 "to go into the general stock." One of these women became critically ill with consumption, and the leaders of Mormonism saw an opportunity to take advantage of her in her worsening state. Rather than allowing her to see her friends and relatives in her final hours, Himes said that they refused her entreaties. Even money purposefully set aside for her burial costs, Mormon leaders claimed for their church. Himes used this story as evidence the leaders of Mormonism "swindled" these women and others "out of their property and . . . from their comfortable homes to endure the perils of a journey of about two thousand miles, by these *ignorant fanatics*."[33]

The way antebellum evangelicals understood the Mormon practice of sharing all property finally led them to see it threatening the social fabric by turning families against one another. The editors of the Presbyterian *New York Evangelist* warned that communitarianism had divided some families, and in others, mothers have been obliged to follow their "deluded husbands," or they "adopt the disagreeable alternative, of parting with them and their children." While traveling throughout the interior of the country, the itinerant evangelical Nancy Towle concluded that rather than producing an Edenic paradise, Mormonism's commitment to sharing property led children to cease following the God-given commandment to honor their fathers and mothers. That upheaval of social hierarchies subverted the God-given relationships of the Bible because abolition of property had caused "every such member . . . [to] forsake, father, mother, wife and children." These attacks on the communitarianism of Mormonism convinced many antebellum evangelicals that the leaders of Mormonism had found a way to subvert the correct workings of the market, a similar struggle to one they would deal with internally.[34]

Evangelicals and the Kirtland Safety Society

All of the charges against Mormonism's economic practices that denigrated the character of Joseph Smith and characterized the ultimate aim of Mormonism as profit-making came together with the rise and fall of the Kirtland anti-banking safety society. The leaders of Mormonism created this bank to address the relatively common problem of lack of currency on the western frontier of the United States, a problem that led Smith to run short of money to pay for the laborers and materials for the large temple being built at Kirtland. He directed some of his subordinates to obtain a charter and raise the necessary capital for their bank. Smith, with his grandiose plans, wanted his bank to be the largest in Ohio. He planned a capitalization of over four million dollars, so he quickly signed up several hundred subscribers. These subscribers had little hard money to commit, so most pledged whatever land they had to the bank.[35]

Many groups and individuals on the frontier in the antebellum period established unsanctioned wildcat banks to provide needed capital for their enterprises. Antebellum Americans often turned to paper bills from unregulated nonbank institutions during periods of economic downturn or when state regulations prohibited legal banks from circulating currency. Known as shinplasters because of the poor quality of the paper money, these bills operated on the fringes of legality and undermined American confidence in paper money. Dismissed in some places, these paper bills often found acceptance in places, such as the western frontier, lacking confidence or quantity of government-sanctioned currency.[36]

The leaders of Mormonism did not wait to see if the state of Ohio would approve their proposed bank charter before beginning operation. They began to print money and offer credit in 1837. Despite the bank's acting like a legitimate financial institution, the inherent difficulties of starting a bank—lack of knowledge and poor funding—combined with political animus led the Ohio Legislature to deny the Safety Society an official charter. Joseph Smith responded creatively by rebranding the bank. No longer a normal bank, he named it an "anti-banking company." Smith and the other leaders of the bank collected all of the already-printed currency and affixed the word "anti" before the word "banking." Subscribers evidently did not embrace this attempt at rebranding because depositors immediately began to attempt to exchange their paper notes for hard currency. Within just a few weeks, the bank ran out of capital. The value of the existing notes plummeted to zero and the subscribers who had put up the bulk of the initial capital lost their entire investment. After limping along for a few month, Joseph Smith publicly disowned the entire enterprise in the late summer of 1837.[37]

Although the Kirtland bank had a relatively short existence, it took on an outsized role in the antebellum evangelical concerns about Mormonism's economic practices. Evangelicals used the bank to reinforce anti-Mormon charges of financial deception in the name of religion, the contemptible character of Joseph Smith, and the project of counterfeiting currency by the leaders of Mormonism. Joshua Himes pronounced the officers of the bank "guilty of downright swindling." He believed that the leaders of Mormonism had planned this conspiracy to defraud their followers for years. Their sinister plan, he believed, began with the establishment of a mercantile house to make the mass of Mormon converts indebted to them. Since Kirtland and its environs had little cash, the leaders of Mormonism paid their workers with promissory notes, or they allowed them to purchase goods on credit. When the debts of these workers came due, few had the money to repay them. Himes argued that Smith then economically exploited the workers through the chartering of his bank. This new bank ultimately had the same effect as the commercial house. It enriched Smith, but impoverished the mass of Mormon converts. This did not surprise Himes, who concluded "as regards the pecuniary transactions of the Mormons . . . Smith uses his power for his own benefits."[38]

Opposition to the Mormon bank and the economic practices of Mormonism bound together evangelicals by giving them the common antagonist of a religious crook. James M'Chesney and David Reese were both prominent New York evangelicals. They disagreed on a number of issues, mostly related to the size and scope of the Benevolent Empire. What these evangelical adversaries could agree on was that the Mormon bank was part of a larger cultural moment of self-aggrandizement. They both believed ignorance had entered the "laudable enterprises" of medicine and politics because of the selfish desire of deceit and knavery. Deceitful individuals in these various professions used advertising and other marketing techniques to prey on weak-willed individuals in order to build up their own net worth and power. M'Chesney and Reese believed the Mormon bank acted in the same fashion, making explicit comparisons between these similarly deceptive movements. Just as politicians used every trick and tool of deceit possible to "gain the ascendency over their fellows by every artifice in their power," the leaders of the Kirtland bank acquired wealth and prestige through the same means.[39]

Assisted largely by the reportage of E. G. Lee, antebellum evangelicals came to understand the actions of the Mormon bank in the context of the antebellum practice of counterfeiting currency. Lee was a Philadelphian who evidently challenged several Mormon elders at a meeting in his hometown. While his precise motivations and personal background are unknown, the text of Lee's response reveals how he characterized Mormonism as a financial fraud for locally specific and religious reasons. Self-identified as a Protestant Christian of some stripe, but apparently not a member of any organized religious group, Lee viewed contemporary Mormonism as "dishonest swindling." To demonstrate the disgraceful conduct of Smith and the other leaders of Mormonism, Lee reprinted a letter by Cyrus Smalling, an excommunicated member of the Mormon Church. In this account, Smalling charged the leaders of Mormonism with opening up a bank to pay off a large number of debts, acquiring a large quantity of bills for "filing and signing." When people began to grow suspicious of the bank notes issued at Kirtland, Smalling commented that Smith used his church to get out of his financial difficulties. Mormon missionaries exchanged Kirtland Safety Society notes in places unaware of their true value at the same time they attempted to attract new converts throughout the nation. Smalling said that people caught on to this subterfuge, and Smith had to search for other solutions. He furthered his deception, according to Smalling, by having 100–200 boxes made. Smith filled these boxes with all the lead and scrap metal he could gather in Kirtland, and then wrote $1,000 on each box. When people arrived to investigate the financial stability of the bank, Smith would show them a bank vault filled with over $200,000. Smalling concluded that if Smith would put all of this work into fashioning these Potemkin lockboxes, then the leaders would manipulate anyone or anything for financial gain. Reprinted by Lee, this account circulated widely in evangelical circles.[40]

Antebellum evangelicals deployed a diverse and sometimes contradictory set of charges against Mormon economic practices. The claims that Joseph Smith was an indolent money digger who used the black arts to locate treasure defined Mormonism's spiritual economy as premodern. By hunting for treasure, Smith participated in a materialistic faith that responded, in part, to the anxieties created by the emerging market economy. The economic order in antebellum American had become more complex, impersonal, and interdependent. Participants in the supernatural economy, like Joseph Smith, recognized that their economic livelihood rested on distant factors far beyond their control. Recovering treasure promised quick wealth and a sense of power. Existing alongside and sometimes uneasily with this premodern characterization was a more modern critique that claimed Joseph Smith was too good at the market. Evangelicals saw Smith's accumulation of wealth driving the creation and operation of Mormonism. His counterfeiting, exploitation, profiteering, and speculation allowed him to exploit the burgeoning national market economy for his own gain.

Evangelicalism Goes Corporate

Much more than religious or economic animosity drove these modern concerns about Smith's malfeasance and the economic practices of Mormonism. Criticisms of Mormonism and its founder on this score echo concerns about evangelicals' own relationship to the market. The overlap between their charges against Mormon economic behavior and evangelicals' criticisms of their coreligionists registered a profound anxiety that evangelicalism had become a big business. Evangelicals charged one another with using the market for their own advantage, just as they had attacked Joseph Smith for religious profiteering. Evangelicals had, by the early nineteenth century, accumulated wealth, developed celebrity preachers, and founded large institutions.[41]

Of particular concern for evangelicals concerned about the direction of their own movement were the obsession with wealth and the quest for celebrity within evangelical churches and the Benevolent Empire, the same charges used against Mormonism. These problems arose because of the very successes of the evangelical movement. Born-again Christians had become a pervasive cultural force by the 1830s. They attracted an enormous amount of wealth, as increasing numbers of its members entered the middle class, as its denominations attracted thousands of converts, and as religious businesses flourished. Churches and revivals became popular entertainment activities as preachers used dramatic displays of theatrical preaching and commercial techniques to engage their audiences. Specific churches became associated with individual preachers, as in the case of Henry Ward Beecher and his Plymouth Church in Brooklyn. Individual preachers consequently became personally popular and drew converts based on their ability to influence people. Evangelical preachers even became some of the best-paid entertainers in antebellum America.[42]

Antebellum evangelicals also dominated other parts of the marketplace through the creation of corporate institutions, like the burgeoning publishing industry. An insatiable desire for printed material combined with technological advances allowed evangelical publishing houses to saturate the country with millions of books, tracts, and newspapers that grossed millions of dollars annually. Evangelical print culture sold so well throughout the country that it had become a kind of publishing monopoly by the 1830s. Antebellum evangelicals acquired this market dominance, in part, by adopting popular styles and methods of writing, publication, and distribution.[43]

The largest institutional part of the business of evangelicalism was the Benevolent Empire. The evangelical surge of the early nineteenth century led to the creation of a myriad of voluntary societies. What started off as small, local organizations dedicated to a single social or economic problem became large, national and transnational associations by the 1810s and 1820, enterprises dedicated to broad-based social and political reform. These efforts included the publication of Bibles and religious tracts, the establishment of Sunday schools, the passage of Sabbatarian laws, the reformation of drunks and prostitutes, and the foreign and domestic missions movement.[44]

The growing wealth, celebrity, and institutionalization of evangelicalism allowed evangelical Christians to reshape the United States in their own vision, but these developments did not proceed without complication and debate. Segments of the evangelical community became concerned about their movement's engagement with the marketplace and the accumulation of wealth by preachers and organizations, in the same way as Joseph Smith and Mormonism did. Their anxieties tapped into decades-old concerns about how wealthy, established ministers and churches understood the relationship between God and mammon. In the years surrounding the American Revolution, a group of ministers opposed to the Congregationalist Standing Order saw seminaries as sites for the raising of vast sums of money to enrich those already in power. As part of their challenge to authority, tradition, and education, antebellum evangelical populists attacked the pomp and preening of the established orthodoxy, mainly the established churches of New England. Mostly Calvinists, these members of these Congregationalist churches had long held privileged positions in New England towns, and their ministers had grown wealthy from state support. To the leaders of this popular religious movement, the Congregational Standing Order represented ecclesiastical tyranny and using religion to profit from faith.[45]

What many evangelical populist leaders criticized these Calvinist clergymen for during the early decades of the nineteenth century was turning religion into a profit-making enterprise, like Mormonism. Elias Smith, a minister within the Christian Connection movement, railed against the wealth obtained by the "priestcraft," missionary societies, and seminaries. He derided the ultraorthodox Andover Seminary as a place where "*large salaries* can be raised, or large sums given per month, for *missionary labors*." Freeborn Garretson made similar comments about Lyman Beecher's obsession with obtaining fame and fortune. This populist Methodist clergymen believed Beecher had made a "trade of the gospel." Garretson accused many of Beecher's colleagues of being failed lawyers, who sought out another high-paying profession. Once settling on the "glimmering profession of religion," they "say they are called to the ministry." He claimed they chose a pulpit not based upon a calling, but on finding a "salary to their inclination." The Baptist minister John Leland composed a poem describing how clergymen had created seminaries as places to channel their sons into lives of wealth and leisure. Describing the "Modern Priest," Leland lyrically wrote that preaching had become a "science and a trade" to make many "grand estates."[46]

These populist criticisms of clerical wealth coincided with a burgeoning evangelical anxiety about the prosperity produced by the emerging market economy. A growing number of evangelicals thought that material gain became sinful when it breached the limits of Christian teaching. But in *The Bible in the Counting-House*, Henry Boardman provided a theological justification for evangelicals who believed making money was not incompatible with their faith. Boardman was the minister of a wealthy Presbyterian congregation, and he taught a pecuniary moderation he hoped would appeal to his wealthy congregants. "To say for example," he mused, "that the Bible prohibits all indulgence in luxuries would be taking very ambiguous and dangerous ground." As his congregation undoubtedly believed, he saw commerce serving an important role in a civilized society. The very existence of luxury goods after all required the employment of thousands of individuals in Philadelphia alone. Simply condemning all luxury and wealth would unintentionally force many individuals into almshouses. Boardman also wrestled with the simple idea of how to define luxury. Ostentatious displays of wealth to one person also might come across as inconspicuous and subtle to another person. What one society has considered luxuries, he believed, "will in turn become common place comforts."[47]

Where Boardman worried was when people would begin to see money as the sole key to success. He thought this misplaced confidence in mammon eroded the foundation of the Christian witness. Financial speculation drew his ire because money "which is hurriedly made, is wastefully expended." People who see the accumulation of wealth as their chief purpose adopt that same sensibility of contest in their social life. Conspicuous consumption, he believed, could be seen as a marker of virtue and lead to sinful fanaticism.[48]

The Congregationalist minister and domestic missionary Leonard Bacon likewise expressed an anxiety about the national market economy by contrasting an honest merchant with the misleading speculator. Merchants transferred commodities from the producer to the consumer, giving an "augmented value to the commodities thus transferred." Speculators did the opposite. They only had an "acquaintance with the arts of panic and excitement, whose hopes of success depend on the skill with which he calculates the expansibility of a bubble and the change of its bursting."[49]

Albert Barnes expressed similar discomfort over the desire for wealth. While much of his preaching and writing praised the profit-making efforts of Philadelphians, this New School Presbyterian also lamented the single-minded focus on money many of these individuals displayed. This "passion" for wealth caused his fellow Presbyterians to forsake their families, schools, and churches to travel west to find increased fortune. Contrasting the deep and firm connections in the East with the shallow and thin associations of the West, Barnes believed the lack of rootedness would cause people to give up on the laws of the Sabbath and to begin to act dishonestly and unfairly toward others.[50]

In addition to a discomfort with the accumulation of wealth, some evangelicals saw examples of vainglorious greed in the form of their own celebrity preachers, similar to the ways they saw Joseph Smith. The Methodist author James M'Chesney saw this problem at his own church, when a new minister arrived to serve the Washington Street Church in Brooklyn. This young preacher, M'Chesney charged, sought to enrich himself through an abundance of personal charm. The popularity of this minister had the consequence of making him unaccountable to any ecclesiastical authorities. When this young minister asked for donations for pet projects or an increase in his salary, no one could deny him or provide oversight because of his popularity. M'Chesney charged that these kinds of ministers would hold, "with a death-like grasp" an ability and a passion to demand money.[51]

Antebellum evangelicals had longstanding anxieties about the ways the fame of individual preachers could make it more difficult for people to hear the Gospel. The Primitivist Walter Scott contrasted the pursuit of celebrity and the truth of the Gospel. He claimed the "chief and leading cause" of the rise of sects was the adoption of men with "extraordinary zeal and self denial, for superior endowments of body and mind, or for exalted and singular acts of piety and benevolence." The popularity of a single minister was, Scott charged, the reason why many churches had the names of the places they began. This kind of celebrity, he believed, made humans the locus of authority.[52]

The concern over the ways celebrity could create sinful motivations in evangelical preachers permeated the western frontier, and in particular, the areas experiencing the growth of Mormonism. The editors of the *Western Recorder*, a religious newspaper for members of the Methodist Church, warned their readers about the effects of preaching with the goal of acquiring fame. Told in the form of a dream, this parable relates that a gospel minister of evangelical principles fell asleep after a long day of preaching. He had a dream about an encounter with a ministerial friend who was damned because he preached the Gospel for the "applause of mortals." Contrasting ministers who preach to please people and become popular versus those who do so for pure reasons, the same editors made a sarcastic list of how to preach to become popular. Popular preaching was showily erudite with a fine delivery. The well-liked minister should also be personally attractive, wear "clothes by the best tailors," and preach sermons people want to hear.[53]

The Financial Power of the Benevolent Empire

But it was the size and scope of the Benevolent Empire, the network of antebellum reform societies, that came in for the most forceful challenges from evangelicals concerned about their movement's direction with respect to the market economy. They saw it turning religion into big business. Because of their growing prominence and increasing economic power, the largest of these societies, the American Bible Society (ABS) and the American Tract Society (ATS), received the bulk of this attention from proponents and critics of the business of evangelicalism. The ABS had begun operating in the second decade of the nineteenth century and by the middle of the century, it had organized the publication and circulation of over 40 million Bibles and hundreds of millions of pages of tracts. The leaders of the ABS believed their efforts could hasten the Second Coming through the universal spread of the Gospel, so they acted with unbridled optimism. The Bible Society showcased their economic prowess in 1853 when they relocated their offices from Nassau Street to Astor Place. The society's new home contained multiple steam-powered printing presses, a bindery, and a salesroom with modern display cases. The directors of the ABS believed this building would provide conspicuous evidence that their organization was the preeminent organization committed to reform in the antebellum period.[54]

Critics of the business of evangelicalism believed the ABS had ceased to act with selfless motives and only cared about money and power. The ABS had acted immorally, they charged, by pressuring its auxiliaries to stop distributing Bibles for free. While the representatives of the society had originally given away Bibles and tracts for the purpose of saturating the country with religious texts, the ABS now wanted its auxiliaries to begin taking payment for tracts and Bibles. An anonymous pamphleteer had traced the ABS's movement toward religious profiteering to the moment it stopped providing Bibles "without money and without cost." In this new mode of distribution, the auxiliaries would request a certain number of copies of the Bible from the ABS. These petitions to the ABS came with the promise of a future donation from the auxiliary society, but these payments always outstripped the cost of the Bibles. An anonymous critic of the ABS used the East Tennessee Bible Society and the Steuben County Bible Society to prove that the society profited handsomely from this new arrangement. The East Tennessee Society had paid the ABS $1,900 for 1,700 books, while the Steuben County group had received over 110 Bibles from the national organization, while sending back $147 to the ABS. While the ABS claimed to be giving away nearly $10,000 annually in free Bibles, this pamphleteer said that the financial numbers provided by the society itself proved this claim a lie. Instead of being a "benefit to the community as it was generally supposed," one disgruntled former supporter complained, the ABS had become "injurious to the public at large" and sat like an "incubus" on the body politic.[55]

While religious profiteering afflicted the entire society, like evangelical critics of Joseph Smith this former supporter of the ABS blamed the managers and directors of the society for a sinful spirit. He described the society's effort to place a Bible in the home of every American as a scheme to "convert" an accumulation of "immense numbers of Bibles . . . into cash as soon as possible." This critic believed accomplishing this effort in as rapid a fashion as desired would only be possible with the aid of a gullible public and a willing consumer base because ABS managers "called on all Christians to aid in this scheme, not only with their own individual funds, but with any that they could raise from their dependents or neighbors." The choice of where to spend money revealed that the ABS was more concerned about pecuniary matters than salvation. The critic of the ABS noted how in the first years of the society, the managers did not focus on using their funds to provide Bibles for the indigent. They instead purchased stock in banks and insurance companies. While this may have been a good financial decision, according to this critic, it demonstrated how the society had departed "from the plans laid originally before the public." The managers would even refuse to accept money if it meant placing limits on their ability to swell their coffers, as they did when they publicly refused a donation of several thousand dollars from one of the British Bible Societies that came with strings attached.[56]

This embrace of unlimited profit, according to the anonymous critic of the ABS, occurred alongside efforts to hide its finances and to spend extravagantly. The organization had received nearly five hundred thousand dollars in donations by 1830, but the anonymous critic of the ABS thought the opaqueness of the institution made keeping track of their finances difficult. Since the ABS claimed a substantial operating deficit without any financial transparency, he wondered who could test the accuracy of this statement. The anonymous pamphleteer used the society's records to perform his own calculations of the financial benevolence of the ABS. He determined the ABS ran a profit of over $170,000 in the operation of "selling Bibles and Testaments" during its existence. While not a substantial sum, he believed it ludicrous the society could claim poverty. After all, he charged, the ABS owned significant amounts of property in stereotype plates, buildings, and land. How the ABS spent money also drew the ire of the anonymous critic, particularly the large salaries paid to the ABS's auxiliaries, agents, and other staff. The ABS even paid all the expenses of auxiliaries, including "postages, fuel, lights, [and] stationery." This critic of the ABS found it convenient that paying these costs allowed agents and other staff to claim low annual salaries, while actually making more than they would in secular enterprise.[57]

This critic of the ABS charged the society with acting like a private business through its marketing and selling of salvation to an audience in desperate need of eternal security. The ABS decided in 1819 to urge their auxiliaries to sell Bibles, in addition to donating them. In his *Exposé*, the author of the critique of the ABS lambasted this decision, arguing that the managers expected their auxiliaries to make a profit from selling the Bible with a "pertinacity worthy of a better cause." The managers of the ABS believed people who paid for their Bible would be more likely to read it because they would be invested in reading it, and not see it as merely a gift of charity. This anonymous critic disagreed. He charged that when the Bible became a commodity, pulpits became book stalls and churches became bookstores. Young itinerants no longer promoted the eternal word of God for its own sake, but they became mere peddlers of goods with sales quotas, he wrote. This critic believed that selling things that perished changed the character of these innocent ministers. They became no better than traveling salesmen, aggressively going from home to home peddling their product.[58]

Auxiliaries further took a business-minded approach to the selling of scripture by dividing cities and towns into potential profit sectors. This became increasingly true as the ABS moved from local auxiliaries to agents paid and supervised by the national office. The anonymous critic found the society not only enlisted auxiliaries and pious young men, but "duly considering the great weight and influence which justly belongs to the female sex in this community, a direct appeal was made to them." Adopting a ravenous appetite for profit, this critic accused the ABS of defeminizing women, turning them into "hawkers and peddlers for the Institution" by convincing them that they were "doing God's service by . . . peddling the Holy Scriptures."[59]

Comparing auxiliaries to book peddlers and clerks worked within changing perceptions of both professions. Traveling around the city, booksellers led a kind of double life. While they often advertised didactic literature, some also offered more salacious materials. Moving around urban spaces gave these individuals familiarity with people in private spaces, and antebellum evangelicals increasingly worried this intimate knowledge of the city would lead peddlers of print to spread licentiousness or commit crime. Male business clerks represented a different kind of threat, as antebellum American society increasingly saw them as possessing masculine and feminine traits. Clerks acted with a masculine heterosexual rapaciousness, while they also had an intimate understanding of female desire. This antebellum critic of the ABS seized on how these newly created clerks lingered and operated on the margins of society as a third sex.[60]

The economic practices of the ABS had sizable successes in spreading evangelical Christianity, but this anonymous critic of the society thought that it came with an insatiable desire to obtain wealth and prestige. The society's constitution forced it to publish the Bible without any kind of commentary that might be used to induce commercial activity. The critic of the ABS cynically knew that the ABS would not "alter or abrogate" the Bible because "this would set the religious community in a ferment, and lose them a great part of the immense influence they had obtained." They then had to devise another plan to continue making money that did not involve publishing popular sectarian literature. Managers of the ABS also schemed to obtain additional funds by raising their status in the eyes of elites who already donated to the "treasury of this Institution." They needed to show wealthy elites that the society "herded not with the poor and lowly of the world." Fashioning themselves as cultural insiders, the ABS inserted correspondence from famous and well-regarded members of society into their fundraising appeals. In these paeans to the ABS, "arch-bishops and bishops, ministers and prime-ministers, earls, dukes, and lords" lavished "praise on the Institution and its Agents." They detailed "the brilliancy of show made at their anniversary meetings, and the fine speeches delivered by the high dignitaries of church and state." As if this preening was not enough, the anonymous ABS critic commented that the inclusion of all these inserts had cost the society over $5,000, money that could have provided many free Bibles to those in need.[61]

In addition to the criticism that the economic practices of the ABS used the market too well, some evangelicals believed the society had skewed the efficient operation of the market through the creation of a monopoly on the publishing, distribution, and selling of the Bible. The evangelical Episcopalian Herman Hooker believed that if publishing became the product of "individual enterprise, the price would fall to the lowest *living* point, and there would be hands and capital enough to engage in producing them at one half they now cost the Church in charity." Hooker put significant energy into critiquing one of the other major bodies of the Benevolent Empire, the American Tract Society. He believed the ATS had created a tax on legitimate religious publishing through its actions and its extravagant spending. In his attack on the tract society, Hooker charged the ATS had become a "bad economy of sacred funds" by enacting taxes on the "honest industry of men engaged in the book business." This society printed and sold their publications "so near their cost" that all "private enterprise and capital must fail in any attempt to publish at similar rates." Hooker did not believe benevolent work had to be conducted in this kind of market-skewing fashion. If they "used the economy that good men should," then the ATS would still "be left with means enough to do a great and successful business," instead of enriching the wealthy. Because of the ABS's economic practices, private sources could no longer sell religious books profitably, so wholesale book dealers looked to popular literature for potential areas of profit, and he considered the increased printing of children's books as "the distinguishing folly of the age" because publishers now had to "appeal to the children through gilt and pictures."[62]

By crowding out legitimate actors, evangelical critics of the Benevolent Empire feared that its monopolistic growth would inevitably lead to a single-minded focus on profit-seeking that would ignore the preaching of the Word. An 1832 convention of Maryland Reformed Baptists issued an address claiming that the Benevolent Empire had created "pharisaical, money-loving, money-hunting, money-begging, mesmerizing, passion-exciting" religionists. This misplaced focus led the various appendages of the Benevolent Empire to show partiality by supporting only those enterprises under their authority. Antimission Baptists thought this not just sinful, but also bad practice. Money flowed from more deserving and experienced preachers to novices willing to accept the authority of the business of evangelicalism. The need for funds to support the Benevolent Empire necessarily caused these young ministers to focus only on places where they could easily collect the funds that the Benevolent Empire required them to produce on a monthly basis. In urban centers, they could attract the most attention and gain additional dues-paying members to the society. The Maryland Baptists contrasted this young coterie's love of money to the example of Christ, who willingly visited the highways and byways to preach the Gospel.[63]

Anti-Mormonism and the Evangelical Relationship to Capitalism

These fault lines within evangelical circles over their movement's relationship to the market meant that evangelical objections to Mormonism's economic practices represented more than just visceral rejection of a heretical faith. Their own checkered history with wealth, celebrity, and the market economy allowed evangelicals to use charges against Mormonism's economic practices to advance their own religious program. Both the charges against Mormonism's economic practices and their use in internal evangelical politics shared a common concern that their respective sinners used faith to make a profit and went beyond the limits of a moral economic system. Both sets of malefactors profited off the weakest members of society and acted like speculators through the immoral production of wealth. The charges deployed against Mormonism then provided a language for evangelicals to express their concern with their own movement's relationship between God and mammon, largely registering in their opposition or support for the Benevolent Empire and through the blaming of their coreligionists for the rise of Mormonism.

Critics of the Benevolent Empire not surprisingly registered their displeasure by frequently noting the similarity of the various voluntary societies to Mormonism. Evangelicals criticized religious entrepreneurs in their own ranks just as they attacked Joseph Smith for strutting around town in fine clothes with a gold-headed cane selling salvation to the highest bidder. The uses of this variety of anti-Mormonism varied based upon topic and inclination, but in general, these individuals had reservations about the way the evangelical movement had acquired power and wealth through the corporate-like activities of the Benevolent Empire. Both loved wealth and fame, engaged in religious profiteering, encouraged spiritual apathy, caused disagreement, and discouraged innovation through their economic practices.[64]

The concern with profit was not the only problem for the antagonists of the Benevolent Empire and Mormonism. Critics also believed shareholders in the business of evangelicalism and the followers of Joseph Smith shared a scheme to enrich themselves at the expense of converts. The Methodist James M'Chesney saw leaders concerned with wealth at the helm of both evangelicalism and Mormonism. He worried the "cause of the Redeemeer has been in great measure under the management of mere religious mountebanks." M'Chesney complained ministers in both groups had made their spiritual calling into a "means for obtaining a livelihood" or "a business." Both acted like charlatans because of their false motives. A love of money resulted in evangelicals "destitute of its power, and knowing but little, if any thing of its experimental influence." While the church may end up with all the outward manifestations of religious success—good singing, quality prayers, and exciting preaching—the "influence of wealth," he argued, will never result in a "thriving spiritual condition." Evidence for the negative consequences of wealth was the faith founded by Smith, according to M'Chesney.[65]

Critics of the Benevolent Empire, like M'Chesney, believed a focus on the accumulation of riches encouraged religious laziness. He believed Mormonism ridiculed "the indolence of many of our preachers." M'Chesney charged that the economic activities of his coreligionists had provided an opening for the growth of Mormonism. Followers of Joseph Smith deliberately contrasted their chaste and frugal lifestyles with those of evangelicals by "pretending to work with their own hands for their support" and boasting of "meeting in cellars and barns, while we have gorgeous and extravagant temples."[66]

A focus on wealth, prestige, and celebrity within evangelicalism also encouraged the rise of Mormonism by pitting fellow believers against one another, according to this Methodist critic of the Benevolent Empire. M'Chesney believed socioeconomic status had become a marker of faithfulness within evangelicalism. The wealthiest became the sole arbiters of truth. The final stage of this obsession with pride and wealth was confusion, bickering, and the ultimate breakup of evangelical churches. The irony of this development, he wrote, was that it was this very kind of selfishness and "proud . . . back-biting" that had allowed the rise of Mormonism and rendered evangelicalism impotent in the face of the growing Mormon threat.[67]

These evangelical critics of the Benevolent Empire further believed members of their own movement had become overly reliant on the tools and techniques of business in their religious efforts. "Knowledge" of the "various branches of business . . . has not saved us," M'Chesney wrote. An "improper confidence, and conduct" with these tools had instead led to a boastful and shameful attitude.[68]

Stakeholders in the Benevolent Empire ironically responded to their critics with the same technique of comparing them to the wealth-obsessed Mormons. Their antagonists believed those opposed or indifferent to the Benevolent Empire had let their own greed, sectarian feelings, or short-sightedness prevent them from participating in a common good, according to proponents of these supranational voluntary associations. A. W. Corey, a leader within the American Sunday-School Union and the American Home Mission Society, argued the religious fanaticism associated with camp meetings and revivals had inevitably led evangelicals to selfishly oppose the work of national religious societies. Among the extremists he named included "the religion of Mormon, the imposture of Matthias, the crusade against the catholics, the madness of sectarianism; so many professors of Christianity, so few imitators of Christ." All these groups, according to Corey, flocked after the latest idea, acted zealously, and desired reformation, while acting selfishly and usurious. Each of these groups displayed the dominant vice of the age, "the making of money, the acquisition of wealth, and the respect which is paid to its possession." While they may have claimed a desire to assist in religious activism, their claims were simply a cover for their selfish obsession with wealth and power. Evangelicals who were inclined toward revivalism and Mormonism "sweat and run, and grunt and ride, and labor and contend, as fishes in a glass for a crumb of bread thrown upon the surface of the water."[69]

Proponents of the ABS often charged opponents of the Benevolent Empire with acting like "ultra-Protestants," being overly sectarian. Henshaw, an Episcopal priest and long-time member of the ABS, claimed that by being tight-fisted with money, ultra-Protestants and Mormonism sowed division. In an 1834 speech before the ABS, he warned his fellow members about the rise of "great and increasing" fears "against amalgamation societies." He believed these sectarian Protestants made a number of specious claims about the ABS and other members of the Benevolent Empire. Henshaw charged that these illiberal individuals misunderstood the intentions of the ABS. These critics charged the ABS for wanting to use its wealth and resources to set itself up as a kind of Mother Church. They were wrong, and through their selfishness, he believed the opponents of the Benevolent Empire used their oppositional attitude to accumulate wealth instead of saving souls. Henshaw compared their "spirit of schism to be as pregnant with evil as the spirit of infidelity." Members of the ABS, he wrote, had no desire to come together to form a compact or association. Their attempts merely tried to create a "voluntary association of the friends of the Bible, without regard to their Ecclesiastical connexions . . . for the sole purposes of distributing" the Bible "without . . . comment." He wanted critics of the ABS to understand this group was much more like "an association of the friends of humanity to feed or clothe the orphans." Henshaw pointed to an example in this address where some British evangelicals withdrew "from the British and Foreign Bible Society because Unitarians were permitted to bear a part in its labours." Henshaw took a more ecumenical approach, refusing to exclude any group willing to support the ABS's project of placing a Bible in every household in the nation. To demonstrate his big tent approach to Benevolent work, he argued that supporters of the Benevolent Empire should be willing to accept money from even the "deluded followers" of Mormonism because once people came into contact with the Bible, then they would see their own need for salvation.[70]

While opponents and proponents of the Benevolent Empire both used anti-Mormonism to adjudicate their relationship with money, both agreed evangelicalism had become too concerned with the accumulation of wealth, like Mormonism. M'Chesney compared what was taking place in "various branches of the business of this world" to the "concerns of the Church; to illustrate her sad condition." In a section containing the ways medicine, politics, or business could become like Mormonism "in conning systems of defraud and intrigue," he discussed the economic developments of nineteenth-century America. M'Chesney thought everyone, "from the preacher in his pulpit, and the bishop over his diocese, down to the humblest of their flock; all were filled with the wild flames of speculation." Cities and towns "were built in imagination, far more splendid than cities of ancient times." He saw "every river or stream" strewn with "splendid places, rail-roads, canals or steamboats . . . carrying the wealthy and happy inhabitants home to their delighted families." This spirit of money-making then proceeded to enter banking and finance. M'Chesney argued they took to these feelings with "such extravagance as was never thought of before, and which we cannot enter into here." All kinds of people emerged to take advantage of this situation, from "brokers, shavers, knaves, and swindlers," who all wanted to destroy and ruin "beyond recovery some of its highest and most brilliant star." Only truth, M'Chesney believed, that came from the "gift of God," would effectively combat the delusions of Mormonism or selfish greed.[71]

Corey, despite his criticism of opponents of the ABS, similarly believed the Benevolent Empire had become too concerned with money. He used anti-Mormonism to highlight how wealth could create bitter disagreements and discord within his own organization. He conceded "it has given birth to many arts; it is highly beneficial, by furnishing opportunity for gratifying the most dignified natural affections." Without private property, he wondered "what place would there be for benevolence or charity?" Corey saw sinfulness taking place when wealth became a "degenerated condition . . . passing the bounds of moderation." "Want" and "appetite for property" became more important than "honor and justice." Money encouraged selfishness, where "every man is for himself— each for his own ends." Corey believed that with this attitude "no charity, friendship, nor consanguinity, can bear a touch upon the chords of self." Friends "become bitter enemies, for slight causes; and men who formerly would seemingly do kind offices . . . the moment the string of selfishness is touched, do revile and hate each other." Seeing how this affected the Benevolent Empire, he wrote how "one boasts of the temperance cause; another, abolition; another, colonization; another, missions; another, a crusade against the catholics." What they all want, Corey worried, was money; "the root after it." He accused his greedy coreligionists of not acting in a disinterested fashion, that is, engaging in religious philanthropy for the purpose of enriching themselves. Those engaged in the Benevolent Empire publish newspapers, magazines, and other religious periodicals, he wrote, but all of them "trumpet the names of the twenty-five cent and five thousand dollar donors, to any or all of the thousand and one devices for getting money." What the "vices of superstition and fanaticism in this age" like Mormonism and the excesses of the Benevolent Empire had in common was a sense that "nothing can be done . . . but by money" and a tendency to do things like "hold *fairs* for the sale of knickknacks, eatables, drinkables, flowers, dolls, ribbons, and all other varieties of vanities—to suppress which true religion is directed." Those fripperies, concluded Corey, are "done under the thin specious veil, of obtaining a charity for a church."[72]

Evangelicals attacked Mormonism's economic practices throughout the antebellum period. They claimed that Joseph Smith was a crook who had turned religion into a big business for the purposes of enriching himself. The evangelical charges that Joseph Smith corrupted the marketplace and corrupted others through his economic actions highlight anxieties that some evangelicals had about their own movement's direction. By the 1830s, the business of evangelicalism had many successes, but some evangelical critics saw too much interest in wealth and celebrity preachers within the church, and the corporate growth of the Benevolent Empire. These attacks provided these evangelicals with a language to work out their own internal tensions regarding the market economy. Evangelicals used anti-Mormonism not because their coreligionists acted so differently in the marketplace from the followers of Joseph Smith, but because they often behaved in exactly the same way.

At the same time as many of these economic criticisms of Mormonism, antebellum evangelicals built on earlier concerns and launched new broadsides about how Mormonism used scripture. They continued to see the Book of Mormon as a made-up and misguided religious text. Antebellum evangelicals also expanded on these criticisms. They obsessed over finding the true author of the Book of Mormon. Many of these concerns about the false nature of the Book of Mormon were the same ones evangelicals had about their own Bible. More and more antebellum evangelicals saw their own Bible as a historical document, and that belief, in combination with the elevation of the belief that any person could read and interpret the Bible for themselves, led some evangelicals to blame their coreligionists for giving rise to the conditions that created false texts, like the Book of Mormon.

CHAPTER 4

"God Has Been Pleased to Give a Revelation to Mankind"

Anti-Mormonism and the Evangelical Interpretation of the Bible

The hunt was on. Antebellum evangelicals embarked on a desperate search for the urtext of the Book of Mormon in the middle of the 1830s. They quickly found an answer in the form of a New England widow named Matilda Davison. She was, according to her evangelical interlocutors, "a woman of irreproachable character and a humble Christian." The Congregationalist minister John Storrs placed most of his hopes in her, believing she could "arrest the progress of what I deem to be one of the rankest delusions ever palmed on poor human nature."[1]

Matilda Davison could do all this and more for antebellum evangelicals. They believed she possessed the original document Joseph Smith used to create the Book of Mormon. If they could acquire it, then evangelicals believed they could definitively prove that Mormonism came from the imagination of Joseph Smith.

Davison was the widow of one Solomon Spaulding. Spaulding had lived in the Western Reserve and moonlighted writing works of historical romance before he died in 1816. Antebellum evangelicals concocted a detailed conspiracy theory, where Spaulding wrote a work of historical fiction, Sidney Rigdon stole it from him, and then Rigdon and Smith used this purloined work to form the basis of the Book of Mormon. To corroborate the accuracy of this account, Storrs asked a fellow minister to go and interview Davison. In a statement made through these male intermediaries, she wrote that the claims of the Book of Mormon "are wholly unfounded." Since it had "impregnated" some of the members of her local church, she "determined to delay no longer doing what I can to strip the mask from this monster of sin, and to lay open this pit of abominations."[2]

Confirming to Storrs that her husband had authored significant sections of what became the Book of Mormon, she told these two evangelical ministers about her relationship with Spaulding. Davison and Spaulding had married young, and then moved to the Western Reserve of eastern Ohio. Spaulding became chronically ill after the move and was no longer able to perform manual labor. Davison remembered he long had a "lively imagination and a great fondness for history," so he quickly took interest in the "numerous mounds and forts, supposed by many to be the dilapidated dwellings and fortifications of a race now extinct." These ramblings led Spaulding to produce a "historical sketch of this long lost race," according to Davison. He wrote this book in an ancient style, similar to the Old Testament, because of the "extreme antiquity" of these ruins. Spaulding intended the book as a "historical romance" to "amuse himself and his neighbors." Dating the creation of this work of fiction to the War of 1812, Davison claimed that her former husband had shared the manuscript with numerous friends and family.[3]

The Spauldings next moved to Pittsburgh, Pennsylvania, where Spaulding connected with a local printer, who wanted to publish Spaulding's work of historical fiction. Davison claimed that Sidney Rigdon, one of the earliest leaders of Mormonism, knew this same printer. Rigdon, according to this conspiracy theory of the human origins of the Book of Mormon, had "ample opportunity to become acquainted with Mr. Spaulding's manuscript and to copy it if he chose." Spaulding died a few years later in 1816 in possession of the manuscript, she said. Skipping forward a few decades in her story, Davison recounted that when the Book of Mormon appeared, "the historical part was immediately recognized by all the older inhabitants, as the identical work of Mr. S., in which they had been so deeply interested years before." Spaulding's brother was with her when she first read the Book of Mormon and could corroborate her account that Mormonism's holy writ was a plagiarism of Solomon Spaulding's work. Friends and family of the Spauldings who also recognized these similarities worried that the general public might see the same overlap, so they worked preemptively to clear Spaulding's name. Her kin, including several prominent local evangelicals, sent Doctor Philastus Hurlburt, an excommunicated member of the Mormon Church, to go to Davison and obtain the original manuscript. Showing Spaulding's influence on the Book of Mormon, these interested parties believed, would "prevent their friends from embracing an error so delusive." Davison concluded her story to these two ministers by suggesting her husband would grieve for the ways the leaders of Mormonism had taken his "historical romance, with the addition of a few pious expressions and extracts from the sacred Scriptures" and construed it "into a new Bible and palmed off upon a company of poor deluded fanatics, as divine."[4]

Although Davison claimed to have plenty of circumstantial evidence connecting Spaulding's work of historical romance and the revelations of Joseph Smith, what she did not actually have was the manuscript in question. She told her interviewers that she thought it might be in a trunk she had left in upstate New York. Hurlburt didn't find it there. He did find a single parchment containing a story about a ship "being driven upon the American coast, while proceeding from Rome to Britain, a short time previous to the Christian era, this country then being inhabited by the Indians." After showing it to several friends and acquaintances of Spaulding, Hurlburt concluded this was the wrong manuscript. He believed there must be another manuscript definitively demonstrating the human origins of the Book of Mormon, so Hurlburt continued his search. Evangelicals never found it. Some evangelicals, like Jonathan Turner, took this inability to find a plagiarized manuscript as evidence of conspiracy. He wondered if Davison "had a trunk full of manuscripts . . . who took them all away but one?" Finding Spaulding's manuscript became a long-lasting obsession for antebellum evangelicals attempting to disprove the Book of Mormon and for Mormons desiring to assert the veracity of their holy writ until Spaulding's text finally appeared in Hawaii toward the end of the nineteenth century. This discovered manuscript bore no resemblance to the Book of Mormon.[5]

Like most conspiracy theories, the one about the Spaulding manuscript reveals much more about the anxieties of its proponents than about any secret agreement to deceive others. Antebellum evangelicals wanted to find Spaulding's novel for the purposes of destroying Mormonism, but the spiritual animosity revealed in the hunt for the true origins of the Book of Mormon also became useful in a larger struggle over how evangelicals themselves would read and understand scripture. Following the earliest years of criticisms of the Book of Mormon, antebellum evangelicals continued many of the same charges they had initially made throughout the rest of the 1830s and into the 1840s. They continued to claim the Book of Mormon was uncanonical and outside the bounds of scripture. Antebellum evangelicals saw Mormonism as trying to fashion a new holy writ in direct opposition to their understandings of the Bible. They also continued to point out the ways, they believed, the Book of Mormon copied the appearance, content, doctrine, and style of the Bible. At the heart these criticisms was a belief among antebellum evangelicals that the Book of Mormon was a product of human imagination. These charges expanded over the course of the 1830s and 1840s as evangelicals learned more about Mormonism and the ways its followers claimed the Book of Mormon came to fruition. The Book of Mormon was still an invented text in these later descriptions, but evangelical narratives of the translation process took on more creative and rococo forms. As a result of their fixation on the true origins of the Book of Mormon, antebellum evangelicals added a new line of criticism that Joseph Smith had plagiarized his revelation from preexisting sources, including Spaulding's.

While antebellum evangelicals developed this more vibrant critique of Mormonism's scriptural practices, their detailed concern with the Book of Mormon reveals much more than just religious intolerance. In a similar way as the critiques of Mormonism's spiritual economy, the antebellum criticisms about the ways Mormonism used and abused scripture resonated within evangelicalism because they faced many of the same debates and dilemmas about the uses and abuses of their own sacred texts. In their initial objections to Mormonism, mostly members of the Stone-Campbell movement criticized the Mormon use of scripture because of their competing claims to pure and unadulterated scriptural practices. Over the 1830s and 1840s, as Mormonism expanded, a larger and wider group of evangelicals advanced the same kinds of criticisms about Mormonism's scriptural practices.

Focused on proving that the Book of Mormon was not an ancient document, evangelicals at the same time grappled with a growing feeling that their own Bible was itself a product of history. They criticized Joseph Smith for introducing a new Bible, while at the same time instigating a flood of new translations of the Bible, an ever-widening variety of Bibles, and numerous theological aids and dictionaries. The overlapping nature of these charges against Mormonism's scriptural practices and internal tensions over how to read and understand the Bible allowed evangelicals concerned about how their coreligionists mishandled scripture to use Mormonism as a foil to mark out the boundaries of how one should correctly read and interpret the Bible.

The use of Mormonism to define acceptable evangelical scriptural practices was not new. Evangelicals, like the leaders of the Stone-Campbell movement, had pursued the same strategy. While Alexander Campbell, one of the leaders of this restorationist sect, blamed man-made religious creeds and ideas for the rise of Mormonism, some evangelicals opposed to the excesses of revivalism used the same tactic to insinuate that the Second Great Awakening had fostered a way of reading the Bible that was ungrounded, irrational, and with the purpose of confirming preexisting beliefs. The consequences of these revivalist scriptural practices, according to these evangelicals concerned about revivalism, included an embrace of religious ignorance, injury to new Christians, and the promotion of bad and novel religious beliefs. Blaming their fellow coreligionists for the ways revivalist scriptural practices had allowed the rise of Mormonism, these evangelicals worked to further a more careful, discriminating, faithful, and harmonious way of reading the Bible. Placing constraints on theological creativity, they believed, would end dangerous evangelical distinctiveness.

The Evangelical Origins of the Book of Mormon

From their earliest encounter with this rival faith, evangelicals depicted the Book of Mormon as a product of contemporary history. They contended the Book of Mormon was crude and contrary to the teachings of the Bible, that Joseph Smith had ransacked the Bible to produce his own holy writ, and that he had invented his religious text out of whole cloth. Later evangelicals in the 1830s and 1840s agreed and built upon these assessments, charging the stylistic elements of the Book of Mormon showed this religious text was the product of Smith's imagination rather than divine revelation. In a lecture delivered to a Wesleyan Methodist Chapel, a British evangelical minister preached "it is evident that the book was written by no more than one man" because the "same low, groveling style, runs through the whole work." This British Methodist contrasted the Book of Mormon with the different styles contained in the Bible, remarking variety "is found in holy writ; but from the beginning to the end of the Book of Mormon, one low monotonous style meets you straight in the face." The Baptist minister David Marks offered an equally unflattering and relatively common criticism about the authenticity of the Book of Mormon, observing that "whereas the early apostles preached the Bible openly with power, the 'Book of Mormon' was written, secretly, and out of sight from all men, except twelve, and preached afterwards." He insulted the book as dull and charmless. Marks concluded Mormonism's religious text has no basis in biblical philosophy, and it "is not confirmed by any miracles, but its authority rests on the testimony of . . . men whom we do not know."[6]

The Affinities between the Bible and the Book of Mormon

Evangelicals built upon their earlier charges that Joseph Smith had copied heavenly sources when writing his new revelation. They believed Joseph Smith purposely copied or modified the appearance, style, text, and doctrine of the Bible, and they even referred to the Book of Mormon as a kind of Bible. Shortly after its initial publication, evangelicals like David Marks referred to the Book of Mormon as a "Golden Bible," and Alexander Campbell said likewise that early Mormons trafficked in "new Bibles." Similarly, Oliver Barr, a minister of the restorationist Christian Connection movement, observed that because a "new Bible presented for our acceptance," Christians must determine if the "Mormon book is either a revelation from God, or one of the basest of impositions." Many critics parsed the precise number of chapters and verses the Book of Mormon contained from the Bible to demonstrate its unoriginal nature.[7]

Evangelicals commented on the significant role the Bible played for Mormons to confirm their belief in the Book of Mormon. The Baptist missionary Alexander Evans claimed Mormons used the Bible extensively in their early missionary efforts to the Native Americans of the Ohio River Valley. He wrote they justified their belief in the coming millennium through appeals to the Old Testament prophecies of Malachi, Zephaniah, and Zechariah. Evans saw the leaders of Mormonism citing Isaiah 29 to demonstrate how the spirit of God could come to an unlearned man, like Joseph Smith. They also, according to Evans, used biblical names, like Zion and Jerusalem, to describe their settlements.[8]

Some antebellum evangelicals worried Mormonism's use of the Bible would confuse Christians. Jonathan Turner believed the "abundant quotations" from the Bible in the Book of Mormon showed the "stupidity, the vulgarity, and sacrilegious proganation" of Mormonism's holy writ in comparison to the "moral light" of the Bible. He expressed concern the "stupid, credulous, and the unwary" might become confused and pronounce the Book of Mormon as a "very good book." Too many people, Turner thought, read the Book of Mormon and believed it "reads much like the Bible." For this reason, he wanted to affirm to his readers "that there is not a single idea in it, excepting such as have been stolen from the Scriptures, which is not wither useless, or ridiculous, or absurd."[9]

Causing additional worry for many evangelicals was the Book of Mormon not only sounded like the Bible, but it also looked like one. Mormonism's sacred writ appeared at a historical moment when the American Bible Society attempted to place a Bible in every home in America. The managers of the ABS relied on two editions of the Bible as part of their nationwide push: the 1829 Minion and 1830 non-Pareil imprints. Printers of both editions bound their volumes in brown leather with twin gold bars impressed on the spine at regular intervals. Joseph Smith styled his Bible in the same fashion. The Book of Mormon and the two editions of the Bible put out by the ABS were nearly the same size, and both had a black label imprinted with gold letters on the spine bearing the volume's name. On a bookshelf, these Bibles and the first edition of the Book of Mormon would have looked nearly identical.[10]

Mormons made much of the theological similarities between the Bible and the Book of Mormon in their writings and their worship services. Sidney Rigdon, after his conversion to Mormonism, began telling people the Book of Mormon was merely an addition to the Old and New Testament. After Henry Perkins, a Presbyterian minister based near Buffalo, New York, publicly accused Mormonism of adopting a new Bible in the late 1830s, Benjamin Winchester, a Mormon leader, responded that the followers of Mormonism were "firm believers in the Old and New Testament." Rebutting Perkins's arguments point by point, Winchester assiduously used the Bible to defend the Book of Mormon as an inspired revelation. He cited the works of Isaiah and Ezekiel to "assert the Book of Mormon to be equal in authority with the Bible." Winchester defended Mormon beliefs and practices as supremely biblical, like the continued presence of miracles and the doctrine of the preexistence of spirits. He asserted that Americans were living in a millennial age. He concluded this vigorous defense by declaring Mormons are "firm believers in the Bible," and that they disfellowship "every person that denies the Bible."[11]

Many Mormon converts reported how they accepted the truthfulness of Mormonism's holy book by reading the Bible and the Book of Mormon alongside one another. Sidney Gilbert mailed his father a copy in 1832 accompanied with a letter testifying that the book had already altered his own eternal destiny. Sidney's father, Eli Gilbert, gave the sacred writ a "close reading . . . and it bore hard upon" his soul. Eli Gilbert read it "again, and again with close attention and prayer." He examined the veracity of the book, "the witnesses, and all other testimony." Eli Gilbert then compared Joseph Smith's revelation with the Bible, a book that he "verily thought" he believed. He concluded the "two books mutually and reciprocally corroborate each other; and if I let go the book of Mormon, the bible might also go down by the same rule."[12]

Joseph Smith liberally used the Bible in his own prophetic sayings and writings. Antebellum evangelicals saw this as incontrovertible evidence of the false and derivative nature of Mormonism's holy writ, while converts to Mormonism saw it as another example of the veracity of their faith. While it is difficult to determine Joseph Smith's earliest feelings about the Bible because many of the accounts of his earliest years of religious creativity were written down years later, the Bible played an important role in his religious project. Smith seems to have grown more comfortable over time with different kinds of modifications to the biblical text that fit his religious visions. He also made more significant changes to the biblical canon because he saw his entire prophetic existence as a continuation of the biblical narrative. Smith reworked biblical material to emphasize the reality of the events and prophecies contained in the Bible, as well as to make room in the biblical canon for additional revelatory materials.[13]

Members of the Mormon faith used similar scriptural practices to prove the trustworthiness of the Book of Mormon as antebellum evangelicals did to prove the reliability of the Bible. Antebellum evangelicals and Mormons modified and used the Bible in a like fashion. Using different kinds of Bibles, various translations, and the increasing number of textual apparatuses allowed Joseph Smith to signal his biblical authority while lacking any kind of formal ministerial training. Access to a wide array of Bibles provided him with the ability to modify and play with biblical texts as needed. Smith's revelations then were not random assortments of teachings, but the result of engaging in the same scriptural practices as evangelicals. On one occasion, Smith had a series of revelations after the death of his son. This series of prophecies bore resemblance to the writings of the Proverbs. This reworking of scripture to meet the felt needs of an individual corresponded to the ways many antebellum evangelicals would have used the Bible during periods of grief and sadness.[14]

The Book of Mormon and antebellum Bibles also shared an emphasis on proving the veracity of their text. Both emphasized the reliability of their revelations through comparable moves. They both used a multiplicity of authorial and editorial voices to verify and attest to the consistency of the text. The Book of Mormon itself consistently referenced the golden plates and their many authors, editors, and preservers. Within Mormonism's holy writ, each of these individuals asserted the accuracy of their efforts.[15]

The Golden Plates

The reliability of Mormonism rested on the physical existence of the golden plates, so evangelicals demanded proof of their existence. They wanted scientific evidence for the truth of Mormonism's holy writ. In accounts appended to the first published editions of the Book of Mormon, testimonies described how three and then eight individuals had the opportunity to view the golden plates. The three witnesses had a supernatural encounter in the forest, where they heard the voice of God, paged through the leaves of the golden plates, and viewed other sacred artifacts discussed in the pages of the Book of Mormon. The eight witnesses had a non-supernatural encounter with golden plates. Smith simply showed them the plates, allowing the witnesses to examine the plates themselves.[16]

Although these witnesses vouched for the existence of the golden plates in both an empirical and supernatural fashion, antebellum evangelicals doubted their accounts. The inconsistency, language, and character of the claimants made their apologetics unreliable, claimed antebellum evangelicals. Alexander Campbell remarked that these professions about the golden plates merely proved that if "Smith wrote it . . . they signed it." He questioned the biases of the eight witnesses who publicly claimed to have seen the golden plates, suggesting that they all were "relatives and connexions" of Joseph Smith. Codified and elaborated in *Mormonism Unvailed*, Eber Howe added that the witnesses could not be trusted to make an honest oath because they did not believe in "a future state of existence." He further claimed they all had a financial interest in the Book of Mormon, like Martin Harris mortgaging his farm for the printing of the book. These pecuniary stakes led evangelicals to charge that it served the interest of the witnesses to confirm the divine nature of the Book of Mormon. They also have "vague and uncertain" testimony, according to Howe, and none of their claims mentioned the time, place, or other circumstances of the revelation. The final piece of evidence, according to this evangelical summation, to make these accounts unacceptable was their ultimate effect. None of these people should be trusted because their public claims had led to the creation of a new religion, "contrary to the revelations of Jesus Christ, as revealed in the Bible."[17]

Antebellum evangelicals demanded production of the actual plates. Campbell publicly challenged Smith or any of the witnesses who "handled . . . the brazen or golden leaves" to produce the plates for inspection. The evangelical Episcopalian John Clark thought it would be "easy . . . were any such plates in existence, to produce them." The Methodist La Roy Sunderland, like many other antebellum evangelicals, referred to the plates as a "pretended discovery," seemingly begging the leaders of Mormonism to make a public exhibition of the golden plates.[18]

Evangelical descriptions over the course of the 1830s and 1840s embellished earlier accounts of the golden plates to criticize Mormonism's scriptural practices as laughable and manufactured. Published in 1834, the widely circulated *Mormonism Unvailed* added many additional details about the supposed discovery of the golden plates. Willard Chase, a Methodist minister in Palmyra, testified Smith's father came to him in the late 1820s to tell him that a spirit had appeared to his son Joseph. Smith's father told him that "in a certain place there was a record on plates of gold, and that he was the person that must obtain them." The younger Joseph Smith was supposed to go to the "place they were deposited" dressed in black clothes and riding a black horse. After obtaining the plates, the spirit told Smith he should leave and not look back. Smith's father told Chase that his son tried to take the book, but "was hindered." Smith saw "something like a toad, which assumed the appearance of a man and struck him on the side of the head." He could not obtain the book because he had not followed the given instructions, according to the spirit. After years of returning to the same place, Smith finally took the plates out of the ground and hid them in a tree. He returned a week later to get them and "on his return," Chase remembered, Smith's father recounted that two men attacked Joseph Smith. The younger Smith fended them off, and once he returned home, Smith asked Chase for his seer stone to help him translate the plates and to build him a chest for the plates.[19]

In addition to more information about the actual discovery of the plates, antebellum evangelicals added more elaborate stylistic details about the appearance of the plates and the methods Joseph Smith used to translate them. The editors of the *Baptist Chronicle and Literary Register* of Georgetown, Kentucky, described how they heard the plates resembled gold "with Arabic characters inscribed on them." When

Smith found the plates, they added that he also found "two stones." He used these tools to "decipher the hieroglyphics of the plates." The Presbyterian Truman Coe described these as the Urim and Thummin, which Joseph Smith could look through and "see the import written in plain English on a screen placed before him." When Nancy Towle, an evangelical itinerant, visited the Mormon community in Ohio, she claimed Mormons told her that Smith received a "pair of 'interpeters' that resembled spectacles" to translate the golden plates. Later evangelicals added that Smith placed his head into a hat containing his seer stone during the translation process. He would then dictate to his scribe the text that became the Book of Mormon.[20]

Echoing their earliest objections, antebellum evangelicals concluded that the story of the golden plates showed the absurd and questionable nature of the origins of Mormonism. The itinerant John Mason Peck described the appearance of the plates as "extravagant." He believed they revealed an effort to pretend to work miracles and to seduce believers. The Baptist minister David Marks allowed, no doubt disingenuously, that he was initially open to accepting the story of the golden plates because he believed that the world too often "rejects truth and judges matters before they hear it." But then, he said he quickly came to dismiss the entire account of a sacred text written by an angel because it came from an "obscure, illiterate, awkward, and unpolished youth . . . [who] had previously been in the practice of telling fortunes and digging in the earth for chests of gold." In *Mormonism Unvailed*, Eber Howe charged that the story of the golden plates "was a farrago of nonsense," revealing the mind of an "atheist" who was making "an experiment upon the human understanding and credulity." Origen Bacheler, a Methodist minister, referred to the Mormon leader Parley Pratt's teaching of the golden plates as an example of "Mormon Fooleries."[21]

Evangelicals thought they could conclusively demonstrate the Book of Mormon as a product of Joseph Smith's imagination because they believed Mormonism's accounts disagreed with each other about how Joseph Smith had discovered the texts. Eber Howe claimed that the accounts about the finding of the golden or brazen plates were "contradictory, vague, and inconsistent." John Clark, an evangelical Episcopal minister and active participant in the American Tract Society, reinforced these charges in a series of newspaper articles in the *Episcopal Recorder* appearing in the 1840s. In one of his many harangues against Mormonism, Clark concluded the statements about the golden plates "were modified from time to time according as their plans became more mature." He contended the objects in question even changed over time, with Smith initially claiming "it was a gold Bible—then golden plates engraved—then metallic plates stereotyped or embossed with golden letters."[22]

As the 1830s progressed evangelicals felt even more confident about dismissing the existence of the golden plates because some of the most educated individuals in the country had pronounced them as frauds and present-day creations. In the immediate aftermath of Smith's translation of the golden plates and before mortgaging his farm to pay for the initial printing of the Book of Mormon, Martin Harris sought confirmation about Joseph Smith's account of the plates. Harris took a scrap of paper given to him by Joseph Smith covered with writing from the golden plates to New York to consult with Charles Anthon, an expert in Semitic languages at Columbia College. Multiple conflicting accounts exist of this meeting, but the accounts contained in the evangelical press contain the same basic plot. In the evangelical apologist Origen Bacheler's account, Anthon interpreted the writing as "a singular scrawl." He wrote that Harris's sheet of paper "consisted of all kinds of crooked characters disposed in columns, and . . . [had] been prepared by some person who had before, him at the time, a book containing various alphabets." Calling attention to his linguistic expertise, Bacheler said Anthon had even figured out the source of the plagiarism. He claimed that "the whole ended in a rude delineation of a circle . . . copied after the Mexican Calendar . . . but copied in such a way as not to betray the source whence it was derived." Those who continued to believe, he charged, "must keep on making fools of themselves, for aught I see; for when men shut their eyes to the light, their case is hopeless indeed."[23]

Appealing to experts was a common way for antebellum Americans to prove or disprove outlandish claims about religion or science. The St. Louis showman Albert Koch attempted to demonstrate the authenticity of a fossil sea serpent by appealing to the same type of educated individuals as Martin Harris had done. He went to Benjamin Silliman, a Yale University geologist, for confirmation. Silliman supported Koch's conclusions, giving Koch the cultural imprimatur to display his find around the country. Because of Anthon's denunciations, Harris and Smith did not have this option.[24]

Antebellum evangelicals long paid attention to the physical aspects of the golden plates as a way to express incredulity about the founding moments of Mormonism. The editors of the *Painesville Telegraph* reflected on the plates, wondering why many people were "duped by so barefaced and contemptible an artifice" that had conflicting descriptions of the plates themselves. One version claimed Joseph Smith and Martin Harris had some gentlemen from the nearby vicinity estimate the value from the weight of the golden plates. Other witnesses, according to these Stone-Campbell editors, described the "plates as being something like eight inches square, the leaves were plates of metal of a whitish yellow color, and of the thickness of tin plate." This account continued with a description of three small rings passing through the metal of the plates, so that the leaves of each plate "were divided equidistant between the back and edge, by cutting the plates in two parts . . . so that the front might be opened . . . by a hinge, while the back part remained stationary and immoveable." This made the entire object "a sealed book," allowing Smith to claim the book "would not be revealed for ages to come."[25]

Further systematic study of the events surrounding the appearance of the golden plates and the Book of Mormon over the 1830s and 1840s convinced many evangelicals that the golden plates made little empirical sense. In *A Little Talk between John Robinson and His Master about Mormonism*, a British Methodist author wondered how Joseph Smith would have carried the golden plates by himself. The master described the size of the plates as "about 7 inches by 8" and about six inches thick, and since "all learned men" knew that the "Egyptian language takes up a very great deal of room . . . as much room as the English, and it is quite certain that, as the Book of Mormon is 600 pages thick," the plates would need at least one thousand pages to hold all of the Egyptian language. Concluding the weight of the plates at over 400 pounds, this Methodist found it unlikely Smith could have hefted the plates alone. These charges that scientific evidence did not confirm the truthfulness of the Book of Mormon were similar to the concerns that many antebellum evangelicals had about their own Bible.[26]

In the same way antebellum evangelicals raised questions about the physicality of the golden plates, they also inquired into the true authorship of the Book of Mormon. Part of the evangelical study of the origins of the Book of Mormon over the 1830s and 1840s involved trying to determine the real author of Mormonism's religious text. They initially pegged Sidney Rigdon as the mastermind behind the Book of Mormon. But in the middle of the 1830s, antebellum evangelicals began to focus on Solomon Spaulding as the true author. Eber Howe's widely translated compendium of anti-Mormon arguments and affidavits stated, "the leading features of the 'Gold Bible' were first conceived and concocted by SOLOMON SPALDING." The Solomon Spaulding theory of the origins of the Book of Mormon described earlier in this chapter became a powerful tool for evangelicals to explain its popularity and to disprove Mormonism. Almost every major work of anti-Mormonism written by evangelicals from the publication of *Mormonism Unvailed* through the 1850s referenced the Spaulding story. Most of these accounts followed a standard structure, where Spaulding "wrote the historical part of the Book of Mormon, or, as it is sometimes called, the Mormon Bible." In one of the earliest of these accounts, found in the *Ohio Repository*, the editor told his readers that Spaulding had penned the account more than twenty years ago without the least intention on the part of the author "of framing a system of delusion for his fellow-men." Joseph Smith had appropriated Spaulding's work for his own nefarious purposes. Evangelicals obsessed with who wrote the Book of Mormon would struggle with the same question concerning their own Bible.[27]

The emphasis on the romantic aspects of the Spaulding story further helped evangelicals explain the popularity of the Book of Mormon. They feared many Americans had become overly obsessed with historical fiction. Antebellum evangelicals saw this kind of sensational literature leading weak individuals away from Christendom. Among them was the English Congregationalist minister Samuel Haining, who often referred to the text as a "wild, romantic tale . . . of mere fiction." The editors of *The Pioneer*, a Baptist periodical reprinted by the *New York Weekly Messenger and Young Men's Advocate*, agreed that the lost Spaulding manuscript provided the Book of Mormon with a "series of extravagant and romantic histories about two sets of people that crossed the Atlantic and lived on the continent," and that "the extravagant fictions" of Smith's plagiarism "outdo the Arabian Night's Entertainment, or the stories of Sinbad the Sailor." They described how it had all the elements of historical fiction, like swashbuckling male characters, militarism, and political intrigue.[28]

The Historicity of the Bible

Though filled with derision and venom, the evangelical questioning of the Book of Mormon reveals much more than reactionary ill will. While evangelicals were not the only group attacking Mormonism's scriptural practices, the intense dislike they had toward Mormonism resonated not just because the Book of Mormon was so different, but because it raised many of the same challenges that had come to surround evangelicals' sacred scriptures. At the center of many evangelicals' concerns in the 1830s and 1840s was an increasing concern with the authenticity of the Bible. As their criticisms of Mormon scriptural practices developed over the decades—as antebellum evangelicals came to emphasize that Joseph Smith had invented the Book of Mormon, whether from his own imagination, the Bible, or from Solomon Spaulding—they viewed Mormonism's religious text as a product of its time and place. Here was a historically contingent text—just as a growing number of Protestants, including increasing numbers of evangelicals, became aware that the Bible might be too. Throughout the 1830s and 1840s, growing numbers of evangelicals had begun to see the biblical translations they used at home and in their churches as riddled with errors and biases. Most evangelical denominations published their own editions of scripture along with theological aids, but those religious texts often came to competing conclusions on vital matters of faith and practice. Achieving an authentic faith faced an additional hurdle arising from the evangelical conviction that individuals should read and interpret scripture for themselves. In a society overflowing with religious texts, that democratic reading strategy created religious cacophony and confusion.

Antebellum evangelicals had their central belief in the trustworthiness of the Bible challenged through a flood of new Bibles, a growing awareness of the historical nature of the Bible, an increasing number of new translations of the Bible, and the unstable authority of the Bible. Bibles appeared in unprecedented numbers and variety in the antebellum period because of increased demand, new technological advancements, and the growth of the national market economy. No American printers published editions of the English Bible prior to the 1780s, but in the years between the American Revolution and Civil War, American publishing houses printed nearly two thousand editions of the Bible or New Testament. All these editions contained the same text of the Bible, nearly all using the King James translation, but there was a significant variety of Bibles available for purchase. In a crowded marketplace, religious publishers attempted to distinguish their Bibles from each other. They published Bibles to sell to specific denominational, demographic, or political groups by attaching terms, like "Self-interpreting," "Comprehensive," "Polyglott," "Family," or "Pulpit" to their title pages.[29]

The number and variety of Bibles in print unintentionally created a sense of anxiety about the Bible in antebellum evangelical circles. In *The Wide, Wide World,* Susan Warner, an antebellum evangelical novelist, fictionalized this experience when she portrayed a young girl named Ellen visiting a bookstore with her mother. After rightly passing by the children's literature, the shopkeeper showed Ellen the Bibles for sale. They came in "various kinds and sizes," but the seemingly endless supply of Bibles overwhelmed her. As "she flew to the place, where a dozen different Bibles were presently displayed . . . Ellen's wits were ready to forsake her" because she had never seen "such beautiful Bibles." She "poured in ecstasy over their varieties of type and binding, and was evidently in love with them all." Her mother told her to "look and choose," but she knew that "it was not likely that Ellen's 'time' would be a short one." Ellen took so long that her mother had to find a chair "to await patiently her decision." The final decision did not come easy to Ellen. She weighed the "comparative advantages" of the different sizes, shapes, colors, and translations of Bibles. The sheer number of different Bibles produced ecstasy, making Ellen forget that there "ever was such a thing as sorrow in the world." It also produced anxiety. When faced with all of these Bibles, Ellen threw "off her light bonnet, and with flushed cheek . . . and a brow grave with unusual care, as though a nation's fate were deciding." For evangelicals like her, the choice of a Bible had eternal consequences because her eternal salvation depended upon reading the Bible correctly. Warner's description of Ellen's Bible shopping suggests the Bible had become a totem for many evangelicals. If the appearance and words of the Bible could so easily be changed to appeal to the preferences of consumers, then it seems likely some evangelicals wondered if it would be that difficult to change some of the weightier matters of holy writ. This was what they believed Joseph Smith had done with the Book of Mormon.[30]

Working alongside this flood of new Bibles to soften evangelicalism's belief in their scripture's authenticity was a growing sense that the Bible itself was a historical artifact. When examined under the gaze of critical scholarship, the revealed word of God seemed more like a product of the past, rather than a timeless guide to answering all of evangelicalism's questions about this life and the life to come. Confessional and theological readings of the text became increasingly difficult to sustain. Antebellum evangelicals ironically aided in this process by embracing historical scholarship about the Bible. They used these tools because they believed these methods would strengthen biblical authority through the identification of historical and textual variations in different translations of the Bible. Through attempts to engage in philological scholarship, antebellum evangelicals hoped to make the Bible more relevant through an identification of the historical flotsam preventing people from fully understanding the Bible. These efforts to strengthen biblical authority had the unintended consequence of challenging biblical and ecclesiastical authority because accentuating the historical, archaeological, philological, and anthropological ways of studying the Bible highlighted the chasm between the ancient and modern world.[31]

Modern biblical criticism, largely emanating from colleges and universities in Germany, made it more complicated for educated Christians to believe in the literal reality of the biblical text. Increasing numbers of Christians familiar with the works of German biblical criticism saw the unity of the Bible and uniformity of its inspiration questioned. This kind of biblical interpretation differentiated between the Bible as the word of God and the Bible as the vehicle for God's word. These critics believed the Bible should receive the same kind of historical and literary analysis as any other text. With the growing idea that the Bible was not uniformly inspired, critics inspired by modern textual criticism found it necessary to investigate questions of biblical authorship, dating, canonization, and inspiration.[32]

While never replacing evangelicalism's emphasis on individuals reading and interpreting the Bible for themselves, orthodox evangelicals absorbed some of these ideas about biblical criticism and concluded historical awareness was necessary for Christians to understand its complexities. Charles Hodge, an evangelically inclined scholar, created an entire magazine dedicated to disseminating cutting-edge biblical scholarship to the widest number of evangelical believers. He believed the historical study of scripture was an essential component of the reformed hermeneutic. Hodge also thought one of the markers of the very goodness of God was the ways He revealed His divine presence in a particular time and place. The study of history could, according to Hodge, check the threat of historical studies that called into question the veracity of the Bible. In his proposal for *Biblical Repertory*, Hodge wrote that he intended the periodical to cover the widest range of historical topics. The magazine's inaugural issue contained an editor's note stating that the mission of the periodical was "principally designed to excite a spirit for Biblical Studies." The magazine would circulate "information on the Criticism of the Text—on the circulating information on the Criticism of the Text—on the Ancient Versions—on Critical Editions." Understanding the historically inclined nature of his endeavor, Hodge advertised that he would present "interesting articles on the manners, customs, institutions, and literature of the East—on various points in Biblical antiquities—and on the Literary History of the Sacred Volume."[33]

James Henry Thornwell, a southern Presbyterian with similar theological views as Hodge, used the same tools of historical analysis to determine the veracity of the Bible. Since the Bible itself asserted to be a true revelation from God, Thornwell argued it could be studied and discussed just like the Koran or the Book of Mormon. To determine what is and what is not a revelation, Thornwell distinguished between natural and supernatural facts. The Bible contained revelations of supernatural facts, like the Trinity or the Atonement. Natural facts included historical narratives and geographical references. Thornwell argued that both the Koran and the Book of Mormon clearly had contradictions and falsehoods in their natural facts, while the Bible could pass this test of veracity.[34]

While Hodge and Thornwell were educated evangelicals who eventually grew fearful of the excesses of the Second Great Awakening, even evangelicals influenced by revivalism took note of the historical nature of the Bible. In a review of a book about "some accurate knowledge of Jewish antiquities," the Methodist editors of the *Christian Advocate* stated that "Biblical students in this country have long and very sensibly felt the want of such a work." They recommended the book to "every . . . minister of the gospel, but [also] useful to all who desire to read the holy Scriptures with full understanding." Since most people did not have the money or language training to read the "books from which it was to be derived," the editors believed this volume would present "this interesting subject" as a "system . . . within reasonable compass."[35]

An awareness of the historical nature of the Bible led evangelicals to append a growing number of theological aids to assist their readers in better understanding the word of God. Reflecting the views of later antebellum evangelicals, the orthodox minister Jedidiah Morse defended Bibles containing these additions as a necessary tool to defend against the rise of false teaching within Christianity. Believers needed synopses, cross-references, and commentaries because, he suggested, Christians needed to understand the Bible in light of scientific, archaeological, and intellectual advances. In *The Panoplist*, Morse told his readers that "God has been pleased to give a revelation to mankind, which without note or comment, is able to make them wise unto salvation." The problem, in his view, was that the Bible abounded with "allusions to manners, customs and facts, which it no where fully explains." Morse went on to say that the "recurrence of unknown characters and hard names, would exceedingly embarrass the reader . . . [and] men are not fond of reading a book, which they cannot understand." Access and cost prevented most Christians from obtaining "various and expensive books of history, travels, and antiquities, where it is to be found." Morse believed it was "to say the least, very desirable" that "common people" should have information about "the general history of the ages and countries in which the Scriptures were written." He argued the "proper use" of these materials would never "supersede the study of the sacred pages, but to facilitate it."[36]

Evangelicals believed these tools of theological explication would have an apologetic and pastoral purpose, but their use ultimately challenged a literal understanding of the Bible. Besides supporting a clearer understanding of the Bible, antebellum evangelicals believed knowing the historical context of scripture would give them the tools to respond to the growing threat that science posed to traditional understandings of the word of God. Geology was the first natural science to threaten antebellum Americans by raising questions about the age of the earth and the existence of a worldwide flood depicted in Genesis. Antebellum evangelical theologians initially felt confident the new field of geology, like discoveries in archaeology and philology, would confirm their deepest held beliefs about the literal nature of the Bible. When geologists concluded that the structure of the earliest rocks could not confirm the Genesis account of a global flood, evangelicals turned to creative scriptural exegesis to explain these scientific discoveries. They accepted empiricism, and what many antebellum evangelicals invoked was a long-day theory, where they claimed that the seven days of the Genesis Creation account were not literal days. They found support for this position in the Bible itself with Hebrew words that did not imply a twenty-four-hour day.[37]

To supplement this historical scholarship, religious publishers added theological tools to their Bibles. These additions appeared before, after, or on the borders of the main text of the Bible, as well as within the text itself. They included concordances, cross-references, maps, annotations, dates, commentaries, and alternative translations of words or passages. John Brown's *Self-Interpreting Bible* and Philip Doddridge's *The Family Expositor* both provided annotations and theological guides for the reader. The goal of these additions, according to Brown, was to provide theological assistance for people who lacked the time or money to devote to full-time Bible study. Doddridge similarly wanted to make the New Testament accessible to those lacking formal education. Different publications aimed to provide a synthesis of these additions. Doddridge's version contained three different English translations of the New Testament and a paraphrase to present the Bible to readers in the clearest way possible. Although designed to present the Bible in its simplest form, Doddridge's Bible required six lengthy volumes to include all the commentaries, paraphrases, sermons, and other additions just for the New Testament.[38]

To facilitate theological and historical awareness, some antebellum evangelical Bibles also contained date entries. On the top of the page of many of the most popular versions of the Bible, religious publishers included dates to tell their readers the precise time of biblical events. Evangelicals could learn that creation occurred in 4004 BC, that David killed Goliath in 1063 BC, or that Jesus preached the Sermon on the Mount in 31 AD. These chronological markers reinforced a sense that the Bible was a product of the past, but the inclusion of date entries ironically furthered more interpretive discord. Evangelical religious publishers and editors did not always agree with one another about the date of certain events, or they approximated the precise time events occurred. This conflict, in tandem with the placement of the dates themselves, unintendedly conveyed a sense of historical uncertainty to the reader of the Bible.[39]

While many antebellum evangelicals believed the attachment of these guides would aid in theological reflection, these additions faced growing opposition from within evangelical circles. Critics of the inclusion of theological aids believed they undermined belief in the Bible because this theological assistance demonstrated to readers that the Bible was a historical document that sectarians could use for their own purposes. Those most committed to a restorationist plea to restore the primitive church, like Alexander Campbell, often led the strongest opposition to these elements. Campbell argued in his own edition of the New Testament that these aids encouraged Christians to read the Bible "detached from the drift and scope of the passage." Well-meaning Christians who wanted to understand the Bible on its own terms, he believed, could too easily become distracted by all of the theological apparatus. In the preface to his own translation of the New Testament, he reminded his readers that "neither words nor sentences . . . have any meaning, but what the scope, connexion, and design of the writer, give them." Campbell believed ignorance of this important hermeneutical principal had "beclouded the apostolic epistles, has introduced more errors into the views, and unmeaning ceremonies into the practice of professing Christians." He argued that "cutting up the sacred text into morsels . . . has greatly contributed . . . [and] any passages . . . have been weakened and obscured."[40]

Having an accurate text of the Bible was important to all evangelicals, but especially to Campbell and other committed restorationists who held the Bible, and its picture of early Christianity, was the sole model for Christian living. Calling into question the veracity of other denominational translations, Campbell commented that "each religious party had sought to secure the Bible within its own sectarian cell." While Campbell lacked any formal linguistic training, he concluded that the King James Version had significant inaccuracies resulting from theological biases, interpretive compromise, and the discovery of new, more reliable manuscripts. Campbell published his own translation of the New Testament in 1826, one that assumed that words could change meaning, resulting in ideas contrary to their original concepts. The King James Bible itself had outdated and incorrect language, and Campbell wanted to strip away the errors of misguided translators and to clarify ambiguous terms to reveal the true message of the Bible. He relied upon many of the same biblical scholars and manuscripts as other evangelicals, but he reached different conclusions. Campbell's translation advanced his own theological agenda, most famously by retranslating the word *baptism* as "immersion." While Campbell believed that his translation would help the reader understand the plain meaning of the Bible, pointing out how errors and biases had crept into the Bible ironically called into question the trustworthiness of religious texts.[41]

In the midst of his attempt to present the Bible as an inviolate, timeless text, Campbell's publication strategies unintentionally reinforced a belief that the Bible was a historically contingent document, like the Book of Mormon. Campbell included theological apparatuses to encourage readers to employ a commonsense reading of scripture. Because of his emphasis on the pure text of the Bible, he was sensitive to the cluttering of the Bible. This awareness led Campbell to eliminate all chapter breaks and verse numbers, which raised questions about the malleability of the Bible. He also dated biblical events, highlighting that biblical characters were historical figures. Although he included most of the editorial material at the conclusion of the volume, Campbell's theological materials complicated his strongly held democratic hermeneutic. He resolved textual questions or theological conundrums by appealing to academic consensus. Claiming that he wanted to bring the Bible to the common man, appeals to learned theologians acknowledged that reading the Bible might require learned instruction and be a little more complicated than he claimed.[42]

Sounding Like the Bible

Adding to the growing anxiety within evangelical circles that the Bible was a historical document that could be manipulated was the appearance of many other kinds of writings that mimicked biblical languages and forms. Antebellum evangelicals encountered numerous tracts and publications written in a biblical style with biblical cadences. As a way to imbue their political and social arguments with gravitas and veracity, some antebellum Americans deployed the language and narrative style of the King James Bible. To make political points that spanned the ideological spectrum, pseudobiblical authors presented the history of America as if it had occurred in the biblical world. They presented their tracts and pamphlets as if they were translations of ancient sources that they alone had miraculously discovered and supernaturally translated. These blatantly political documents showed antebellum evangelicals the Bible could be a living text through its incorporation of contemporary political matters into timeless religious principles.[43]

Antebellum evangelicals not only encountered emulations of the Bible, but also other texts claiming to be new sacred writs, like the Book of Mormon. The most well-known of these documents for evangelicals were the apocrypha and the Koran. A flood of Catholic immigrants, a rising number of missionaries worldwide, a fascination with the Orient, and a growing interest in comparative religion put antebellum evangelicals in contact with these other sacred revelations. A number of indigenous religious movements also claimed to have new scriptures. Besides Mormonism itself, these groups included both the Shakers, Millerites, Hicksite Quakers, and others. In 1843, the Shakers published *Holy, Sacred and Divine Roll and Book*. Revealed to Philemon Stewart, a Shaker living in the United Society's village at New Lebanon, the text numbered more than four hundred plates and resembled the spirit-filled messages of this period. Stewart claimed that an angel identified as Al'sign te're Jah appeared to him and dictated a series of testimonies. He claimed the angel then appeared to him a few weeks later to confirm the authority and authenticity of the revelations. This Shaker revelation also explicitly identified Stewart as a prophet of God, who had received messages of the same status as the Bible.[44]

This Shaker text overlapped and interacted with the Bible. *Holy, Sacred and Divine Roll and Book* spoke directly about its heavenly origins, affirmed the central message of the Shaker Gospel, and confirmed many of the essentials of the Christian Gospel. It developed religious ideas and contained proverbs for living, quotes from the Bible, and observations from the past. Appearing during a period of intense religious manifestations including visions and revelations, the *Sacred Roll* reinforced its revelatory nature by using similar strategies as the Bible and the Book of Mormon. The *Sacred Roll* also acted as a kind of commentary on the Bible. Instructions found in the text directed readers to place *Sacred and Divine Roll* alongside the Bible in order to provide spiritual edification for Shakers. Representing a divine revelation, the text situated itself as a new Bible, a supplemental revelation needed for the corrupted Christian Bible. To demonstrate the veracity of this Shaker revelation, the second part of *Sacred and Divine Roll* contained the testimony of an array of spiritual figures, like ancient prophets and angels, to show the divine origins of the text.[45]

What worried evangelicals was that many of these groups with new religious texts, like the Millerites, Shakers, and Mormons, had close ties to their own churches. The Shaker community at New Lebanon, for instance, sent several missionaries to western New York because they saw it as fertile soil due to the evangelicals' successes in the Burned-over District. The antebellum efflorescence of evangelicalism in general had given religious groups the freedom to proclaim a new revelation, and it ironically created a set of conditions that led some even to demand the appearance of a new revelation to compete in a thriving spiritual marketplace. The unity of Christendom promised by the preaching and revivals of the Second Great Awakening seemed distant. The freethinker Frederick Evans suspected antebellum evangelicals had created this denominational cacophony by cutting off the revelatory voice of God. Echoing the writings of Mormon converts, Evans believed only a new word from God could cut through denominational chaos. Since God was a God of order, he foresaw that Christian unity and progress could only come through a new revelation. What these alternative religious revelations like Mormonism showed antebellum evangelicals was that Americans had a favorable disposition toward new Bibles, that they could confuse these texts with the orthodox Bible, and that the content of the Bible itself was unstable.[46]

Evidentiary Basis for the Bible

The increasing assaults on the authenticity, accuracy, and singularity of the Bible entered and ramified an evangelical interpretive framework growing simultaneously more reasonable and more chaotic. To meet the challenge that revelation was historically contingent, antebellum evangelicals embraced an evidentiary theology aiming to show the rationality of belief and necessity of revelation. Evangelicals applied principles of inductive science rooted in the methods of Baconian practices to defend the truth of the Bible and to make their reading of the Bible in accordance with logical principles. Antebellum evangelicals came to understand that greater understanding of the word of God came through observation about a set of particular facts. Only after they had organized these facts in a systematic fashion did evangelicals believe they could draw larger conclusions.[47]

These evidentiary-based arguments became so ubiquitous by the 1830s that they acquired a formulaic character, as evidenced by their initial use against Mormonism by Alexander Campbell and sustained use by other evangelicals. In this set of claims about the authenticity of religious texts, evangelicals differentiated between external and internal arguments. The antebellum use and development of evidentiary Christianity also encouraged evangelicals to believe and to practice a more reasonable form of Christianity. Internal arguments for belief became popular in evangelical circles because they fit comfortably alongside revivalism and devotionalism. They reinforced an understanding that experience alone could confirm the authority of the Bible. Embracing sentimentality, evangelicals emphasized the character of Jesus as proof of the divine origins of Christianity. They recounted Gospel stories, with a focus on Jesus as the prime example of human excellence and sacrificial suffering. Many antebellum evangelicals worried the Bible alone could no longer sustain a reader's attention, so publishers and ministers focused on moral narratives, rather than works of doctrine, to compete with novels, historical fiction, and other popular literary works. Using an apologetic strategy, evangelicals also fully embraced the historical veracity of all the prophecies foretold in the Bible. Eschewing concerns with a growing awareness of the past, evangelicals found these miracles credible because of reliability and trustworthiness of their witnesses and the authors of the New Testament.[48]

Alongside evidentiary Christianity and undermining a unified way of reading scripture, antebellum evangelicals believed Americans should read the Bible in a populist fashion. They cast aside ecclesiastical traditions and clerical traditions for the right to open the Bible and think for oneself. This kind of democratic move away from the longstanding way of reading scripture supported a literal interpretation of the Bible. Antebellum evangelicals believed the Bible meant what it said. The literalist hermeneutic aided in mass conversions, social transformations, and ecclesiastical organization, but it came at the cost of validating everyone's religious beliefs and fostering religious discord.[49]

The problem was that growing historical awareness demonstrated to many evangelicals the ways a simple commonsense method of reading the Bible could lead to disbelief and disunity through differing interpretations. William Miller, the eventual failed millennial predictor, began his ministerial career with deist inclinations. Miller adopted the widely held commonsense literal hermeneutic to resolve personal doubts about biblical inspiration. He believed a person possessing only basic literacy could interpret all parts of the Bible. Miller even self-consciously studied the Bible for a dozen years without the aid of any intermediary influence, like teachers, creeds, or scriptural commentaries. Upon completion of this hermeneutical experiment, he concluded the Bible was harmonious and understandable. It led him to believe he had uncovered biblical prophecies relevant to contemporary events. Since standard modes of biblical interpretation had failed to uncover these hidden messages, Miller found it necessary to create an entirely new religious sect, the Millerites. While he praised himself for coming to religious conclusions by only reading the Bible, Miller unintentionally created an entirely new religious movement that sold thousands of newspapers, tracts, and books; promoted Bible classes and Sabbath schools; and broke publicly from the Baptist denomination in 1845.[50]

Reading the Bible More Reasonably

To meet the growing concerns about the authenticity of the Bible, the rise of a historically aware interpretive framework, and a theologically cacophonous hermeneutic, a group of evangelicals came to blame revivals for encouraging too much theological independence. These evangelicals critical of revivalism even saw this hermeneutical creativity leading to the rise of Mormonism. They called for a more reasonable, constrained understanding of the Bible. This response, many evangelicals critical of revivalism concluded, would alleviate what they believed was one of the major threats to belief in the authenticity of the Bible: the theological excesses and rebellion emanating from the revivals of the Second Great Awakening. The managers of the American Sunday School Union addressed this tension in an 1827 pamphlet directed toward young children and their parents. In *Eyes and No Eyes*, these directors educated Christians about how they should read their Bible through the contrasting attitudes of two boys named Thomas and Henry. Thomas and Henry's uncle had given each of them a Bible. Both "were very much pleased with their Bibles, and read them very often . . . but they were quite as different in the way they read their Bibles." Henry read it for the "pretty stories" of the Old Testament, and he was "very fond of the parables which Christ told to his disciples and the Acts." Henry's uncle worried that reading the Bible in this fashion led Henry to "read the Bible only as a history book" because he could never remember the didactic purposes of the biblical stories. What caused his uncle the most grief was that young Henry read about the "birth, sufferings, miracles, death, and resurrection" of Jesus "very carelessly, without thinking about them, or desiring to know their meaning." By only reading the Bible as full of "pretty stories," young Henry would ultimately never learn the "evil consequences of forgetting the will of God" or how sinners could be "cleansed or washed from their sins in the blood of Christ, which he shed upon the cross."[51]

Henry's uncle feared his nephew read with a dangerous curiosity. Many evangelicals compared an overly inquisitive interest in printed material to alcoholism. One would never be able to consume enough. Novels, narratives, and other interesting texts would so titillate readers that they would find the Bible dull by comparison. The irony was evangelicals used exciting devices and stories to interest readers. Evangelicals concerned about revivalism worried the intriguing aspects of the text would become more important than the Christian aspects. Readers would have an immediate reaction to the text, but they would ultimately lose interest because they had never embraced the full meaning of the Bible.[52]

While Henry demonstrated a juvenile reading of the Bible, Thomas showed the proper, deferential attitude and method for reading scripture. About his personal Bible study, Thomas remarked that "there are many . . . things which I cannot make out, but I am sure they cannot be put there for nothing." His uncle told Thomas that he was glad that his nephew read the Bible "carefully, and not merely to amuse yourself." Thomas's uncle wanted to be sure that Thomas would read and interpret the Bible through an established, conservative framework. The uncle told Thomas that "when you are reading those parts of the Bible which appear to you most difficult, mark what you wish to have explained." His uncle said they would then sit down together, and Thomas's uncle would explain the difficult passages.[53]

The Reverend Charles Buck responded to the same growing concern about the authenticity of the Bible and an anxiety about unfettered theological interpretation and advocated a similar kind of careful, guided hermeneutic free from the theological creativity of the Second Great Awakening. He thought intense emotions naturally resulted in invented theology at odds with orthodox Christianity. In sections concerning experience and enthusiasm contained in his widely read theological dictionary, Buck characterized enthusiasm as "any impression on the fancy, or agitation of the passions, of which man can give no rational account." He feared many preachers predisposed to revivalism used charisma as a tool to bring about repentance and conversion. Evangelicalism, for Buck, had lost its grasp on reason. Counterfeit experience, he believed, might result in "imaginations heated and delighted." Buck concluded more moderated and reasonable scriptural practices could oppose exactly these imaginations.[54]

Anti-Mormonism and More Constrained Biblical Interpretation

Evangelical critics of revivalism used anti-Mormonism to articulate a vision of reading scripture that stood in contrast to revivalist scriptural practices, which they believed relied too much on personal desires and emotion. They used religious prejudice toward Mormonism to blame their coreligionists with reading the Bible in an incorrect and dangerous fashion. Embracing the same kinds of scriptural practices as Mormonism led evangelicals critical of revivalism to charge their coreligionists with falsifying and inventing religious doctrine. Because of this fanciful and harmful way of reading and understanding scripture, evangelicals critical of revivalism used anti-Mormonism to articulate a biblical hermeneutic that understood and read the Bible in a more careful, more discriminating, and more faithful and harmonious fashion.

While blaming Joseph Smith and many early leaders of Mormonism for engaging in ungrounded, irrational, and self-serving scriptural practices, antebellum evangelicals critical of revivalism blamed their coreligionists for practicing a similar kind of hermeneutic. The Presbyterian

Jonathan Turner attacked evangelical churches who believed without proof as practicing a similar search for "imagined truth" as the founder of Mormonism. Comparing the scriptural practices of Mormonism to those churches most heavily influenced by the revivals of the Second Great Awakening, he claimed the "wonderful spasms, visions, traces . . . experienced by Sidney Rigdon and company in Ohio are no more proof of the divine authority of their doctrine" than the "enthusiasm" of revivalism. Feelings of contentment signaled the prophetic nature of his revelation. Turner sarcastically suggested to "other churches, who are in the habit of practicing upon the same principle" that they should "commit Smith's rule to memory." These other religious groups who, like Joseph Smith, believed "on mere human testimony" included the followers of the "Kentucky Revival," Turner's term for the organizers and participants in the Cane Ridge revival.[55]

These evangelicals concerned about revivalism argued the scriptural practices of Mormonism and revivalists not only lacked a solid foundation in reality, but also relied on excitement and feeling as the primary marker of trustworthiness. Turner called both groups "spiritual pleasure-seekers" who looked to an "internal sign, or impulse, or emotion" for spiritual revelation. These internal feelings and signs, Turner argued, would "relieve or confirm the tedious process of thought, and indicate to them the path of duty and faith, not only by the convictions of reason and conscience, but also by the impulse of passion." This kind of mentality led individuals to work "their minds up to as high a pitch of excitement as possible." Whatever truth they then want to affirm, "that side of any question around which their feelings kindle, and glow, and burn most readily, and most furiously, is of course the side of truth." Using a critique of Mormonism to attack this revivalist way of understanding scripture, Turner wrote that the "Mormon prophet says that the Lord told him how to go through this whole process to perfection while translating the gold bible." He says the process of each is the same: "study it out in your own mind, and then pray." If it is right, "your bosom shall burn within you," Turner argued. Thousands, he believed "are now practicing upon it . . . and other thousands who are in a fair way to be there soon."[56]

Evangelicals critical of revivalism saw both Mormons and revivalist preachers reading the Bible without any grounding in common sense. While discussing the scriptural practices of Mormonism and revivalism, Turner considered the "two general modes of interpreting written language." The first was "to let it speak to plain common sense for itself."

The second mode of interpretation, Turner argued, involved reworking scripture to meet your own theological proclivities. He described this as pinching the text "by the nose, with our expounding forceps, until it squeals, and then interpret the squeal." He charged both groups with professing "to adhere only to the former, but . . . in reality practice both modes, as occasion requires." By claiming to read the Bible only through the lens of common sense, Turner believed this gave Mormonism "great power over the ignorant; and especially where a mystical or restricted interpretation of scripture has prevailed, they can produce a strong reaction in their own favor."[57]

Turner did not just correlate the actions of evangelical revivalists and Mormonism, he explicitly blamed his coreligionists for the advent of Joseph Smith's mode of scriptural interpretation. He believed the obvious secret was that revivalists had allowed the "dreamy visions of Joe Smith." Because they had tacitly permitted appeals to personal feeling in the understanding of scripture, individuals could more easily "dispense with Jesus Christ and his doctrines." He told his readers not to complain about Mormonism's reading of the Bible in this emotional and narcissistic fashion. Mormonism had, by engaging in these kinds of scriptural practices, practiced a similar kind of working on the "credulity of their hearers," which "they finally succeed in breaking down all the powers of rational inference, and thus prepare them for the missions and pilgrimages of the prophet." Evangelicals worried about Mormonism should "not complain of Joe Smith." Turner argued Smith had only brought to fruition what revivalists had already done. He wrote that Smith gathered the "fruits of a harvest from seed sown by themselves and fostered and ripened by their care." Revivalist scriptural practices, the "loose and floating opinions of this sort may, and often do, tend to increase popular excitement." While these practices may have some limited successes, they create "one class utter skeptics and atheists, to make another large class doubt whether . . . God does exert any moral influence upon the world." Revivalist scriptural practices prepared "greater multitudes to believe that all their emotions and feelings, however mischievous and absurd, come directly from God," wrote Turner.[58]

These evangelicals critical of revivalism further compared their revivalist scriptural practice to Mormonism in the ways both used biblical texts to advance their own personal proclivities. Seeing both groups as engaged in fanatical practices, Turner was not surprised they had similar scriptural practices. He warned evangelicals that the world had seen people who read scripture like this before; they included "Matthias, Jemima Wilkinson, and Ann Lee." Individuals reading to prove what they wanted to believe would always exist, so the real issue was when "such facts and events are ascribed directly . . . to God" and proved by "internal revelations, visions, raptures, ecstasies, of all sorts . . . ascribed to the direct influences of the Holy Spirit." Mormons and revivalists both ascribed all of their "transient states of internal commotion to the fiercest agency of the Spirit of God," Turner wrote. Too many Christians, he thought, used these revivalist scriptural practices to measure the "daily influences of the Spirit of God upon their minds." They did not measure their spiritual growth "by the degree with which they are enabled to discharge all of their duties to God and man, but by the amount of pleasurable or happy feelings which they are enabled . . . to excite in themselves." These kinds of scriptural practices that sought personal satisfaction, whether in Mormonism or revivalism, actually led to a negative outcome. They created an unsecure faith for converts, where "today they are in ecstasies; tomorrow, in despair."[59]

Evangelicals concerned about revivalism used these deliberate comparisons with Mormonism to charge their revivalists coreligionists with fashioning ignorant, unorthodox, novel, and harmful scriptural practices. This revivalist tendency to rely too much on personal whims led evangelical critics to see some of their coreligionists trumpeting ignorance and a lack of religious education as the marker of true religion. When comparing the fanaticisms of the Cane Ridge revival to Mormonism, Turner claimed both were "starved for want of facts." While the "people generally have homilies, doctrines, and dogmas enough ever at hand," what those most likely to experience the extremes of revivalism or the "wonderful phenomenon among the Mormons" had in common was "lukewarm and lazy" professions of faith. Turner described advocates of revivalism and Mormonism as satisfied with their unlearned condition. When describing the rise of humbugs, like sectarianism or Mormonism, the Methodist David Reese likewise thought both flourished by downplaying "a learned ministry," condemning "all study as a preparation for pulpit efforts," and denouncing "literary and theological knowledge, as though ignorance were indispensable to piety or usefulness."[60]

Using elaborate allusions, antirevival evangelicals saw their coreligionists as single-mindedly fixed in a state of ignorance. James M'Chesney compared this narrow way of reading the Bible, which he associated with Mormonism and revivalism, to a "pair of favourite

Grey Squirrels" that he kept as pets. They "were so tame that I could play with, and handle them at pleasure" until one of the squirrels escaped "out of the cage, ran on a shelf where stood a bottle of Aqua Ammonia, which by some means he broke, and got himself completely saturated with its contents." M'Chesney had "no other remedy than that of dipping him in water . . . but instead of receiving my proffered friendship kindly, and submitting to this treatment . . . he snapped at me." M'Chesney used force to "apply water, so as to save his life." He saw this squirrel acting with the same stubborn ignorance as Mormonism used scripture. M'Chesney called it a "picture to the life . . . of a blind, deluded, infatuated, and beastly heart."[61]

This revivalist focus on minute matters of theology that came from a personal, emotional reading of scripture could harm the faith of new Christians, according to these evangelical critics of revivalism. The Methodist James M'Chesney warned his Methodist audience that "the enemy of your soul will try to detain these new Christians." The devil would try to get them to look closely into the doctrines, governments, and customs of the Presbyterians, Baptists, Methodists, or the Anglicans. It gave them too "limited" or "private" view of interpretation. M'Chesney thought this view of scripture would render "one people or nation more peculiar to God." He believed that Satan would convince these new Christians that their everlasting salvation depended on determining which group was correct. M'Chesney argued denominational distinctions did not matter to new Christians because they had little preparation or religious training for these kinds of theological discussions.[62]

Those concerned about revivalism used anti-Mormonism to criticize their coreligionists for engaging in scriptural practices that fostered contentious and divisive theology. A Methodist minister in England argued that Mormonism forced believers to accede to their "religious peculiarities." Stevenson asked, "[S]uppose I believe in all the grand doctrines of the Book of Mormon, such as the fall of man, the restoration of the world by Jesus Christ . . . and a few others." Would he still "be saved, if, at the same time, I do not believe that Jared went over to America[?]" By asking if he did not believe in Mormonism's literal account of the lost tribes of Israel coming to the new world, he characterized Mormonism as legalism, a danger he saw lurking among "Churchmen, Dissenters, Primitives, and Wesleyans." Turner likewise believed that bad theology would encourage skepticism among new believers, and that this excessive way of reading scripture would lead converts to doubt all "revivals of pure religion."[63]

As he compared the consequences of revivalism and Mormonism, Turner thought the scriptural practices of both could sow confusing and harmful beliefs. Both movements, he believed, could make people feel "that their eternal salvation . . . is suspended on a metaphysical cobweb." This feeling of indecision will lead them to "never rest easy until they think they see clearly what that cobweb hangs on." He thought people would listen and believe Joseph Smith "because they prefer belief to doubt," which was the same argument he made earlier in *Mormonism in All Ages* about the ways revivalism fostered powerful, charismatic religious figures. Turner thought when matters of scripture became "magnified into great fundamental truths" by discordant scriptural practices, then "doubt is more intolerable than absurdity." Mormonism, he believed, was not unique in taking "all possible advantage of this condition of things." It had merely exploited the condition created by revivalism and other fanaticisms. Reese likewise considered humbuggeries, like Mormonism and revivalism, as leading to disagreement over religious questions of original sin, natural ability, regeneration, and limited atonement. This led to a contentiousness, where groups who believed differently thought "my doxy is orthodoxy;—your doxy is heterodoxy." Because competing Christians profess "steadfastly to adhere to the same standards, while each appeal to the same authorities for their different explications of the common creed," Turner believed that disagreement was inevitable.[64]

The similar scriptural practices of Mormonism and revivalism also led to bad theology, according to the evangelicals concerned about revivalism. Referring to the Cane Ridge revival, Turner charged that learned religious professors twisted the Bible to defend the view that the "convulsions in Tennessee were the result of the Spirit, because they operated as the Saviour promised the Spirit should operate." He believed these revivalist thinkers had adopted rogue interpretations of the Bible, as Mormonism had. Turner charged them with forgetting that Jesus "did not promise that the Spirit should set the world to twitching, jerking." While he accepted that promoters of revivals were correct in their belief that "the operations of the Spirit will change from age to age," their views constituted "vain imagination, credulity, and dogmas of men." Self-serving scriptural practices, Turner wrote, will change "much more than the Spirit of God does."[65]

Turner specifically challenged the way these revivalist thinkers understood the work of the Holy Spirit in the New Testament, like the events on the Day of Pentecost found in the New Testament book of

Acts. He wrote how "we read that the Spirit was then poured out in power." Disciples spoke in tongues and "were greatly amazed at what happened." Revivalists misinterpreted this event, making much more out of it than the authors of the Bible intended. Turner argued that "the precise number that were affected with shouting, bellowing, trembling, twitching, barking, hysterics, catalepsy, and nightmare" was not large.[66]

Revivalist scriptural practices, which Reese lumped in with other kinds of humbugs, like Mormonism, could also lead to the creation of new religious beliefs. Moving beyond the natural restraints of the Bible could promote any kind of personal or denominational interest. Reese did not think it was possible to "imagine an imposture that is too obscene, base, or infamous" if the intent is to "make proselytes." Right before he discussed Mormonism as a humbug like ultra-Protestantism, Reese concluded the worst "impostures which shock the sensibilities of the more refined portion of their community, owe their existence and perpetuation to the reception which the more polished humbugs receive."[67]

Evangelicals concerned about the ways the Second Great Awakening enabled too much theological improvisation in the 1830s and 1840s fashioned a religious critique of their own movement that used anti-Mormonism to further scriptural practices that would limit the variety of translation, place constraints on theological creativity, call for an end to Christian partisanship, and be more faithful to the text of the Bible. Calling for less inventiveness, more constraints, and a spirit of harmony within their own movement's scriptural practices was not inaugurated with Mormonism. Their experience with Catholicism gave many antebellum evangelicals a ready language to respond to the new threat of Mormonism. Hundreds of thousands of Catholics migrated to the United States in the first decades of the nineteenth century and a sizable number of native-born Americans converted to Catholicism during the same period. Catholic newspapers appeared in every major American city. The editors of these Catholic newspapers unapologetically claimed that they alone had an authoritative understanding of the word of God. Unlike antebellum American evangelicals, these Catholic editors presented themselves as having qualified interpreters to collect and translate the scriptures in the form of priests.[68]

Influenced by the power of these attacks and vulnerable to Catholics who claimed that they had superior grasp of biblical revelation, antebellum evangelicals critical of revivalism defended their use of the Bible by calling for a less varied, more constrained, and less narcissistic way of reading the Bible. Archibald Alexander provided the template for this position in the 1820s, when he argued the apocrypha did not belong in Protestant Bibles. Some Bibles in early American continued to contain the apocrypha. Alexander published a 400-page treatise on the ways the "Bible is complete, containing all things necessary to guide the faith and practice of every sincere Christian." Although Catholics had added books to the canon, Alexander believed Christians could reject these easily because "they were not written in the Hebrew language, but in the Greek, which was known not to the Jews, until long after inspiration had ceased." Alexander mused that if Christians could retroactively add books to the canon, what would prevent them from introducing "Herodotus, Livy, or even the Koran itself." Alexander concluded with a guide for how Christians could determine if a book belonged in the canon. A book of dubious authenticity, like the apocrypha, would contain internal contradictions; romantic stories; ahistorical terms, events, or words; false doctrine; or misquotations from the Bible. He further concluded that the providence of God showed that the New Testament was complete. This process of analyzing both the internal and external evidence of a purported sacred text was the same one that evangelicals used to undermine the Book of Mormon.[69]

Scriptural practices with less diversity, Alexander believed, would work against the theological cacophony threatening antebellum evangelicalism. He believed Christians should determine through "research, which requires time and labor . . . the foundations on which their religion rests." This kind of attention required a knowledge of history and an aversion to theological populism. He prophesied the "doctrines of men will disappear; and the dogmas of the schools and the alliance with philosophy being renounced, there will be . . . an increasing tendency to unity of sentiment." Christians would forget "a thousand knotty questions." They will no longer permit themselves "to engage in fierce and unbrotherly contentions, about matters of little importance."[70]

These methods of reading scripture articulated vis-à-vis Catholicism influenced how antirevival evangelicals used anti-Mormonism to further a more careful, more discriminating, less creative, and more harmonious and faithful set of scriptural practices. Fearful of the theological excesses embedded in the hermeneutical principles of the Second Great Awakening, these evangelicals critical of revivalism pressed their goal through an emphasis on the reasonableness of theology. Antebellum evangelical theologians increasingly relied upon natural theology and rational evidence to prove the authenticity of Christianity. They appealed to internal and external apologetic arguments to prove the trustworthiness of the Bible, which was exactly how evangelicals challenged the reliability of the Book of Mormon. Jonathan Turner, Origen Bacheler, Alexander Campbell, and others used this language of evidentiary Christian reasonableness to undermine belief in the Book of Mormon. While believing they disqualified Mormonism based upon a lack of evidence, these evangelicals' apologetic strategy had the consequence of reinforcing a belief that Christianity had to prove itself as rational through appeals to common sense.

Evangelicals concerned about revivalist scriptural practices used anti-Mormonism to argue that members of their own movement needed to read the Bible more carefully. Turner, in *Mormonism in All Ages*, lumped together the followers of Joseph Smith and revivalism as both mistaking "understanding all that was said by Christ and his apostles *to their hearers*, as of course said to them." He charged both "impostors" with claiming a "*literal* interpretation" of the Bible through their assertion of the visible manifestations of the Holy Spirit, like speaking in tongues and supernatural healings. Turner asked the followers of Mormonism and his own coreligionists to read more carefully in the Bible and look for "any past or future sign."[71]

Turner explicitly called for evangelicals to read the Bible with a careful eye to "rational evidence." He concluded this was the "great work" of evangelicals, to substitute "reason and faith for credulity and belief without reason." More judicious scriptural practices would "arrest at once the fatal career of the skeptic and the fanatic." Christians, if they "discriminated more, and doubted less," would show "more intellect, and secure to themselves more good." Turner compared the correct reading of the Bible to "an apothecary's drug; if the labels are wrong, it is worse than nothing." He blamed religious teachers in the United States, who "ought neither to assert nor believe any thing in religion, until it is absolutely demonstrated, however unimportant." The British Methodist Stevenson argued likewise that "keeping the commandments of God is necessary; but faith must go before." Saying the Bible needed to be read in a less creative fashion, Stevenson thought "keeping of the commandments before faith, is like planting a tree with its branches fixed in the earth, and its roots waving in the air; or something like putting the coach before the horses."[72]

Evangelicals critical of revivalism also used Mormonism to call for less creative and varied scriptural practices. In his argument for a more rational and careful way of reading the Bible, Turner wanted to emphasize that these more discriminating scriptural practices should be done in a faith-centered fashion. He emphasized that "faith is cordial belief on rational evidence, and belief in anything whatever, on any other ground, is not faith, but folly, or madness, or presumption." In this section where Tuner explicitly compared the scriptural practices of revivalism and Mormonism, he wrote that "those who teach men to believe on any other ground, teach Mormonism, and not Christianity." He even heaped blame for the rise of Mormonism on the "extreme frequency with which" Christians "are called upon to believe in matters of faith, without having the grounds of rational belief placed distinctly and clearly before them." Turner accepted that making these kinds of scriptural errors was common because of "limitation of mind and the uncertainties of language." He hoped that if "religious belief could be chained rigorously to reason," then "fanaticism, and infidelity too, would soon be consigned to the moles and the bats."[73]

Attacks on Mormonism's scriptural practices finally allowed these concerned evangelicals to call for a more unified and harmonious set of scriptural practices. Attempting to come to some sort of peaceful theological coexistence was important to these evangelicals because they identified these intramural disagreements as an important factor in creating a fertile environment for the appearance of the Book of Mormon.

Mormonism first allowed evangelicals critical of revivalism to promote a more unified and constrained reading of the Bible through the downplaying of theological particularities. The British Methodist minister Stevenson sketched out the way that evangelicals could survive the Mormon "enemy . . . one that aims at the destruction of them all" through the avoidance of a sectarian way of reading the Bible. Since Mormonism wanted to "lay every section of the Christian church on a level with the dust . . . [and] erect a temporal empire, to the exclusion of everybody but themselves," his defense contrasted with Mormonism's strict way of reading the Bible. Stevenson hoped that "every sect of Christians holding the grand doctrines of the Bible, should begin in earnest to love each other fervently, to pray for each other faithfully." Evangelicals all shared a common enemy that aimed "at the destruction of them all." While Mormonism had struck a "bold, though feeble blow at our common Christianity," Stevenson believed it aimed to "lay every section of the Christian church on a level with the dust." Only through unity and ignoring small differences would Christianity be able to survive.[74]

The Methodist James M'Chesney also saw the unity of Christendom coming to fruition only through the downplaying of theological particularities as the antidote to the Mormon threat. In his *Antidote to Mormonism*, he spent much of the first chapter arguing that disinterested love would provide the best defense against Mormonism. While the words and actions of Mormons demonstrated a lack of concern for others, he warned evangelicals that they would fail if they continued on this same path. M'Chesney thought Mormons and fanatical evangelicals shared a common tendency to praise God with the same mouth that they used to slander and destroy their opponents. Instead of caring for others, they spent all their time "looking for miracles, signs, and wonders." M'Chesney warned his Methodist Episcopal audience that they needed to hold on to this "fixed principle of love" lacking in Mormonism. Unlike Mormons who considered themselves the aggrieved, "peculiar favorites of God," evangelicals needed to follow the Great Commission and pray for those who persecuted them. If evangelicals would eventually adopt a more reasonable and loving spirit, then all Christians would obtain the wisdom to distinguish between the voice of a "sheep and a goat." Drawing this contrast with Mormonism allowed M'Chesney to remind his readers that "the devil cannot counterfeit disinterested love."[75]

With his focus on humbugs within his own movement, David Reese thought a less discordant scriptural practice would have a variety of positive religious outcomes. He believed it "absurd" to think that uniformity of religious belief was ever possible. Reese stressed peaceful coexistence within antebellum evangelicalism. It would improve missionary efforts by not needlessly dividing up the field of missionary work. Reese wrote that he had seen some successes when religious groups downplayed theological specifics. He hoped that more and more evangelicals were falling in "love with their religion than with their sect." This embrace of a broad, common creed was what he thought of as "enlightened Christianity." Reese believed Christians who most effectively responded to "Popery, infidelity heresy, error or sin . . . do so in the name" and on behalf of this broad form of Christianity.[76]

Evangelicals believed the Book of Mormon was a poor imitation of the Bible and that it had sprung from the head of Joseph Smith. Since their earliest moments of encounter, they denigrated it in the strongest terms as a plagiarism of both God and man. Filled with intense venom, these denunciations of Mormonism's scriptural practices reveal as much about evangelicalism's own internal politics as it does about their intolerance toward Joseph Smith's religion. Antebellum evangelicals expressed a mounting concern with the grounds for the authenticity of their own faith. Growing numbers of evangelicals had begun to see the biblical translations they used at home and in their churches as riddled with errors and biases. As people who believed that the Bible contained essential spiritual truths, they required an accurate translation and understanding of scripture. Genuine faith faced an additional hurdle arising from the evangelical conviction that individuals should read and interpret scripture for themselves. In a society overflowing with religious texts, that democratic reading strategy created religious cacophony and confusion. Evangelicals increasingly worried over the 1830s and 1840s that groups like Mormons could pass as orthodox because no one had the standing to challenge their way of understanding the word of God. Evangelicals critical of revivalism responded to this chaos by fashioning a religious critique of Mormonism that sought evangelical peace by limiting the variety of translations and by placing constraints on theological creativity.

The charges that Mormonism read the Bible in a wrong and dangerous fashion comprised just one component of a broader antebellum rejection of Mormonism. Like their attacks on Mormonism's religious economy, antebellum evangelicals attacked the followers of Joseph Smith with a cornucopia of criticisms. These charges always represented something more. They revealed and heightened tensions and divisions within antebellum evangelicalism itself. The use of anti-Mormonism in evangelical infighting came to a climax surrounding the establishment and growth of the Mormon city of Nauvoo in the late 1830s and early 1840s. Evangelicals found spiritist, martial, and sectarian forms of fanaticism in this new Illinois city. The irony, of course, was similar forms of fanaticism existed within the evangelical movement itself. A group of evangelicals concerned about the radical nature of the revivals of the Second Great Awakening used the anti-Mormonism surrounding Nauvoo to fashion a calmer faith that fit in more comfortably with the surrounding society.

CHAPTER 5

"Mormonism, Whether Found . . . in Kentucky, or at Nauvoo"

Revivalism and the Rise of Mormonism

On a spring evening in 1842, Henry Caswall walked along the banks of the "noble Mississippi" with the mighty river flowing smoothly "undisturbed by the slightest ripple." He was anxious because he had just seen human nature "in a novel aspect" through the "absurdities of Mormonism" in the city of Nauvoo. After spending several days in this new Illinois city, investigating the shape and direction of the Latter-day Saints, he came away convinced Christians needed to respond to Mormonism in a different fashion. A new response by Christians, Caswall claimed, would ultimately determine whether this religious rival would succeed for a little while, and "then sink into obscurity; or whether . . . it shall extend itself sword in hand, until . . . Christianity shall be levelled with the dust."[1]

When Joseph Smith purchased land along the Mississippi in the late 1830s, a number of antebellum evangelicals became increasingly concerned about the variety of fanaticisms practiced by Mormonism at Nauvoo. Through a comprehensive set of charges, antebellum evangelicals characterized Mormonism as practicing a spiritist, martial, and sectarian faith. They had long criticized Mormons for displaying a spiritist fanaticism through their associations with the dark arts and through their promotion of the miraculous workings of the Holy Spirit, and over the 1830s and 1840s, they continued to build upon these objections. Mormon fanaticism at Nauvoo, evangelicals argued, also displayed militant elements that boded a variety of dangerous consequences. Antebellum evangelicals finally labeled Mormons at Nauvoo as practitioners of a sectarian fanaticism and aggressive exclusivity.

Those polemical charges reveal antebellum evangelicals had more than just a reactionary attitude toward a new religious rival. At the conclusion of his book about the Mormon prophet, the Anglican professor Henry Caswall told Christians they needed to move beyond merely articulating the heretical theology and practices of the Latter-day Saints. Instead of expecting people to see the falsehoods of Mormonism through well-crafted critiques, Caswall hoped that evangelicals would see that their own movement experienced the same three varieties of fanaticism that appeared at Nauvoo. As Mormonism continued to grow, seemingly unchecked, more evangelicals followed Caswall's lead, so that over the 1830s and 1840s evangelicals concerned about the excesses of revivalism concluded their own movement bore significant blame for the rise and shape of Mormonism. Focusing their charges primarily on the revivals of the Second Great Awakening, these evangelicals critical of revivalism accused their coreligionists of encouraging a radical spiritism, a militant ethos, and a destructive exclusivity within their own movement.[2]

The Spiritist Fanaticism of Mormonism

Antebellum evangelicals charged Mormons at Nauvoo with practicing a spiritist fanaticism. They found it ludicrous that followers of Joseph Smith believed God interacted with them on a regular basis. For evangelicals, the radical spiritism of Mormonism involved both the occult practices described in chapter 1 and the work of the Holy Spirit. Over the 1830s and 1840s, they sustained initial objections that accused Joseph Smith of religiously using rituals, incantations, animal sacrifices, prayers, and religious books to hunt for fortune, and they extended these charges to emphasize the Latter-day Saints' continuing belief in the workings of the Holy Spirit. Later evangelicals focused less on these origin stories as quirky anecdotes of a new religious group, and they paid more attention to the ways the followers of Joseph Smith actually participated in and perpetuated a belief in supernatural healings, speaking in tongues, and raising people from the dead. Antebellum evangelicals believed, in the representative words of the Methodist minister La Roy Sunderland, that Mormons declare "to act under the infallible inspiration of God, and to have the power to work miracles." They "profess to have "intercourse with the angels of God, and affirm that they frequently see them, and have messages from God through them." Evangelicals like Sunderland thought that by continuing to believe in spiritist fanaticism, Mormonism resulted in foolish faith, blind belief, and physical danger.[3]

Mormons walking on water was one of the most widely circulated stories among evangelicals seeking to ridicule Mormonism's spiritist fanaticism. Throughout the middle of the 1830s, evangelical editors reprinted the story of a "Tragical Event," where a Mormon elder from Missouri summoned "disciples . . . to a pond, on the waters of which . . . [this] gifted elder announced that he should walk and preach." In evangelical accounts, editors recounted how this Mormon minister, who in some accounts was Joseph Smith himself, prophesied "great things," but before his expected miracle, residents decided to "secretly . . . make mischief." These cunning individuals traversed a shallow pond, where they "soon discovered a line of plank laid in a particular direction completely across the pond, sunk about four inches under the surface of the water." Leaving everything else undisturbed, the local troublemakers "decided to prevent the miracle by sawing the plank in half." When the expected day finally arrived, the Mormon congregation "placed themselves in an amphitheatre on the surrounding slopes," and the Mormon elder stepped out on one of the planks and fell into the water. Unable to swim, the Mormon preacher, these evangelical editors recounted, "sunk, and long before the confounded assembly were in a condition to afford him relief, perished a victim to his impious presumption."[4]

In addition to the spiritist fanaticism of Mormonism eliciting foolish behavior, antebellum evangelicals saw the embrace of manifestations of the Holy Spirit resulting in blind belief. Truman Coe, a Presbyterian minister who lived among Mormons for more than five years in Kirtland, came away from his experience with the Latter-day Saints thinking that their fundamental principle of belief was that "God continues to hold intercourse with the saints on earth by visions and revelation." Elaborating on earlier objections about Mormons claiming to have the power to perform feats of physical daring, Coe recounted they also believed the Holy Spirit gave believers the power to drive out demons, handle serpents, drink poison, and heal the sick. Evangelicals thought such unreasoning belief meant Mormons also always had a convenient explanation for the apparent failure of the Holy Spirit to respond to their supplications. Mormons had a "salve at hand when any miracle fails," according to Coe, because "nobody can have any evidence of these wonders but those who have Mormon eyes and Mormon ears."[5]

While evangelicals criticized Mormonism for the ways they attempted to prove their miracles, these techniques were familiar to antebellum evangelicals. Leaders of Mormonism used the same methods to verify contemporary supernatural occurrences as those used by evangelicals to vouch for the miracles recounted in the Bible. Evangelicals and Mormons both appealed to the reasonableness of faith, logical proofs, and the testimony of sensory evidence. In *A Dialogue between Joseph Smith and the Devil*, Parley Pratt made the point that if the few witnesses to the New Testament are to be believed, then the thousands of witnesses to the healings and miracles of Mormonism should also be believed.[6]

The justifications for the truthfulness of Mormon miracles, according to antebellum evangelicals, could take on an outlandish quality. The American Sunday School Union leader Harvey Newcomb told his readers about a "*curious circumstance* that has transpired among the Mormons in Chatauqua county" when a new Mormon convert received the "gift of tongues." After quickly becoming one of the "brightest ornaments of the church," another "young man arose and broke out in an unknown language" during a Mormon worship service. The first convert, Mr. Robinson, pretended to be able to interpret. During his attempts, he confessed to his fraud. According to Newcomb, Robinson admitted he had not experienced any manifestations of the Holy Spirit since his baptism, that "the tongues spoken by me are of my own invention," and that as far as he knew all of Mormonism "was a farce."[7]

Antebellum evangelicals worried because it seemed that the spiritist fanaticism of Mormonism put the movement's converts in physical and spiritual danger. After the Mormon migration to Missouri in the early 1830s, the editors of the *Christian Secretary* remembered that the Mormon emigrants arrived in their village "on foot, without overcoats or baggage" because they "professed to be living examples of the power of faith." The Latter-day Saints had told these Missouri evangelicals that "the Lord kept them warm during the winter, and also furnishing them with clothing . . . by substituting new ones while they slept." The obvious conclusion of such spiritist fanaticism, evangelicals thought, was the death of Mormon converts. Coe remembered a young man "lying on a bed of sickness" who sent for Joseph Smith and other Mormon elders to come and heal him. "After praying over him, anointing him with oil in the name of the Lord," Smith "commanded the disease to depart." The Mormon leader then pronounced the young man healed, and he ordered him to rise and walk. Probably "stimulated by the circumstances and by high expectation," according to Coe, this youth rose up and attempted to walk, but he quickly became faint, "betook himself to the bed again, and grew worse." Coe concluded with a wry observation that the man's health improved dramatically only after a doctor finally came to visit him. In a similar, but more depressing story, Coe relayed that a young woman "lying at the point of death with the measles" called for Mormon elders to come and lay hands on her, but after they did as she asked, she "very soon afterwards . . . was a corpse."[8]

The editors of the *Christian Advocate and Journal* told a similar story about a female convert named Mrs. Hodge from Illinois. Hodge became sick in April 1839, and Joseph Smith's father "was formally called upon to heal the deceased woman." He laid hands on her and prayed for her healing. According to this account by antebellum evangelicals, she immediately "smiled, moved herself in the bed, and her mother, greatly rejoicing, came to her, lifted her up, and the whole family . . . declared in great triumph to their neighbors the miracle which had just been wrought." After Smith's father left, these evangelical editors claimed the excitement subsided and the "sick lady, in a few brief hours, was much worse than before." Smith's father came back to heal her again and again, but "all was vanity." Hodge's mother begged for Joseph Smith himself to appear, and when he did, Smith commanded the disease to depart. The disease was "deaf to his mandate, and on the third day afterward the mortal remains of this lady were laid, in the silent tomb." These evangelical editors concluded that "such are the boasted powers of this grand imposter."[9]

The Militant Fanaticism of Mormonism

Mormonism represented not just a rhetorical threat to evangelicals. They also feared the Latter-day Saints had embraced a militant fanaticism. The Nauvoo Legion, established in 1840, drew much of this criticism. Many evangelicals at first did not know what to make of the Nauvoo Legion, with some evangelicals seeing it as a defensive organization. As they learned more about the actions and powers of the Nauvoo Legion, though, antebellum evangelicals came to see it as a threat to peace and order. Since Joseph Smith had complete authority over the Nauvoo Legion, evangelicals concluded that it functioned as his personal fighting force. The Delaware Methodist Amos Wickersham described the Legion as "six or seven thousand men" of "the most efficient and best drilled corps in the Union." When the Nauvoo Legion appeared at the laying of the cornerstone for the Nauvoo temple, an evangelical reporting to the *Christian Advocate* called the Legion's presence a "most imposing scene." The Presbyterian editors of the *Religious Monitor and Evangelical Repository* further warned their readers that "every one of a certain age is called on to bear arms; and the 'legion of the Lord' is drilled twice a week."[10]

The Nauvoo Legion imbued all Mormon civic celebrations with a martial character, according to evangelicals. In an account of a July 4th celebration, the editors of the *Western Christian Advocate* described this fete as "a kind of military celebration." Joseph Smith presented himself in the "appearance of a prophet . . . dressed in military costume, riding a fine horse, and surrounded by quite a respectable staff . . . mounted . . . and armed with rifles, pistols, and knives." The editors of this evangelical periodical saw Joseph Smith commanding "fifteen military companies under an ecclesiastical organization, with an assembly of spectators variously estimated at from five to eight thousand." At another civic event, the construction of the Mormon temple at Nauvoo, the editors of the *Christian Advocate and Journal* remarked that Smith appeared "besides a lifeguard of twelve men, mounted, dressed in white." These men had taken an oath to protect their prophet "even unto blood" because they believed that Smith was "the inspired organ of the divine commands, and the grand centre of all this strange pageant!" In a final example of the civic militancy of Mormonism, Tyler Parsons, a Congregationalist from Boston, recounted a "splendid parade," where a group of "Mormon ladies" presented the Nauvoo Legion "with a splendid national silk flag . . . under roar of cannon." Parsons further witnessed one of the Mormon leaders giving a speech that prophesied a "day of retributive justice," with "the blood of the innocent flow[ing], and . . . the groans of the dying as witnesses for Jesus." At the front of this assembled army was a "Cohort of 500" followed by "Lieutenant-General Smith, Major and Brigadier Generals, with their aid[e]s . . . general staff-band-cohort of 500-ladies, eight in breast," and once the Mormon women delivered the flag to Joseph Smith, Parsons said Smith "received it . . . [on] behalf of the church and defence of Jesus," and the founder of Mormonism declared "so long as he had command of the Legion, that flag never should be disgraced."[11]

Mormons described the military power represented at Nauvoo in almost the exact same way as evangelicals, but they reached the opposite conclusions about its meaning. Describing the laying of the cornerstone of the temple in Nauvoo in militaristic ways, the editors of *Times and Seasons* emphasized that displays of their strength would ward off future persecution and prevent Mormonism's demise. These descriptions of the Nauvoo Legion worked to unify the Mormon people and emphasize their identity as God's chosen people. Editors of this Latter-day Saints newspaper remarked "none but Jesus could or would accomplish such things as we behold." Completion of the temple at Nauvoo also represented the indwelling of God in the Mormon community, according to these Mormon writers, demonstrating that Mormons were "highly favored of God." The very items Mormonism itself saw as markers of providential safety, antebellum evangelicals felt as existential threats.[12]

Evangelicals believed the inherent militancy of Mormon theology prompted violent behavior. Evangelicals began to deploy these criticisms in greater depth after the Missouri War of 1838, when a conflict broke out between Mormons and local residents. In this heated context, an evangelical "Disciple" asked rhetorically whether or not "Mormons claim America as the land promised them, in the same sense as Canaan was promised to the Jews anciently?" because if they do, then will it "become the duty of every Mormon as soon as they feel themselves able, to attempt to drive out these Gentiles from the land of promise?" For this evangelical "Disciple," the Mormon belief system meant that that the very "essence of Mormonism" was to "carry conviction to the hearts of unbelievers on the points of their bayonets, and eventually to preach their doctrines from the mouths of their cannon."[13]

Antebellum evangelicals feared a variety of dangerous outcomes emanating from the warlike nature of Mormonism, false conversion prominent among them. Through their military organization, the Methodist minister Daniel Kidder warned, the leaders of Mormonism could frighten off religious competition through "the pomp and circumstance of military parade." He concluded the awe-inspiring nature of the Nauvoo Legion served "as a means of astonishing the natives, and of drawing in a class of adherents that could be secured in no other way." La Roy Sunderland, a Methodist minister, compared the converts of Mormonism to victims. He believed the leaders of Mormonism hoodwinked converts, forcing them into a "course of irreligion and crime, under the penalty of death." Jonathan Turner concluded Mormonism's "desire for power and aversion to restraint" led to "credulity and infatuation."[14]

Evangelicals also warned Mormonism could overthrow the state or federal government in a direct or indirect fashion. First in Missouri in the early 1830s and later in Nauvoo in the 1840s, evangelicals theorized that Mormon communities would undermine state and federal governments by withholding tax revenue. Ezra Booth, the Baptist critic of Mormonism, believed the efforts by Mormon leaders to establish a trading depot in Missouri were merely a tactic to deprive the federal government of revenue. This withholding of incoming funds from the West meant the federal government would lack the monies to secure the western frontier. Playing into longstanding fears of a Mormon-Indian alliance, Booth believed this financial maneuver would result in an increasing number of Indian raids on evangelical communities in the West, and ultimately the destabilization of the entire western frontier.[15]

Antebellum evangelicals, like Booth, believed Mormons had allied and intermarried with Native Americans. They had turned native in their worship, according to Booth. Describing their emotionally expressive worship services in ethnocentric and racist terms, he thought they became like Native Americans by speaking in unknown tongues and making strange sounds. It became difficult, Booth claimed, to distinguish between Mormons and Indians, as Mormons assumed "the visage of the savage." Booth concluded the entire Mormon proselytization project served to recruit Indians for warfare. He charged that Mormons appealed to Indians by telling them conversion would allow them to reclaim their lands from white settlers. This was a ruse. Booth luridly stated that Joseph Smith commanded Mormon men to intermarry with Native American women in order to take their land.[16]

After the Missouri War of 1838, evangelicals, like Robert Baird, increasingly believed Nauvoo stood as the epicenter of Mormonism's attempt to create a "kind of empire in the West." A correspondent writing in an August issue of the *New York Evangelist* concluded Mormonism "has literally environed itself with threatening military munitions at Nauvoo." Describing their political efforts as "mobocratic," evangelicals viewed Mormon efforts at winning elections as secretive and violent. Antebellum evangelicals thought Mormons voted according to the dictates of Joseph Smith in a kind of "religious and political despotism." The very rights of "life, liberty, and the pursuit of happiness" would not be safe in their hands, according to this evangelical newspaper.[17]

In the most infamous suspicion that Mormons might be plotting a coup, evangelicals accused Joseph Smith of plotting the assassination of Lilburn Boggs, the governor of Missouri, after someone shot him at his home in May 1842. A Stone-Campbell editor asked whether or not "Gen. Joseph Smith, Jr. . . . found it necessary to detail a body guard on account of a very general impression that he hired ruffians who attempted to assassinate Gov. Boggs?" This evangelical believed that since Mormonism commanded assassination "in the case of dissenters from the Mormon faith. . . . is it not the design of the leaders of Mormonism to establish a Western Empire?" Some evangelicals believed Mormonism posed a militant threat to the state and federal government by giving people the wrong allegiances. La Roy Sunderland, in his description of Mormonism, charged the followers of Joseph Smith with assuming the "prerogatives" of their own faith "over the consciences of Men." He added a further charge that Mormonism "authorizes and sanctions physical resistance to the laws of the land," and that the leaders of Mormonism demand "independence above the authorities of the nation."[18]

The Sectarian Fanaticism of Mormonism

The final danger posed by Mormonism's fanaticism at Nauvoo, according to antebellum evangelicals, was sectarian warfare. This charge of exclusivity acquired force as a wider array of evangelical denominations participated in anti-Mormonism over the 1830s and 1840s. La Roy Sunderland saw sectarianism as one of the defining features of Mormonism, writing that adherents claimed theirs to be the only true church. He further wrote that Mormonism believed "all others are of the Anti-Christ, and exposed to God's eternal displeasure." Jonathan Turner concurred, writing how all of Mormonism's converts "are perfectly sure that their dogmas, and those of their teachers, are true." Primitivist evangelical Walter Scott also worried the "pomp and farce, the foundation of a third Temple at Nauvoo . . . supported by the Nauvoo Legion of 600 men" didn't seem to concern most Americans, even though "any one, with the least particle of reflection, must perceive that unless the career of these outlaws is speedily checked," the Mormons "will involve the far West in a ferocious and exterminating war." One British Methodist agreed Joseph Smith aimed to "lay every section of the Christian church on a level with the dust." This Wesleyan claimed Mormonism intended to destroy all Christians—"Dissenters, Primitives, and Wesleyans"—by breaking down "the wall" of orthodoxy, "and on its ruins . . . they mean to erect a temporal empire, to the exclusion of every body but themselves."[19]

According to antebellum evangelicals, sectarian fanaticism was the logical outcome of Mormonism's radical exclusivity, which grew more pronounced as the movement gained a larger following. As one Baptist minister expressed the matter, Mormons believed they alone profess "a deeper a more ardent love to God, and professed to set up a higher standard of devotion than other denominations." The Presbyterians Jesse Townsend and Elisha Camp saw most of the teachings of Mormonism as "sectarian assertions." Antebellum evangelicals thought Mormons' belief in their own righteousness encouraged them to demean other religious groups. Truman Coe wrote how Mormonism contends "the God worshipped by the Presbyterians and all other sectarians, is no better than a wooden God."[20]

Sectarian fanaticism also emanated from the overly emotional character of Mormon religiosity, according to antebellum evangelicals. James M'Chesney concluded Mormonism denied scriptural authority by "secretly throwing its sacred pages into contempt." He believed Mormonism favored some over others, betraying the principle "that God is no respecter of persons." Mormonism, M'Chesney concluded, views the "only ones that are favorites of heaven are those who submit to Mormon Baptism." Jonathan Turner likewise argued Mormons claim to let the text speak for itself, but they then interpret it for their own needs. Turner argued "bodily agitation and sympathetic convulsions are . . . one of the sectarian chills which precedes and induces the Mormon fever." He claimed it "is still one of the most energetic forces in recruiting their ranks."[21]

These sectarian convictions of exclusivity made the followers of Joseph Smith a bigoted, unscriptural, and proud people in the minds of antebellum evangelicals. Truman Coe's takeaway from his time with the Latter-day Saints was they considered themselves the "exclusive favorites of heaven." Mormonism, he charged, believed the rest of the religious world consisted of "natural brute beasts that knew nothing." James Eels, an evangelical missionary, wrote to Joshua Leavitt that Mormons pridefully believed in the veracity of their teachings. These Mormons, he wrote, have "perverted intellect, disordered piety, unfurnished minds, with no sound principles of religion, inclined to the mystical and dreamy." With this inordinate self-esteem, converts to Mormonism were "genuine fanatics" who would "seize upon any thing, no matter how crazy or absurd, that will gratify their restless, crazy piety, and bolster up their exorbitant, spiritual pride."[22]

A posture of exclusivity had consequences. In the minds of antebellum evangelicals, sectarianism led the leaders of Mormonism to condemn others and to control their followers. At one of Mormonism's prayer meetings, Henry Caswall remembered a Mormon minister voicing a prayer of thanksgiving to God for saving them from the sectarianism of the larger religious world. A different Methodist charged that the leaders of Mormonism, "in order to present success . . . must pretend that the Churches are all corrupt" by attacking Christianity as full of "antiquated forms." Daniel Kidder concurred that Mormonism, because of its belief in the law of God given through a prophet, "consider the different Christian denominations of the present day as offspring of the great whore of Babylon." Their belief that no one can be saved who does not believe in the Book of Mormon had created "jealousy and difficulty between them and their neighbors."[23]

The Spiritist, Martial, and Sectarian Fanaticisms of Evangelicalism

Beyond registering the intolerance of antebellum evangelicals, their attacks on Mormons came in reaction to tensions within the evangelical movement itself. They suffered the same kind of spiritist, martial, and sectarian fanaticisms within their own ranks that they found within Mormonism. Similar anxieties had driven their initial objections to Mormonism, and over time evangelicals critical of revivalism became convinced that the excesses of their own coreligionists had fostered the rise and shaped the character of their religious rival. Such evangelical critics used the specter of Nauvoo to reinforce their criticisms of the spiritual excesses of the Second Great Awakening. Just as the heyday of camp meetings seemed to be waning, this group of evangelicals critical of revivalism became increasingly comfortable attacking the very elements that had made it so successful. These evangelicals saw revivalism fostering unrestrained enthusiasm and radical supernaturalism. An increasing number of these evangelicals also criticized the militant ethos of camp meetings and evangelical religiosity, so popular among Methodists, Baptists, and other evangelical Christians. Finally, they believed, some evangelicals had embraced a bitter sectarian zealousness that had manifested during the Second Great Awakening.[24]

The Consequences of Spiritist Fanaticism

Evangelicals critical of revivalism feared the spiritist fanaticism emanating from their own movement had created the conditions for the rise and growth of Mormonism. Since the early nineteenth century, the likes of Asahel Nettleton, Grant Powers, and John Fanning Watson had warned that unrestrained religious enthusiasm could lead to the rise of celebrity preachers and demagoguery. Evangelicals in the 1830s and 1840s took these anxieties a step further to lay out the specific consequences for the spiritist excesses of the Second Great Awakening. Building on a long history of concern about popular supernaturalism, these evangelicals charged that revivals fostered the rise of the radical spiritism of Mormonism through an expansion of what constituted miraculous occurrences, fostering a love of excitement, encouraging the rise of authoritarian leaders who make use of popular prejudice, weakening ecclesiastical institutions, spreading false beliefs about the nature of the Holy Spirit, and creating religious confusion.[25]

While evangelicals universally lambasted Mormonism's association with popular spiritist beliefs, they had embraced popular forms of spiritism in the recent past. Evangelicals had long believed in a world filled with spirits, where God worked in mysterious ways not always easily explained through natural means. The use of magical objects allowed them to navigate the difficulties of the quotidian, and charms, rituals, and incantations promised an end to drought, the amelioration of disease, and protection from darker forms of magic. If the widespread acceptance of supernaturalism had waned within evangelical ranks by the 1830s, many still accepted the continuing work of the Holy Spirit, and experienced prophetic dreams and visions, in which they believed God communicated with them in an intimate fashion. Baptists, Methodists, Presbyterians, and members of the Stone-Campbell movement claimed divine communications from heaven through the indwelling of the Holy Spirit. The revivalist Charles Finney, for example, conversed with Jesus in October 1821. While Finney made it clear his experience took place entirely within his mind, his supernatural experience existed on a spectrum along with the more physical supernatural experiences of spiritism.[26]

The anxieties of Finney demonstrate that some revival participants believed they had a supernatural experience because their encounter bore all the markings of a miracle. Whether through the encouragement or castigation of revival preachers, converts concluded that God had pricked their conscience and revealed their sinful ways. He had spoken directly to them, just as described by Finney. As camp meetings grew in number, size, and intensity, a growing number of antebellum evangelicals attributed the continuing belief in the workings of the Holy Spirit to such gatherings.[27]

The debate over spiritist fanaticism within evangelicalism manifested itself in the question over what constituted a miraculous event. Many antebellum evangelicals considered a wide variety of events in miraculous terms. Many antebellum evangelicals wondered if miracles could simply be unexplained events or if they had to violate natural laws. The capacious definition of the former allowed spontaneous healings, tongue-speaking, and visions to all fall under the rubric of miracles. Finney described miracles as divine interference that set aside or suspended the laws of nature. A capacious definition of the miraculous did not include revivals for Finney. He deliberately excluded what happened at revivals from the miraculous because some antebellum evangelicals deliberately viewed their manifestations in supernatural terms. Barton Stone, one of the founders of the Stone-Campbell movement, viewed miracles in the same way as Finney did. Horace Bushnell, by the 1850s, believed evangelical ministers called so many things miracles that the term had simply lost any real meaning. He worried evangelicals considered any exciting event a divine intervention into human affairs.[28]

Evangelicals concerned about the character of revivalism in the 1830s and 1840s elaborated this criticism of camp meetings and their organizers to charge that these outdoor meetings enabled the rise of the spiritist fanaticism of Mormonism. The Presbyterian Jonathan Turner charged revivalism with the emergence of Mormonism by placing it alongside other fanatical movements throughout history. Catholicism, Islam, Shakerism, the "Kentucky Revivalists," and some evangelical groups, he believed, were "agents of credulity and delusion" who loved "whatever is new, strange, mysterious, or marvelous." Turner claimed evangelicals and Mormons both embraced "the gift of tongues, or prophecy, healings, miracles." Both also professed "peculiar intimacy of intercourse and communion with God." He believed most of the leaders of Mormonism and the camp meeting revivals "have been content to be regarded only as the virtual viceregents of God; others . . . have affected to be Gods themselves."[29]

Turner surveyed a series of hypotheses for the "impostors" of Mormonism and the camp meeting revivals before zeroing in on radical spiritism as the primary cause of both. He did not see them as lunatics because the histories of the "Pagan, Mohammedan, Catholic, and Protestant world" demonstrate "that if those are maniacs, it is only because they belong to a race of religious madmen who have more industriously and systematically prosecuted the regular trade in credulity and delusion." Turner thought "their madness . . . singular and eccentric when compared with the more prevailing, settled, and popular phrensy of their fellows." He also dismissed human depravity as a cause for Mormonism and spiritist fanatical forms of revivalism because they "can find fools enough to believe them." What Turner concluded as the "subordinate principle" for both Mormonism and the revivalism of the Second Great Awakening was a "love of excitement" of anything that is strange or mysterious. Turner worried radical spiritism was a slippery slope, as "a marvellous and mystical church dogma, with its attendant ranting eulogies, is tolerable [for the mass of people]; but a stump speech, a good tragedy, a horse-race, or a mob is first-rate." He concluded that "enthusiasts, fanatics, and impostors, find both hearers and believers, provided they can muster absurdities enough to draw them together."[30]

Evangelicals critical of revivalism believed popular revivalism had the unintended consequence of giving rise to authoritarian figures who propagated spiritist fanaticism, like the Mormon prophet. Authoritarian figures represented a natural consequence of the democratic tendencies within revivalism. Despite the democratic tendencies of much of the Second Great Awakening, ministers who could appeal to and persuade people acquired authority. Within Methodism specifically, itinerant ministers, class leaders, and lay exhorters all acquired the power to influence thought and behavior. The populist tendencies of the Second Great Awakening ironically led to calls for greater patriarchal authority. As antebellum economic changes eroded domestic authority of white men, some authoritarian preachers used the language of democracy to call for increased submission from other groups, like African Americans and women. These threatened patriarchs who hated free-market capitalism and bourgeois evangelicalism desired independence among white men while reducing others to dependence.[31]

Antebellum evangelicals had long seen Joseph Smith as a religious figure with significant power and sway over his followers. The missionary of the American Home Missionary Society, Benjamin Morris, described, in a typical fashion, Smith as holding "unlimited influence, and his declarations are as the authority and influence of the word of God himself. He is a complete despot, and does as he pleases with his people." When David Reese included Mormonism with other humbugs, including phrenology, ultra-temperance, ultra-abolition, ultra-Protestantism, and ultra-sectarianism, what bound these hoaxes together were their ability to muddle fact and fiction. Reese believed this confusion made it more likely for their victims to fall prey to the manipulation of tyrannical authorities.[32]

These evangelicals opposed to the excesses of revivalism saw the radical spiritism of the Second Great Awakening leading directly to the rise of Mormonism. Henry Caswall believed camp meetings represented prime opportunities for the likes of Joseph Smith because they had people "engaging in a mode of worship which consisted chiefly in alternate crying, laughing, singing, and shouting, accompanied with gesticulations of a most extraordinary character." He described these revivals becoming more and more heated with the rise of convulsions, rolling exercises, jerks, barks, and people "peculiarly gifted in prophecies, trances, dreams, rhapsodies, visions of angels, of heaven, and of the holy city." Caswall characterized this form of worship as "deliberately chosen by persons . . . who desired to be considered extremely spiritual" and consisting "in feelings, impulses, and experiences, rather than in the exercise of a living faith." It effectively made camp meetings, Caswall concluded, a "new form of superstition." Thus would "an infallible ruler . . . soon arise to lead captive those who had made a great boast of their liberty."[33]

Caswall would have never identified himself as a participant in the events of the Second Great Awakening or as an evangelical. He had sympathies for revivalism and directed his writing at American evangelicals. Many evangelicals quoted his treatises on the state of religion in the United States. This English Episcopalian distinguished between genuine revivals and spurious revivals. Serious, "sober," and right-thinking people like himself saw genuine revivals as consisting of "deep seriousness and a great tenderness of conscience." Most often the consequence of "faithful, solemn, and direct preaching," genuine revivals encouraged listeners to live a "steady and consistent" religious life. Caswall experienced genuine revivals while pastoring congregations in Ohio. Spurious revivals, he worried, had become all too common through the growing popularity of camp meetings. The "avowed object" of these revivals was excitement, in Caswall's mind. They produced a "fever" on the public mind "which is mistaken for religious fervor."[34]

Evangelicals also concluded that a paucity of organized religious structures at camp meetings encouraged the spiritist fanaticism of Mormonism because it gave free rein to the private judgment of individuals. Caswall did not think Mormonism would have emerged in England because the "mature religious institutions of the mother country would have opposed a bulwark against its progress as a fanaticism." With an anti-American bias, he believed fanaticism had found fertile ground in America because the "great mass of the community, being destitute of official guides, were influenced by accident or by caprice in their choice of religious teacher." Since Americans did not have "authorized expositors . . . [or a] consistent scheme of doctrine," according to Caswall, it was not surprising "that numerous wild forms of religion soon held extensive sway." Ground zero for this lack of religious guidance was the growing number of revivals and camp meetings in the western part of the United States during the early part of the nineteenth century. These camp meetings had long made people "accustomed to have their nerves excited by violent preaching and singing" and those in the throes of revivalism experienced the "most extraordinary attacks of enthusiasm," Caswall believed, which encouraged people to trust in themselves and believed "miracles, ecstasies, visions, and revelations." He feared these developments because the "powers of rational influence had thus been almost entirely broken down in the minds of the enormous masses of the population," making it "easy" for Joseph Smith to "persuade them that the Spirit was abundantly poured out upon them" when the Mormon prophet and "his accomplices succeeded in working up their hearers."[35]

In addition to causing people to place religious trust in their own personal feelings, the spiritist fanaticism of evangelicalism, Jonathan Turner thought, provided fertile soil for the growth of Mormonism by fostering a series of false impressions about the influence of the Holy Spirit at these revivals. These included the "ordinary effects of popular eloquence . . . as ascribed to the influence of the Holy Spirit," "bodily agitations or sympathetic convulsions," or "internal revelations." The leaders of the Cane Ridge revival, like many other impostures, had made "bodily agitation and sympathetic convulsions" the "clearest signs" of the Holy Spirit, just as Joseph Smith had done. These examples of the Holy Spirit included the rolling exercise, the jerks, and the barks. Turner noted those most troubled by "these affections" were "young enthusiasts" and "lukewarm and lazy professors." Turner worried this reliance upon individual emotional experience resulted in people following "the man who can most excite them with new and strange things" and that people would be unable to distinguish the true voice of God and give them the impression they had achieved their own salvation. This kind of religious confusion, he believed, took place "among the Mormons, at Kirtland Ohio," where they received "wonderful manifestations of Divine favor." The "sole design of such teaching" of spiritist fanaticism, according to Turner, was to make some skeptics and atheists, "to make another large class doubt whether . . . God does exert any moral influence upon the world," and to "prepare still greater multitudes to believe that all their emotions and feelings . . . come directly from God."[36]

Antebellum evangelicals finally believed an obsession with manifestations of the Holy Spirit within revivalism enabled the rise of Mormonism by causing confusion. Well-meaning evangelicals who embraced the exertions of the Second Great Awakening caused a similar excitement as Mormonism. Both constituted an "outrage upon the common sense of mankind." Turner claimed "it is Mormonism, in all ages and all churches—Mormonism, whether found . . . in Kentucky, or at Nauvoo." They work "up their hearers, by one stratagem or another, to their most excitement, and then of informing them that the Spirit is poured out upon them." Evangelicals who used these radical spiritist techniques, according to Turner, "should not complain of Mormons for doing the same thing." Smith had merely perfected what had come before him.[37]

The Consequences of Militant Fanaticism

In addition to spiritist fanaticism, evangelicals critical of revivalism warned that camp meetings had fostered a fanaticism for militarism that encouraged the rise of Mormonism. The political and social popularity of military heroism in antebellum American promoted aggressive, martial, and honor-filled values. Presidents Andrew Jackson and Zachary Taylor had gained celebrity through their embodiment of rugged masculinity. They led Indian removal efforts, proving grounds to demonstrate one's patriarchal ability to protect women. The milieu created by Mexican American War and the violence surrounding the annexation of Texas likewise centered an American belief in the redemptive power of violence.[38]

Combative manliness characterized antebellum evangelicalism and Mormonism. A violent ethos infiltrated both movements in the Mountain Meadows Massacre, an event taking place about a decade after the collapse of Mormonism's Nauvoo. Evangelicals leading the group of western travelers and the Latter-day Saints they encountered in Utah resembled each other in several ways. The leaders of each group engaged in extralegal violence in the interest of religious expansion. Methodist migrants and Mormon settlers each believed God had chosen them to build a spiritual refuge in a promised land. Their efforts at building Zion, both groups of religious migrants believed, could hasten the millennium.[39]

Particularly in the South, evangelicals owed their religious success to the adoption of a martial ethos at camp meetings. This militant behavior—casting the conversion of unbelievers as a military campaign, embracing physical violence against their opponents, participating in bellicose rituals, enforcing discipline, and fostering arrogance—was what evangelical critics of revivalism saw as dangerous excesses, and they further linked evangelical aggressiveness to the fanatical militancy of Mormonism.[40]

Evangelicals critical of revivalism deplored the tendency of camp meetings to depict religion as a kind of military campaign, a holy war to rescue the souls of men. Revivalists battled the dark forces of Satan at camp meetings. They used the language of spiritual warfare in attempts to recruit and maintain converts. Relying on martial images from the Old Testament, New Testament, and John Bunyan's *Pilgrim's Progress*, preachers spoke of using weapons and conquering territory when discussing spreading their faith. Revivalists publicly shamed individuals in order to spur on a feeling of their sinfulness. They reminded congregants of their own military service and appealed directly to army veterans as a way to reinforce their manly credentials. Francis Asbury, one of the leaders of American Methodism, spoke of camp meetings in these martial terms, describing the meetings variously as forts, fortifications, warships, or military crusades to keep their foes at bay and to defend Christendom. Such language fell discordantly on the ears of ministers critical of revivalism like Henry Caswall, who faulted camp meetings because they relied on "harsh denunciation" and the "extreme force of language and energy of action."[41]

The martial spirit of the camp meetings also took shape through their demands on the personal behavior of participants. Camp meeting revivals often demanded individuals embrace a code of conduct while in attendance. These rules functioned like a code of military justice. Regulations prohibited the intermingling of sexes during worship, drinking on camp grounds, and other kinds of behavior in violation of the code of conduct. The managers of the camp meetings assigned individuals to keep discipline. The English evangelical Andrew Reed described these as "separate committees . . . appointed to preserve order." This select group regulated everything, including the use of fires, access to drinking water, and the order of worship services. Wearing badges and led by a captain, this guard patrolled the periphery of the campsite to keep order, and they had the power to throw rule-breakers into a camp jail. Reed, an English Congregationalist who thought revivals had a use on the frontier, believed this kind of religious surveillance kept strict order and "the temptation for disorderly behavior was cut off." He claimed he saw nothing "indecent and lewd," or any "wine or spirits on the grounds."[42]

Other evangelicals, those generally critical of revivalism, believed strict oversight of personal behavior at camp meetings ironically encouraged and facilitated martial fanaticism. George Elley, a Stone-Campbell minister, blamed revivals for breeding bad behavior that necessitated a kind of military surveillance. He may have found the behavior of Methodists particularly egregious because the Methodists so readily attacked tradition, a watchword of the restorationist movement. Where Reed saw the guard keeping discipline and order, Elley found "excess riot," drunkenness, intermingling of the sexes, and a lack of decency. He asked his readers to think if they would want their sister, wife, or daughter, to become like the "unfortunate female . . . thrown into convulsions by the excitement of the altar," who was "as perfect a phrenzy as ever racked the frame of a maniac, borne along in the strong arms of several able men . . . writhing beneath her delirium." All of the "inhuman and indecent Doctors of Methodism" leered at her, and she was only left unmolested because some of the camp guard took her "into an adjacent tent, and there held until spasm after spasm had completely exhausted her . . . frame; and she lay, a helpless . . . mass." The revivalists then discarded this young woman, leaving her to recover from "the violence which she had now passed."[43]

The criticisms of the hot-tempered nature of camp meeting revivals fit within the changing gender norms of the antebellum period. Camp meetings encouraged introspection, expressive emotion, physical intimacy, and submission to higher authorities. These actions signaled to the wider world a loss of self-mastery, one of the cardinal sins for men in antebellum America.[44]

Evangelicals critical of revivalism further fretted that the martial ethos of camp meetings could result in aggressive arrogance. Elley described the "stout and crabbed managers" of one camp meeting acting "with as much military swagger as they can put on . . . preening about," like they are "consequential and as deed-daring as so many Falstaffs." Albert Dod, a dogmatic Princetonian evangelical, articulated the same concerns about a militant strain within revivalism. He blamed the efforts of Charles Finney for propagating this martial "spirit" within revivalism. Dod found a hypermasculine "swelling, strutting consciousness of self-importance" in "almost every page" of Finney's famous work on revivalism. His book lacked humility, according to Dod. It had a "spiritual pride and arrogance" through the imparting of "infallible information." Finney reveled in aggressive statements in the book, like "let hell boil over if it will, and spew out as many devils as there are stones in the pavement." Finney, Dod worried, trained young revivalists to act with this martial spirit. Once these young men left Finney's tutelage, according to Dod, "they come out, they look about . . . and start as if the devil" was everywhere and in need of defeating. Finney and his foot soldiers allowed "no symptoms of compassion or pity." They believed sinners alone should be held responsible for their actions. Dod thought Finney's aggressive arrogance could result in "additions of his own to the scriptural code of morals." Comparing him to the prophet Matthias, Dod wrote that Finney condemned "tea, coffee, tobacco, evening parties, ribbons, and many other things." Finney was just as confident, according to Dod, in supporting "his false standard as . . . in denouncing those who transgress it, and in launching against them the thunderbolts of divine vengeance, as if it had been communicated to him by express revelation."[45]

These evangelicals concerned about revivalism also charged that the militant sensationalism of revivalism made authentic conversions more difficult. Horace Bushnell claimed camp meetings betray "a certain hardness and rudeness, a want of sensibility to things that do not lie in action." He said evangelicals "hold a piety of conquest rather than of love . . . a kind of public piety that is strenuous and fiery on great occasions." Bushnell indicted his coreligionists for counting "nothing a conversion which did not explode like a rocket in mid heaven, and the number of these explosions was accepted as the gauge of all progress." Calvin Colton, a Yankee evangelical turned Episcopalian, agreed that camp meetings had become overly concerned with vanquishing the enemy. Colton believed the only way revivals had succeeded in attracting a large number of converts was by talking about victory and inculcating "violent excitements," so camp meeting managers pushed their hearers "to the greatest extreme," according to Colton, as they "frighten, shock, paralyze the mind" with the weapons of "scenes of horror."[46]

What evangelicals concerned about revivalism saw were not just parallels between their own movement and Mormonism, but they believed the militant nature of camp meetings had directly enabled the rise of Mormonism. Jonathan Turner denounced the "*military* authority" faiths used to acquire believers and to sustain their efforts. He found "terror" inevitably leading to "increase the general credulity and fanaticism of mankind." While words often convinced people to accept religious belief, Turner compared Mormonism and revivalism through their use of "well-disciplined" armies. A "cannon's mouth," he believed, had a power to make people listen to religious arguments. Like Muslims and Catholics, groups he regularly compared to Mormonism, radical revivalists used swords to make their arguments "and the halter" to silence "all objections."[47]

Some evangelicals over the course of the 1830s and 1840s concluded evangelicalism had unintendedly fostered sympathetic feelings for the followers of Joseph Smith by committing violence against them. This representative example from a few years prior to the founding of Nauvoo demonstrated the negative consequences of the militancy of evangelicalism. After a group of Missourians expelled Mormonism from Jackson County, some antebellum evangelicals did not blame Mormonism for the conflict. They instead heaped scorn on westerners for acting with a socially conservative vigilantism. This struggle over the militant behavior of antebellum evangelicals was part of a larger contest over American religious nationalism, being waged between a popular and populist frontier revivalism and a nationalist-minded, eastern missionary endeavor. More moderate eastern evangelicals often characterized their western coreligionists as uncivilized.[48]

The militant fanaticism shown toward Mormonism became a way for some eastern evangelicals to depict the actions and faith of their western counterparts as distasteful and ill-advised. The editors of the Presbyterian-inclined *New York Observer and Chronicle* called the actions of the people in Jackson County "high-handed." They charged that these westerners acted with the same principles as those adopted "by the Georgians in the case of the Cherokees." These Presbyterian editors found those residing in Jackson County "wholly at war with the genius of our institutions." The editors of the *Religious Intelligencer*, a newspaper dedicated to promoting Bible and missionary societies, reprinted the same article as the *New York Observer and Chronicle*, but they added a solemn note. They deeply regretted "that such an occurrence should have taken place." Though these Connecticut evangelicals seemed happy that the residents of Jackson County "cleared themselves of this fanatical sect, they have doubtless done more to promote the cause of Mormonism than they could have done in any other way." The approbation many evangelicals felt for these westerners was such that the editors of the Kentucky-based evangelical newspaper, the *Western Luminary*, went out of their way to describe the behavior of the residents of Jackson County as "disgraceful to the character to a civilized and Christian people."[49]

Western evangelicals responded to their eastern counterparts' criticism by defending their actions in Missouri toward Mormonism. Isaac McCoy, a western Baptist missionary, published a corrective to people who thought "the Mormons are here persecuted on account of their peculiar notions of religion." He then offered a defense of the actions of the residents of Jackson County, Missouri. McCoy claimed Mormonism had designs on gaining possession of the entire county. This was a providential belief, according to McCoy, where God would actively assist Mormonism in dispossessing Missourians of their land. McCoy then laid out in great detail how Mormonism ignored laws, engaged in mob action, and provoked violence. McCoy made it clear that no westerners had acted violently toward the followers of Joseph Smith; they had only sought to defend themselves.[50]

Eastern evangelicals likewise used the events surrounding the 1838 Missouri War to blame their violent western coreligionists with aiding and abetting the rise of Mormonism. This armed conflict between Mormonism and citizens of northern Missouri had gestated for several years before erupting in August 1838. Some non-Mormon westerners tried to prevent the Mormon community from voting because they feared their political power. A mob then burned down the home of a Mormon resident a few months later. Joseph Smith responded by arming several hundred Mormons, who responded by burning the homes of some of the leaders of the non-Mormon vigilantes. Armed violence continued on both sides until the governor Lilburn Boggs issued what became known as the Extermination Order, which said Mormonism needed to either be exterminated or driven from the state. The mass of Mormons fled to Illinois as a result of this threat.[51]

Antebellum evangelical depictions of the 1838 Missouri War revealed the same tensions between eastern and western evangelicals as the 1833 conflict. Eastern evangelicals continued to depict western settlers as unrefined. The editors of the *Christian Advocate and Journal* wrote that the violence perpetrated by westerners did nothing but harm the weakest members of society. The editors of this eastern evangelical periodical hoped the arrest of several Mormon leaders would appease the "wrath" of the western mob. The opposite took place. "The prisoners being secured, the mob entered the town and perpetrated every conceivable act of brutality and outrage," they wrote, which resulted in "forcing fifteen or twenty Mormon girls to yield to their brutal passions." They considered it "particularly heart-rending to see old gray-headed fathers and mothers, young ladies and innocent babes, forced at this inclement season to abandon their warm homes."[52]

Other antebellum evangelicals heaped blame on both evangelicals and Mormons for the violence perpetrated during the 1838 conflict. H. L. Dodds, a Methodist minister serving as an itinerant minister in Missouri, charged Mormonism with instigating the conflict, but thought non-Mormons in the West responded in too violent a fashion. From a relatively close vantage point, he claimed "Mormons committed the first depradations in the character of a mob." After further attacks by Mormonism, Dodds believed "the defiance of the law" of Mormonism "kindled a flame in the bosom of every patriot." He thought the country would be "soon in arms, and things began to wear gloomy, an awful aspect; vengeance seemed to be determined on both sides." Dozens died in the conflict, but Dodds thought "there is no doubt but both parties are to blame," and he rejoiced "that it is the determination of the officers to punish all who have acted as a mob on both sides."[53]

A final group of evangelicals faulted the leaders of Mormonism for this "civil war" in the West. The editors of the *Zion's Herald* initially grew concerned over a series of meetings throughout the area to oppose Mormonism, commenting "these proceedings are a disgrace to any civilized community." The editors of this mission-minded magazine believed "as long as men do not disturb the public peace, let them quietly enjoy what religious sentiments they please, or none at all." But the growing size and power of Mormonism convinced them to find fault with the leaders of Mormonism. The editors of the *New York Evangelist* likewise titled their account of the Missouri conflict "The Mormons Again Making War," disseminating a rumor that Joseph Smith led a company of over 100 men for the "purpose of getting those persons who do not belong to their church to sign a paper that they will not molest them." As evangelical descriptions of the events continued, they inflated the numbers of those involved to nearly two thousand Mormon "fighting men" with more on their way from outside the United States. The editors of the *Christian Secretary* reported that the Mormon converts acted with religious order, receiving "orders in the name of Lazarus, the Apostles, and Jesus Christ to fire." At the end of the conflict, evangelically inclined newspapers like the *Christian Reflector* underscored the "delusion which induced many well-meaning people to leave their peaceful homes, and risk their lives and property under the control of a few misguided leaders."[54]

The Consequences of Sectarian Fanaticism

Evangelicals critical of revivalism finally believed that some of their coreligionists shared with Mormonism a common sectarian fanaticism. Disestablishment of religion following the American Revolution and the efflorescence of the Second Great Awakening gave Americans seemingly limitless religious choice, but the surfeit of options came at the cost of provoking vicious infighting within the evangelical movement as older denominations and newer sects competed for converts. In print, sermons, and through the work of voluntary societies, antebellum evangelicals battled about correct forms of worship, social order, ecclesiastical organizations, personal conduct, as well as a host of other doctrinal matters. Such exclusivism not only caused interdenominational fighting, evangelicals critical of revivalism believed, but also intra-denominational tension and facture, as happened within Presbyterianism in the 1830s when different camps emerged in this denomination arguing about the use of emotionalism, populist rhetoric, and the apparatus of revivalism. While both claimed to follow the teachings of scripture and a plain reading of the Bible, disagreements descended into bickering, fighting, convening dueling synods, dispossession of church property, and, ultimately, an 1837 schism giving tens of thousands of Presbyterians a new church home. All of this spiteful exclusivity within evangelicalism led evangelicals critical of revivalism to see the excesses of the Second Great Awakening fostering feelings of prejudice, exceptionalism, and arrogance that had encouraged the advent and growth of Mormonism through its bigoted and misguided way of understanding the Bible. The opposition to Mormonism itself even became a tool of sectarian conflict, where antebellum evangelicals could further their own cultural, political, and social goals.[55]

A cacophony of religious opinion was what Joseph Smith claimed drove him to search for religious truth. Smith wrote in accounts of his first vision that after his family moved to Manchester, New York, in 1818, an "unusual excitement on the subject of religion" began. While it began with the Methodists, he said it "soon became general among all the sects in that region of the country." "Stir and division among the people" followed these revivals. Individuals contended for different sects, and while they had zeal and great love for converts who joined their evangelical churches, when the "converts began to file off . . . it was so that the seemingly good feelings of both the Priests and the Converts were more pretended than real." He recounted that this religious chaos made it "impossible for a person young as I was and so unacquainted with men and things to come to any certain conclusion who was right and who was wrong." The "laboring under the extreme difficulties caused by the contests of these parties of religionists" led Smith to the woods near his house to ask of God for wisdom.[56]

Evangelicals critical of revivalism first focused on the irrational attitudes of hostility that emanated both from evangelicalism and Mormonism. David Reese described sectarian fanatics, who included some evangelicals and Mormons, as examples of "ultra-sectarianism." He believed both groups acted with "bitterness and censoriousness, with which some religionists anathematize all other sects but their own." Reese provided four examples of this kind of bigotry operating in both Mormonism and radical evangelicalism. Sectarian fanatics, according to Reese, could first publish religious materials "designed to show that the *ism* of another sect 'is not Christianity.'" Those holding on to this zealous kind of exclusivity could also adopt and propagate "the opinion, there is 'no other true church on earth,' but that sect which claims his name among its members." Taking aim at the more populist strains within evangelicalism, Reese uncovered a third example of this intolerant sectarianism that "condemns all study as a preparation of pulpit efforts, and denounces literary and theological knowledge, as though ignorance were indispensable to piety." Finally, sectarian fanaticism manifested itself in the ways certain religious groups prescribed salvation. Taking aim at groups preaching the necessity of immersion for the forgiveness of sins, Reese said this final group "unchristians all whose baptism has not been administered by immersion." What Reese believed these fruits of sectarian fanaticism had in common was a revanchist spirit that invested religious groups with a belief in their own exceptionalism. He described how these ultra-sectarians would then create groups of "*heresy-hunters*," who guard with "lynx-eyed vigilance against heresy in their particular denomination." Encouraging sects to be "arrayed against other sects" and "ministers of the same sect . . . to watch one another," these sectarian defenders searched "sermons, speeches, pamphlets, or books" for any examples of someone expressing their ideas "in any other than the stereotyped phrases of the Confession of Faith or the expositions of this creed by the old masters in scholastic divinity."[57]

Such fears of the power of prejudice were not rhetorical for evangelicals critical of revivalism as Mormonism expanded beyond its western New York home. When Mormonism eventually entered New York City, it did not surprise David Reese that it quickly gained a foothold among evangelical churches most inclined to an aggressive exclusivity. A Mormon minister, he remembered, had found a "professed minister and Christian congregation who . . . allowed the Sabbath to be outraged and their temple of religion desecrated by the public propagation of the mysteries of Mormonism." Those evangelical churches given over to ultra-sectarianism, according to Reese, drank in wisdom from his "golden bible!" Henry Caswall agreed the prejudicial "divisions and subdivision of professed Christians" caused the emergence of Mormonism. He pointed out that Smith himself claimed early in his ministry that if God had a Church, "it would not be split into factions." Whether or not Smith made this prophecy did not matter to Caswall. What was important, he believed, was that this same bigoted spirit "contributed immensely to the growth of Joseph's heresy." A lack of unity in the religious world and the exclusivist posture of evangelicals led to a confounding of the natural powers of the mind "by a dense fog of commingled truths and sophisms, in which there is neither darkness nor light." He believed this confusion naturally resulted in an "eager desire" to yearn for "Catholicity," but the "true Church is seldom presented in its fullness and with its proper claims, appearing like a small sect, among larger sects, and with its feature veiled by . . . prejudice and misapprehension." It was not shocking to Caswall then that "Smith, or any other new prophet, assumed the place of the Church and professes to teach on divine authority" because people naturally preferred belief to doubt. Mormonism exploited sectarian fanaticism by "engendering distrust in all other denominations, and by holding itself up as the only sanctuary to which men may flee for the solution of their doubts."[58]

Evangelicals concerned about revivalism believed sectarian fanaticism could also result in the rise of new religious rivals because of its theological demands and exclusivity. Caswall blamed the Stone-Campbell movement, in this context, for the rise of Mormonism. He argued Campbell had laid down a "scheme of 'Church' government . . . which approximated in some respects to the doctrine of the apostolical succession." The problem for Caswall was these "opinions spread like wildfire . . . [and] numerous enthusiastic persons were soon preaching them to crowded and breathless congregations," and Campbell required all men to conform to this order. He concluded that the Stone-Campbell movement had "prodigious success" because it labeled its opponents heretics, but their exclusivist demands and lack of ecclesiastical structures led Caswall to believe "Campbellism" formed "one of the main ingredients of Mormonism."[59]

Besides blaming other evangelicals, these evangelicals concerned about revivalism also blamed members of their own churches for fostering the Latter-day Saints through bigotry and unbiblicism. David Reese placed Mormonism's sectarian fanaticism alongside ultra-temperance reformers, ultra-Protestants (those most dedicated to antipopery), proponents of phrenology, practitioners of homeopathic medicine, and ultra-abolitionists. He referred to them all as humbugs of religion. They shielded their true desire to obtain the exclusive loyalty of their followers through the "dogmas of the systems they embrace." James M'Chesney concurred with Reese, agreeing that "in no point does darkness feel so secure in holding its ground, as in sectarian selfishness and bigotry." Sectarian fanatics "can never bear contradictions—their path must not be crossed by any one . . . they make a show of uncontrovertible light." In addition to Mormons, M'Chesney also identified these bigoted zealots within evangelicalism itself, and arguing that these evangelical groups considered themselves the "high favourites of heaven." All of these sectarians envied one another, and "endeavouring to turn their opponents, ruin to their gain; and with a blind zeal that is full of partiality and hypocrisy, they dive on, rejoicing in their shame." M'Chesney concluded that such sectarian fanaticism "perfected" itself in Mormonism because the followers of Joseph Smith displayed "an entire want of Charity—want of patient love . . . in every feature." Evangelicals critical of revivalism found that evangelicals under the sway of sectarian fanaticism too often cared too much about petty disagreements, a prejudicial sprit that allowed the rise of Mormonism. Calling Mormonism one of the grossest delusions of "human ambition," the prominent Presbyterian and student of religion in America Robert Baird thought that the same prideful spirit had infected evangelicalism. Combatting a feared decline in evangelicalism, Baird wanted American orthodox Christians to know that even though the main evangelical churches—Episcopalians, Congregationalists, Baptists, Presbyterians, and Methodists—fought, these churches agreed about more than they disagreed. He stated that "on no one point are all these churches more completely united . . . than on the doctrine of the supremacy of Christ in his Church." Despite his optimistic characterization of American religion, Baird's work betrayed a concern about the harmony of religion in America through his weighing of American religions against orthodoxy. Turner, writing along similar lines, thought the "the influence of modern sectarian animosities, jealousies, and rivalries, upon both the origin and progress of Mormonism, is sufficiently apparent."[60]

Sectarian fanatics, according to evangelicals critical of revivalism, also encouraged Mormonism to see itself as an exclusive group because of an unbiblicism or hyperbiblicism. This was a similar kind of criticism that the initial evangelical objectors had leveled against Mormonism when they accused Smith of selectively reading and using his holy writ. When David Reese wrote about the humbugs of the antebellum period, he characterized all of these groups as consisting of people who practiced the same kind of selective religiosity. These humbugs and extremist believers thought they knew more than the Bible because they believed some particular activity, unmentioned in the Bible, was sinful. Going beyond the Bible encouraged these ultraist-movements to draw boundaries where none existed. Reese cited the refusal of temperance societies to speak to anyone who "adheres to the doctrine of expediency." Turner similarly believed sectarian fanaticism had led vast multitudes of people to believe the substance of Christianity was in the "outward forms and metaphysical distinctions about which the sects are most inclined to wrangle." He thus charged sectarianism with creating space for Mormonism by confounding the God-given reason Christians could use to understand the Bible. Instead, he worried, nothing would be left, but a "fog of commingled truths and sophism, amid which there is neither darkness nor light." He believed the leaders of Mormonism had taken advantage of this "condition of things, by engendering distrust in all other sects, and holding up their own, as the only refuge to which men may at once flee."[61]

Evangelicals critical of revivalism thought Mormons, like the adherents of revivalism, practiced a sectarian fanaticism that led them to embrace a literalist hyperbiblicism. Reese charged both Mormons and the adherents of the Second Great Awakening with pledging their lives, fortunes, and sacred honor for every "jot and tittle of their new scheme." This kind of devotion meant even when a "humbug can be shown to be full of error and evil, no benevolence of motive or kindness" can convince those who "have embraced the humbug." Hyperbiblicism also encouraged bad behavior because people responded to the "stupidity of the victims of delusion" by attacking them "personally instead of attacking the false philosophy and pseudo-philanthropy." Reese concluded that this unchristian persecutorial response made antihumbugs intolerant, which "has been fatal to their success." While reason "may not work against fanatics," he believed sectarian fanatics only served to "propagate new theories," giving new religious ideas fresh vigor "under the blows of intolerance and they multiply by dissection."[62]

These evangelicals concerned about the revivals of the Second Great Awakening found hyperbiblicism could lead to a fanatical sectarian kind of peer pressure that would result in blind belief. Turner thought that nothing was "more childish, and more truly contemptible, than either to believe or disbelieve any religious system, merely because our associates, or those around us do," but he found that "it is probable that Christianity itself is frequently received, at least nominally, and almost uniformly rejected, on this ground, and on this ground alone." "Moral sympathy," he wrote, gives "ridiculous power to the social authority," for both writers "for or against the truths of Christianity." For sectarian fanatics, even the "mere 'dictum' of congenial tempers" leads "the stripling wight and the hoary debauchee" to read a "few passages from Paine, or Voltaire, or Gibbon, or Hume, or Fanny Wright" and "they swallow down all they read, because these skeptics say so, and because it chimes in with their own moral sympathies." Even "the valorous sticklers for orthodoxy, among twenty belligerent sects, each read the 'dictums' of their favorite Joe Smiths, and believe them for precisely the same reason," and Turner charged that these orthodox "chime in with the ruling spirit of their daydreams of sectarian supremacy." He hoped evangelicals could do better, but if they could not "receive and interpret the Scriptures on better grounds than these, we had better pack off to Nauvoo" and become like the Mormons.[63]

Nonevangelical groups also made the link between the sectarianism of evangelicalism and Mormonism. Antebellum Catholics saw Mormonism as the logical extension of evangelicalism because of the latter's zealous blind belief. Responding to a Methodist attack on Catholicism, the editors of *The Catholic Telegraph* lumped together Methodists and Mormons as examples of "self-righteous radicalism." The fact that each of these groups proclaimed their own orthodoxy sowed discord and made it more difficult for Christians to unite as "one body of people." Because of their emphasis on freethinking and opposition to institutional religion, the editors of the *Free Enquirer* saw the consequence of the "various Christian sects" maintaining "constant warfare against one another" led to the persecution of Mormonism in the West through these aggressive attitudes. They commented "the more zealous the Christian, the more destructive his measure."[64]

Evangelical groups even used the term *anti-Mormon* to advance their own sectarian agendas. As the perceived political power of Mormonism increased, a majority of antebellum evangelicals deployed the term to describe those arrayed against Mormonism's growing power. When the political power of Mormonism waned, and it seemed as if some evangelicals had violently persecuted Mormonism, the term became a way to engage in sectarian conflict.

One group of evangelicals embraced the term *anti-Mormon* in the 1840s to discuss and organize their opposition to the Mormon threat. Editors of the *New York Evangelist* heard how "political parties [in Illinois] have nearly given up their distinguishing characteristics for the purpose of forming a union to defeat them [Mormons] at the polls." These citizens of Illinois, according to this eastern evangelical periodical, banded together to form an "anti-Mormon Convention" to deny Mormonism the opportunity to possess "every civil office." The editors of the *New York Evangelist* around the same time as the building up of Nauvoo also advertised an "Anti-Mormon Almanac" for sale that purportedly revealed the "views, numbers, doings, and designs of the strange sect of the Mormons." An English individual, identifying as "Anti-Mormon," wrote a tract criticizing Mormonism in 1846, a moment when Mormonism had made significant inroads on the British Isles. While mostly a pastiche of earlier criticisms of Mormonism, this publication argued "the harrangues of the Mormon preachers abound with allusions to the Christian doctrines, and are well calculated to confuse and deceive the minds of unlearned hearers." When investigated, this "Anti-Mormon" argued "the pretension or foundation on which the whole fabric is reared, is found to be unevangelical." He concluded that "no preaching that does not bring sinners to Christ, and lead them to trust entirely in him, and personally applying to him for pardon, sanctification, and redemption, is evangelical."[65]

Antebellum evangelicals also used the term *anti-Mormon* to denigrate other evangelicals as sectarians, usually when the power of Mormonism seemed to be waning. Some of the opposition to anti-Mormons as a group reflected growing concern in antebellum America that single-issue reform organizations had overly adversarial qualities and did too little to spread the Gospel. Anti-societies had begun within the evangelical movement itself in the early 1800s as a weapon to do battle against specific sins and vices. By the 1820s and 1830s, the ubiquity and defensiveness of these societies led many antebellum Americans to see them as overly antagonistic and radical. While focused opposition allowed these anti-societies to more easily single out and shame sinners, increasing numbers of antebellum Americans connected them to radical social movements, like abolition or temperance.[66]

This backdrop of anti-societies as aggressive and contentious allowed some eastern evangelicals concerned about revivalism to use the term *anti-Mormon* as a sectarian weapon to tar their western counterparts with charges of sectarian violence and deceitful conduct. When narrating the buildup to the 1838 Missouri conflict, the editors of the *Christian Secretary* discussed the thousands of anti-Mormons gathering to combat Mormonism, something these Connecticut Baptist editors saw as encouraging "a general battle." The editors of the *Christian Reflector* went further, making an extended political, sectional, and theological criticism of these "anti-Mormons." These New England editors referred to them as "demi-savages" who "are exceedingly intolerant." The anti-Mormons, according to these New England evangelicals, were "*refuse* Kentuckians and Tennesseeans, intermixed with Virginians of the same caste." These northeastern evangelicals saw these "anti-Mormons" through the lens of slavery; they embraced a sin of sectional pride, with a prejudice against all other people, "especially those belonging to the free states." In addition to their designs for slave power, these evangelical editors believed they have "personal pride to an excess, which leads them . . . to envy his success and hate his person." These westerners also had loose morals, according to these eastern editors, preferring "plunder to fair means . . . because rapine gratifies their propensities to force, indolence, and acquisition." William Lloyd Garrison unsuprisingly picked up on this same argument in the *Liberator* in the events surrounding the 1838 Missouri War. He charged the real reason westerners had persecuted Mormonism was not "because they were bad citizens." Garrison instead claimed Mormons were "*more sober, more industrious, more moral, and more thriving than their neighbors*." Non-Mormon westerners persecuted them because they had the "misfortune to be Yankees,—that is Northern men."[67]

These New England evangelicals further found trouble in the way these "anti-Mormons" misrepresented Mormonism. These westerners had called the Mormons villains and thievish, which these eastern evangelicals found laughable because of the poor character of the anti-Mormons. The anti-Mormons had played on racial fears in order to excite the "slave States," according to the editors of the *Christian Reflector*. These New England evangelicals found plenty of reason "why the Anti-Mormons should have hated their rivals," like disagreements over property in Missouri. While reason existed to dislike the actions of Mormonism, the editors of the *Christian Reflector* found the "massacre at Horne's [*sic*] Mill" shocking and "ought to be rung throughout Christendom." Referring to the attack of a Missouri mob that resulted in the death of seventeen Mormon men, women, and children, these New Englanders blamed anti-Mormons for the violence and were shocked how the mob plundered Mormon possessions.[68]

Western evangelicals used the term *anti-Mormon* to justify their actions against Mormonism. Just a few years after the events of Haun's Mill, the western evangelical missionary John Mason Peck embraced the term *anti-Mormon* to defend against these eastern-originated attacks against westerners. He described the Missouri conflict in generous terms to westerners. Peck wrote how "the Mormons of Caldwell, legally organized, turned out to preserve the peace; and the Anti-mormons . . . armed and embodied themselves for the same commendable purpose." Rather than casting blame solely on westerners, Peck claimed "mingled fear and hatred . . . produced plunderings, burnings, and bloodshed," which did not cease until the actions of the governor stopped the violence.[69]

The martial, spiritist, and sectarian fanaticisms shared by evangelicals and Mormons led evangelicals critical of revivalism not only to repudiate the excesses of revivalism, but also to articulate a new vision of evangelical identity. Campbell and some of the other initial opponents of Mormonism used their criticism of the Latter-day Saints to further a religious agenda that attempted to excise some of the more enthusiastic members from his group. Evangelicals concerned about revivalism had similar goals. They wanted to roll back some of the more radical elements of evangelicalism because they associated them with the emergence of Mormonism. This shared belief in the unintended fanatical consequences of the Second Great Awakening was why after his three days in Nauvoo, Henry Caswall ironically concluded that "it is instructive . . . to watch the demeanour of those who have succeeded in establishing a spiritual dominion." He believed if "the Churches of England and America" possessed the activity of the Mormons, then they would no longer have to worry about losing members to Joseph Smith.[70]

Many of these evangelicals concerned about the progress of revivalism ironically looked to Mormonism as a model. They hated Mormonism, but they also believed that evangelicals needed to become a little more like the Mormons. If evangelicals adopted some of the practices of Mormon institutionalism, like missionaries, education, and infrastructure, rather than continuing to hurl attacks at Mormonism, then evangelicalism might finally be able to dominate the country.

CHAPTER 6

"Apprehension for the Future"

Anti-Mormonism and the Building of Evangelical Institutions

Antebellum evangelicals sustained an anti-Mormon rhetoric that charged Latter-day Saints with embracing strange and dangerous social patterns, immoral business dealings, heretical theological beliefs, and fanatical religious practices. Whether for the purposes of excising their own movements of radical elements, articulating an appropriate relationship between God and the market, or laying out how one should read and interpret the Bible, different groups of antebellum evangelicals used anti-Mormonism to fashion a faith to their own liking. Although antebellum evangelicals came up with innumerable reasons to dislike Mormonism, they paradoxically found quite a lot to like about them. They described their piety, their desire for religious knowledge, their efforts at spreading their faith, and their religious infrastructure in glowing terms. Antebellum evangelicals commended the spiritual desires and devotion of the followers of Mormonism. Missionaries of Mormonism provided examples to antebellum evangelicals of religious success and zeal. Antebellum evangelicals finally gazed longingly at Mormonism's impressive temples as a pattern to be imitated. Acknowledgment of the attraction of Mormonism became more pronounced as antebellum evangelicals critical of revivalism became convinced their own movement had become ignorant, impassive, and impotent. Their own shortcomings had left them unable to respond to the threat of this new religious upstart, according to this view. These critics of revivalism found a solution to reinvigorate their movement by following as a pattern the very faith they had spent years denigrating.

Evangelical Admiration for Mormonism

Even during their most hate-filled religious polemics, antebellum evangelicals expressed affection for the piety of the followers of Mormonism. Those evangelicals admiring the devoutness of Mormonism distinguished between the leaders of Mormonism, who they considered hypocritical crooks, and the mass of Mormon converts, who they viewed as misguided believers. They described converts at various points throughout their encounter as devoted, kind, curious, and faithful. The Presbyterian James Eels noted how converts to Mormonism "profess a great deal of piety, and in this respect they equal the Mahometans." They were not like their leaders, whom Eels saw as imposters. He noted that most Mormon converts "abound in prayers and other acts of devotion." The Presbyterian Truman Coe, who had spent several years living near the Mormon community at Kirtland, likewise described most followers of Mormonism as "very sincerely devoted, and possibly very sincere Christians." The Mormon converts who had come to Kirtland from around the world he described as having "high expectations" to find religious truth on their pilgrimage to Ohio.[1]

Not only did antebellum evangelicals praise Latter-day Saints for their religious piety, but they also viewed converts to Mormonism as good people, overflowing with kindness and benevolence. The editors of the *Western Christian Advocate* described Mormon converts as "polite and affable to strangers." They willingly shared their faith, according to these evangelical editors. Truman Coe remarked how the "common people are industrious [and] good neighbors." The editors of the *Home Missionary* simultaneously attacked Mormon converts as wicked, while praising them as "honest-hearted." Remarking on their interpersonal relationships, the editors of the *Christian Register and Boston Observer* saw Mormon converts having a "truly self-sacrificing spirit among them."[2]

Other evangelicals likewise respected the ways the followers of Joseph Smith worshiped fervently and engaged in a quest for religious knowledge. Truman Coe described Mormon converts as having such zeal that if "sober Christians . . . had half the zeal of these misguided Mormons, the world would tremble, and the millennial day would speedily be ushered in." The Reverend Daniel Kidder believed the emissaries of Mormonism had a "zeal worthy of a better cause." The editors of the *Home Missionary* enviously found the mass of Mormons "who believe their system are ready to make any sacrifice of time, of means, of bodily effort."[3]

These same pro-Mormon feelings led evangelicals to comment positively about the ways the followers of Mormonism diligently sought religious knowledge. The piety of converts to Mormonism surprised Coe when they delighted "in the duty of prayer" and were "conversant in the Bible." Describing the same group of Mormons at Kirtland, the editors of the *Christian Watchman* depicted them as abounding "in prayer and other acts of devotion." The editors of the *Home Missionary* likewise praised Mormon converts for their regular and sustained Bible study.[4]

Religious education became an important part of Mormonism's community of faith, according to antebellum evangelicals who spent time in Kirtland and in Nauvoo. James Eels described his visit to the Kirtland temple in the *New York Evangelist*, where he took notice of the seminary constructed on the second floor. This demonstrated to him that "the Mormons appear very eager to acquire education." Eels described how they employed a Hebrew teacher and seventy men "are eagerly engaged in the study." An evangelical writing in the *Western Christian Advocate* similarly witnessed converts to Mormonism studying Hebrew with "great zeal. "He wistfully noted these men pursued "their studies and attend to nothing else." The editors of an evangelical publication in Connecticut linked the continued growth of Mormonism in their neighborhood to members' quest for religious knowledge. They were not surprised that "more joined them." Not only did they have religious fervor, but "the people are said to enjoy, from their infancy, weekly instruction from the pulpit."[5]

The activity of Mormon missionaries received positive attention from many antebellum evangelicals. Evangelicals saw them as successful and savvy messengers of their faith, and they credited them with much of Mormonism's successes. This admiration for Mormon evangelizers began very early in the evangelical Mormon encounter. The editors of the Stone-Campbell publication the *Geauga Gazette* extensively discussed how three missionaries had successfully converted over fifty individuals to Mormonism. One of these converts, Sidney Rigdon, was a leader within the Stone-Campbell movement, and these restorationist editors viewed Rigdon's conversion as a masterly religious work. Alexander Campbell himself saw Mormon missionaries as so effective that they had convinced many restorationists in eastern Ohio that Campbell himself was a follower of Joseph Smith.[6]

As Mormonism expanded beyond its initial hearth and spread westward, antebellum evangelicals saw much of its successes resulting from these missionary efforts. Writing in the *Christian Secretary* in 1833, a resident from Ohio looked longingly at the activities of a group of Mormon missionaries in the town of Bluffdale. They had attracted "audiences, numerous beyond all former example." Their preaching created a "powerful excitement in favor of their doctrines." The town had previously experienced a series of revival, resulting in a "large and flourishing Baptist church." This evangelical observer described these missionaries as attractive, eloquent, and with an oratory "best calculated to produce deep and powerful impressions on the minds of [their] hearers." The author of this piece noted people listened to these missionaries for over three hours without getting bored because their charisma was "the eloquence of a deep and powerful feeling." These evangelical editors praised the oratorical style of these missionaries, writing that "when denouncing the speedy vengeance of God upon the unbelieving world," the missionary's body "was bent forward, his eyes seemed almost to flash fire, and the deep and shrill intonations of his voice vibrated on every heart." Mormon missionaries were successful, these evangelicals believed, because their members professed a "deeper and more ardent love to God, and professed to set up a higher standard of devotion than other denominations."[7]

Mormonism's temples also drew positive attention from antebellum evangelicals. The homes of Mormonism's most sacred rites and rituals sparked the antebellum evangelical imagination at both Kirtland and Nauvoo. Evangelical publishers discussed the construction, architecture, consecration, and use of these buildings in ways that betrayed an otherworldly fascination with them.

Joseph Smith ordered the construction of the first Mormon temple in Kirtland, Ohio, in early 1833. Smith believed this building would become the site for the establishment of God's kingdom on earth. The temple, Smith claimed, would host religious services, provide a center for the creation of the Mormon people, and become the seat of local government. It would also function as an educational institution where members of Mormonism could study the Bible, learn Hebrew, and meditate on the prophecies received by Joseph Smith. Smith and several other Mormon elders dedicated the temple in the spring of 1836. Several hundred followers of Mormonism attended this dedication, describing it as replete with manifestations of God's spirit.[8]

As the construction of the Kirtland temple neared completion, evangelical publishers described this rising Ohio religious edifice in spectacular and striking terms. Truman Coe emphasized this "huge stone temple" was "50 feet high, and 60 by 80 on the ground" with an inscription reading "the House of the Lord, built by the Latter-day Saints." All this cost over $40,000, according to this Presbyterian. The Presbyterian editors of the *New York Observer* provided the fullest account of the Kirtland temple in early 1836, one that would influence many later descriptions. These editors told their readers the Kirtland temple was a "large edifice, built of sand-stone, sixty feet by eighty on the ground, and forty-four feet high." They further noted the temple had an "imposing appearance" because of its height of two stories with a large steeple on top.[9]

When describing the inside of the Kirtland temple, these antebellum evangelicals depicted all of the activities occurring within this sacred space. The building had two floors. The interior of the building had a large auditorium-like space with a raised dais on one side. These elevated sections, according to these evangelical editors, could hold "three persons." On the other side of the building, twelve pulpits existed to hold apostles, which these evangelicals informed their readers was what "they term their teachers." All of the seats on the first floor could be rearranged to accommodate the varied uses of the temple. The editors of the *New York Chronicle* noted the "centre of the house, between the pulpits, is to be divided by a large veil, made of canvass, to extend from the top to the bottom of the room." There was much about the Kirtland temple they did not understand, noting with a gleeful suspicion the leaders of Mormonism did not like to share much information about this building.[10]

Antebellum evangelicals became preoccupied with the Kirtland temple in their descriptions of Mormonism in Ohio. The Presbyterian James Eels described the temple as of no "earthly order of architecture." Eels used words like "gothic" and "showy" to describe the style of the Mormon temple. He believed the architectural elements of the Kirtland temple existed to "strike the senses and attract curiosity."[11]

William West, an individual from Trumbull County, Ohio, an area full of restorationists of the Stone-Campbell variety, had a Janus-faced relationship with the Kirtland temple. While West's time in Kirtland led him to believe it was necessary "to call upon the citizens of these United States, to arouse from your slumbers for the enemy of truth is abroad in the land," he also found the temple enticing. He included a detailed description of the site in Ohio as part of his book about the rise of Mormonism. West described the building in a similar fashion as other eastern evangelicals. He said it was "forty rods long" and "twelve rods wide," costing more than $30,000. He noted the builders of the temple had used stone on the building, with an outside finished in hard cement and a number of "gothic" windows. West described the interior of the temple as "sublime" as the "vails are unfurled . . . to enjoin sacred reverence." He described a pulpit "in the west end for the Melchizedek priesthood, composed of four seats parallel with each other." Seats in the rear at this end, according to West, "are elevated and each seat calculated for three officers and accommodated with a suitable desk." On the front, "there is the initials of his office in gilt letters; the desk of the front seat consists of the leaves of the communion table upon which are the initials of its occupants in letter of stain."[12]

Underscoring a voyeuristic fascination that antebellum evangelicals had with the Kirtland temple was that this religious building also functioned like a museum. West spent twenty-five cents to go through the temple on a tour. He loved it so much the first time that he went back the next day to see the spectacles inside again. Joseph Smith had purchased four Egyptian mummies and a handful of papyri from a Barnum-like traveling salesman and promoter, Michael Chandler, in 1835. When Smith viewed the scrolls, he told his followers one papyrus contained the writings of Abraham and another, the writings of Joseph. The leaders of Mormonism evidently displayed these four mummies and a cache of records inside the Kirtland temple. West loved seeing these items, writing that the leaders of Mormonism said the mummies "were Egyptian, but the records are those of Abraham and Joseph and contain important information about creation and the fall of man; Smith is to translate them."[13]

The grand architecture, sacred rites, and museum-like quality of the Kirtland temple helped antebellum evangelicals explain Mormonism's popularity. When the Presbyterian Truman Coe saw the Kirtland temple and its mummies, he believed they functioned to bring in people with "high expectations." The editors of the *Zion's Herald* claimed Mormonism's "elegant temple" worked to "deceive the hearts of many of the simple." Alexander Campbell saw the temple as a temptation. It appealed to people's "extravagant desires," he believed, and it held "out a bait to some morbid appetite, until the bit was in their mouth and the saddle upon their back." Campbell sadly believed people would continue to "forsake the path of duty for the gratification of curiosity." Mormonism had hoodwinked its converts by laboring "assiduously to keep up the delusion by claims of miraculous power, and mysterious visions, and the novelty of a splendidly decorated and gorgeous temple," he concluded.[14]

After the leaders of Mormonism moved to Nauvoo and began to construct a new temple, antebellum evangelicals immediately turned their attention to this new religious building. They viewed it with similar esteem as the Kirtland temple. Construction began in 1840 with plans for a temple that would have the same basic design as the Kirtland temple with its fusion of New England meetinghouse and Gothic styles. Joseph Smith had much more ambitious goals, however, for the temple in Nauvoo. He planned it to be three times larger than the one at Kirtland with a wider variety of religious rites taking place inside. The temple at Nauvoo would contain a meetinghouse, a school, and serve as the site for a wider variety of sacred religious rituals. These ceremonies would include baptism of the dead, endowment ceremonies, and the eternal sealing of families. As in Kirtland, all of these sacred rites provided salvation for individual members of Smith's movement, while also tying them into a larger community. Construction of the temple took over five years to complete. Leaders of Mormonism consecrated it only after the assassination of Joseph Smith, and it saw use for only a few months before the departure of Mormonism to the western part of the United States.[15]

Antebellum evangelicals described the Nauvoo temple with similar language as the Kirtland temple, but in more attractive and grandiose terms. Reflecting the size and scope of the Nauvoo temple, they saw the one in Illinois as more threatening and imposing. The editors of the *Christian Secretary* commented during the construction of the Nauvoo temple that they believed it would soon become "the most magnificent structure in the West." The architecture, these evangelical editors wrote, was "entirely original—unlike anything in the world, or in the history of the world—but it at the same time chaste and elegant." A visitor to the Nauvoo temple writing in the *Christian Advocate and Journal* compared the façade of the Nauvoo temple to Greek Revival style buildings of Girard College in Philadelphia. Both buildings, according to this evangelical, represented "artificial curiosities." These evangelical editors believed the aesthetics of the building alone would appeal to the interest of religious seekers. They figured that "even were the Mormons to abandon the city, as it is asserted that they will . . . it will continue to be of importance, unconnected with the false religious tenets of its inhabitants."[16]

The Nauvoo temple, like the Kirtland temple, drew converts to Mormonism, in the minds of antebellum evangelicals. The Presbyterian Jonathan Turner referred to the temple as "splendid." Henry Caswall likewise described it as the "finest edifice west of Philadelphia." The Reverend Tyler Parsons believed the Nauvoo temple had the same extravagance as Solomon's temple. Parsons also saw the temple full of secrets he desperately wanted to reveal. When he visited Nauvoo as construction was underway on the temple, Parsons reported that a Mormon guide told him, "in this house the Lord designed to reveal unto his Church things which had been kept secret from the foundation of the world." The temple was unfinished when Parsons visited, but he still viewed the "great baptismal font" at the very center of the temple. The font impressed him, describing it as measuring almost twenty square feet and four feet deep, resting on the "backs of twelve oxen, as large as life, and tolerably well sculpted."[17]

What happened inside the Nauvoo temple also piqued the interest of antebellum evangelicals. The rituals taking place inside and inaugurated at the Nauvoo temple both shocked and excited antebellum evangelicals. After telling of the giant baptistry in the basement of the Nauvoo Temple, with twelve sculpted oxen supporting it, Milton Badger described Mormonism's practice of baptism of the dead. He wrote "individuals are instructed that they can get their friends out of perdition by being baptized on their account." Telling this story with a voyeuristic glee, Badger claimed that he saw one man who "had been baptized 13 times for his deceased children, because they were not Mormons." He said he heard of another follower of Joseph Smith, "about 80 years old, who was baptized for George Washington and La Fayette; then for Thomas Jefferson." Badger concluded incredulously the same person applied "on behalf of Andrew Jackson! But they told him the General was not dead yet, and so he waits a while."[18]

The final aspect of the Nauvoo temple seducing antebellum evangelicals was its public power. While a threat and a danger, it also made evangelicals obsess about it. The restorationist minister Walter Scott worried the building of the temple along the banks of the Mississippi, if not stopped, was a slippery slope. If no one halted the building of the temple, then what would happen when "they become ten times as strong, and perhaps delude the Indians into the support of their scheme?" Mormonism, unless "the career of these outlaws is speedily checked . . . will involve the far West in a ferocious and exterminating war." This would only be the beginning, as Scott believed Mormons would ultimately use their institutional power to hasten the Second Coming through violence.[19]

Evangelical Apprehension for the Future

Antebellum evangelicals critical of revivalism admired the piety, education, mission work, and religious infrastructure of Mormonism not only because they felt the need to acknowledge Mormonism for its successes, but also because they saw many of the same institutions lacking in their own movement. They believed evangelicalism on the brink of failure because of their own inactivity in these same areas, particularly in the West.

Large evangelical organizations described the western portion of the United States as given over to atheism, deism, infidelity, Mormonism, and other "changes of error . . . rung by confident and zealous adherents." Although the leaders of the American Tract Society believed it would be easy to have contempt for these groups, they also stressed groups like Mormons could not be ignored. "When a single class among them numbers more than a thousand organized churches," they wrote, "and another boasts more than a tenth part of our entire population in her corrupt communion," evangelicals had to take notice. The leaders of the ATS saw these groups "invading our sanctuaries and proselyting men of influence, and all are industriously sowing the seeds of error by the press and the living teacher." When that happens, they concluded "it becomes considerate . . . to pause and inquire whereunto all this may grow, in a land as open to the assaults of error as to the teachings of truth."[20]

Antebellum evangelicals concluded by the 1840s that the western part of the United States was strategically vital in their efforts to convert the world. Antebellum evangelicals had begun to make a concerted effort to evangelize the West beginning in the early 1800s. They had established schools, sent missionaries, built churches, and printed newspapers, but their attempts consistently ran into a variety of difficulties. Efforts to convert the West faced challenges recruiting ministers, competition between denominations, and tensions over leadership between eastern and western evangelicals. Western evangelicals disagreed with their eastern counterparts over funding and evangelization strategies. Western evangelicals believed easterners treated them in a subservient fashion and did not understand their real spiritual needs. Because they believed their geographical location gave them a more pure and unadulterated religion than their eastern counterparts, western evangelicals wanted to create and control their own religious institutions.[21]

Evangelicals believed the religious conquest of the West was necessary because it could lead to mass conversions and hasten the Second Coming of Jesus. Some critics of revivalism believed the excesses of the Second Great Awakening on the western frontier could prevent these millennial events from taking place and leave evangelicals unable to meet outside religious competition. Lyman Beecher publicly worried that without more religious effort, Catholicism would spread unopposed as it continued to convert the growing numbers of foreign immigrants in the region. Beecher believed the entirety of the West under threat from these other groups, and if evangelicals did not arrest this danger soon then the "religious and political destiny" of the entire nation could collapse. He thought the West would play a significant role in the spiritual future of the nation because it was "the great central power of the nation," and its backsliding would affect the "cause of free institutions and the liberty of the world." Bushnell and other critics of revivalism feared evangelicalism might fail in its providential mission because of a lack of education and piety, a lack of missionary effort, and too little religious infrastructure.[22]

A consistent theme among eastern evangelicals critical of revivalism was the irreverence and ignorance of their western coreligionists because of a lack of Christian effort and piety in the West. It was their own lack of effort that, they claimed, had a role to play in the rise of Mormonism's strength at Nauvoo. Benjamin Morris, a missionary active in the AHMS, criticized western evangelicals for their apathy in a letter to his AHMS colleagues. It seemed to him "as if they designed their spiritual eyes shut forever." He blamed the lack of evangelical success in the western part of the United States on "indifference, and inconsistency of Christian conduct . . . too much manifested by those who call and think themselves Christians." Morris charged these western evangelicals with holding "back the power of the gospel" in Illinois, indicting his coreligionists for allowing the rise of Mormonism and putting out "the fires of evangelical piety." The leaders of the ATS similarly blamed the poor media consumption of western Christians for making them susceptible to false teaching. Western evangelicals, they believed, read too much from the popular press, studying "the grossest licentiousness and the boldest infidelity." Once western evangelicals succumbed to these kinds of unorthodox teachings, these leaders of the ATS believed it weakened parental authority and the desire to read the Bible or other works of spiritual edification.[23]

In addition to a lack of piety, a growing number of evangelicals believed their coreligionists in the West lacked education or a desire for learning. Calvin Colton, a disaffected northern evangelical turned Episcopalian, used theological education as a cudgel to attack the excesses of revivalism. Revivalism, Colton claimed, "created a wide spread and insatiate appetite for religious novelties" and a "general instability in the character of our religious world." Since revivalists believed "no religious training can be good or right," according to Colton, they would attempt to "dislodge" converts "from all habits of thinking" they had "established under the best religious guardians and teachers." The only way forward, according to Colton, was for "the sober, the enlightened . . . the truly zealous ministry of our different denominations, who have seen and deplored these evils . . . to assert, and to wield their own appropriate influence." Agreeing with Colton in a more forceful fashion, the Methodist La Roy Sunderland wrote a letter to young ministers that said the "early Christians did not think that, because the apostles of our Lord were inspired . . . their successors in the sacred office would not need the helping hand of the Church in training them." Too often, Sunderland believed, the Methodist Church said if a person has the "gifts, grace, and a sound understanding," then it is enough. Asking young clergymen how they can expect to teach what they have never learned and how can they study the Bible without receiving education, Sunderland stated "the Bible and ecclesiastical history unite in the testimony that . . . a *theological education* . . . [is] an indispensable prerequisite for persons entering . . . the Christian ministry." Christians were not the only ones who believed religious training was necessary. Referencing groups he later compared to Mormonism, Sunderland characterized the "Mohammedans, Jews, and even the heathen" as having "a sense of the *importance of knowledge* in all persons previously to their becoming ministers of religion."[24]

Evangelical missionary organization consistently worried about the religious illiteracy of westerners because of a lack of Bibles. The leaders of the American Bible Society thought providing Bibles cheaply throughout the West constituted one of the "most happy methods of introducing religious conversation in families." The problem, according to the leaders of the ABS, was that too few in the West were "accustomed to this, the most important of all conversation." What they found concerning was that by the middle of the 1830s too few Bibles "are found in this land of Gospel light and religious freedom who openly deny the importance of possessing the Bible." A greater distribution of Bibles would "prevent the spread of Infidel, Roman Catholic,

Mormon, and other deadly errors, which are exerting their unhallowed influence in the . . . extended regions of the West," according to this evangelical organization. They believed the very future of the "social, civil, and religious" institutions could be "preserved in their purity" if this paucity of education was reversed.[25]

Many of the most ardent supporters of the home missions movement had likewise grown concerned about the future of their own efforts in the West by the 1840s. Agents of the AHMS wrote at length about the growing size and strength of Mormonism's Nauvoo, explaining its successes as the result of a lack of missionary effort in the West. Writing in 1841, a missionary from Iowa noted the only way to "cope effectively" with the "new form of error" of Mormonism was an "intelligent ministry." This AHMS official wondered "where are these ambassadors, while this compound of ignorance and blasphemy is destroying the souls for whom Christ died?" The missionary wanted the "unemployed ministers of our land, who are in circumstances to admit of their removal to such a field of labor," believing they should follow the "*example* of self-denial zeal set them by the teachers of this falsehood." This AHMS domestic missionary concluded there would always be ministers of some kind in the West because "people every where want and *demand* the Gospel." With so few ministers in the West, he concluded that "we need very much indeed several able and experienced men."[26]

The leaders of the AHMS described the state of their efforts in the West in 1842, wondering aloud what would happen if the evangelical movement no longer supported missionaries in the "duty of bringing our whole country under the power of evangelical religion." Echoing Lyman Beecher's *Plea for the West*, the AHMS believed the religious status of the West was the linchpin for the religious "destiny of the nation. The "battle must be fought" there, they believed, "to decide whether this land is *now* to be occupied for Christ." The leaders of the AHMS wanted to send more missionaries and teachers to the West now because it was a "great mistake" to think evangelizing the West would be "just as easy ten years hence as it is now," because if the "friends of evangelical truth do not furnish missionaries," they warned, "Mormonism, Popery, [or] Atheism" will."[27]

Since the leaders of the AHMS understood the Mississippi Valley as the crucible of these missionary efforts, they concluded their organization required additional resources and a different missionary disposition. The West needed additional ministers to meet the growing population. The managers of the AHMS believed the "peculiarities of western character" also required a different evangelistic attitude. They saw it as a place to make bold experiments and an environment where "the terrorist selects the West as the appropriate soil in which his system will luxuriate." Sectarianism would not only fail in the West, they believed, but it also would prevent further evangelization and it would embarrass all evangelicals. According to these AHMS leaders, sectarianism was particularly virulent in the antebellum West. Each village and settlement in the West, these individuals argued, had a point early in their history where "the need for Gospel institutions and influence is deeply felt." The problem was that if it was "not supplied, some distracting influence takes the form of religious novelty or spurious excitement."[28]

In this same 1842 annual report of their missionary efforts, the leaders of the AHMS believed the "absurdity" of Mormonism's claims so obvious that "the delusion must have melted away." They lamented the "facts seem to be quite otherwise." This home missionary organization concluded the reason for Mormonism's success in the western part of the country emanated from a "zeal always burning, and a sanctity which excites a reverence in the mind of many, they all make and will make proselytes." What was needed, this domestic missionary society believed, was the sending of "men of nerve and faith to occupy this territory." The leaders of the AHMS thought ten to twelve domestic missionaries "in the right stamp . . . sustained so they might give themselves wholly to the work" might "exert an influence which this world has no arithmetic to compute."[29]

While antebellum evangelicalism established an institutional presence in the West through benevolent organization, missionary efforts, newspapers, and seminaries, evangelicals critical of revivalism worried the religious infrastructure of the West was weak and crumbling from the standpoint of the forms and styles of religious buildings. The specific ways antebellum evangelicals described Mormonism's temples fit comfortably alongside changes occurring within Protestantism about the nature and style of religious worship. By describing these buildings as Gothic and showy, these antebellum evangelical witnesses to Mormonism's sacred buildings reflected an anxiety about the future of their own movement's religious aesthetics. American religious denominations of all type embraced Gothic building styles by the middle of the nineteenth century. Alongside the use of high church architecture was an increasing reliance on crosses, candles, and choirs during religious services. Protestants embraced this religious style in part because they feared the growing number of Catholic converts. Accepting the Gothic style also allowed them to lay claim to a longer religious tradition that made evangelicalism seem more sentimental and expressive. Church design could be beautiful, antebellum Protestants believed, because by embracing a seemingly older style of church building, they could finally set themselves apart from competing denominations.[30]

The embrace of the Gothic style by antebellum Protestants had a dark side in the form of anti-Catholicism. American Protestants attacked Catholic sanctuaries as mummery, enchantments, and priestcraft. Using the same language deployed by antebellum evangelicals against Mormonism's temples, American Protestants argued the Protestant embrace of the Gothic invasion challenged Christian orthodoxy and encouraged Catholic conversions. The problem with this kind of church style, according to these Protestant critics, was it imprisoned people in sensory experience and feeling. This was the same argument made against the revivals of the Second Great Awakening.[31]

While antebellum Protestants saw Gothic cathedrals overwhelmingly in negative terms, they also could not stop building them or visiting them. Like William West and other evangelical tourists to the Kirtland and Nauvoo temples, American Protestants casually attended Catholic cathedrals in their local communities or made stops to see them while traveling. Antebellum Protestants described these Catholic buildings in similar ways as evangelical depictions of Mormonism's temples. The cathedrals, they said, had beautiful and alluring features. What happened during Catholic masses, antebellum Protestants described in dramatic, reverent, and sublime terms. Some Protestants even gave money for the building of Catholic cathedrals. Antebellum evangelicals, even while filled with religious animus, found Catholicism's and Mormonism's buildings as successful because of the way they fulfilled the deepest religious desires of people.[32]

Institutional Anti-Mormonism

Some antebellum evangelicals critical of revivalism concluded by the founding of the Mormon Nauvoo that the evangelical opposition to the followers of Joseph Smith had failed. Evangelicals leading this assault against Mormonism assumed that by the 1840s their assaults on the heresies of Joseph Smith should have relegated the movement to a historical footnote. Doubt had begun to enter into these anti-Mormon polemics. Horace Bushnell, writing in 1847, believed the western part of the United States was at a dangerous precipice. It could relapse into barbarism at any moment, he believed, because of the continued growth of atheism, Catholicism, and Mormonism. He worried specifically about how the Latter-day Saints had gathered in "thousands of disciples . . . [built] a populous city, and . . . [erected] a temple, rivalling in grandeur, even that of the false prophet at Mecca." Bushnell saw the religious destiny of the United States like that of the Israelites during the time of the Judges of the Old Testament; evangelicals were on the verge of backsliding. The Methodist La Roy Sunderland decided the strategy of trusting "the good sense of the people" as a barrier "against the spread of notions so silly and so utterly opposed to reason, to scripture, and well known matters of fact" had not worked. The consequence of rationally laying out the case for the falsehood of Mormonism, he believed, was that "while we have been sleeping the enemy has scattered his tares amongst us, and thousands have been duped by this insidious foe." Writing about Nauvoo, the Presbyterian Jonathan Turner worried that "intelligent" readers would not believe his remonstrances "against errors which do not and cannot exist in a land of light and bibles." All these readers needed to do, he concluded, was to have a "knowledge of the daily arrivals at Nauvoo, from all the quarters in the union." Alexander Campbell wrote in 1843 that if people could not learn about the "monstrous impiety" of Mormonism from what already appeared in his writings, then no "human tongue" could ever teach them. The power of Mormonism's influence was such that Caswall wondered if the "Christian reader will feel that he has now had enough" and would desire to find some other method of response.[33]

The only way evangelicals could effectively oppose Mormonism was by looking in the mirror. Caswall and these other evangelicals critical of revivalism concluded "when the present generation of deceivers and of dupes shall have gone to their graves, a new class of Mormons may have arisen." When Caswall asked himself how Protestants should "effectually avert the calamity" of Mormonism, he answered that they should encourage "the feeble and infant Christian institutions already existing in that wonderful land which Mormonism, even now, claims as its own." The Methodist Reverend Daniel Kidder likewise agreed that "the numbers attached to the Mormon community . . . give cause of apprehension for the future." He wrote how important it was that the "inhabitants of this country, and of our great west . . . should fully understand this subject, and their duty with respect to it." Pushing back against the aggressive response of some evangelicals, he believed the patient use of truth and reason would be the only successful way to respond to Mormonism. He called for the "pure principles of the gospel" to be "disseminated and practiced, and there will be nothing to fear."[34]

Since anti-Mormonism had proved unsuccessful in the minds of these evangelicals critical of revivalism, they focused on a series of institutional changes within evangelicalism as the solution to the threat of Mormonism. Individuals like Caswall called for a "learned clergy in the rising cities of the west," "zealous missionaries," and a building up of the religious infrastructure of the church. The irony about these areas chosen by Caswall and other moderate evangelicals was the inspiration for these items came from Mormonism itself.[35]

The evangelical use of comparative religion to engage in self-reflection was not surprising. Other religions helped antebellum evangelicals make sense of their place in the world. Through this cosmopolitan outlook, many evangelicals saw inadequacies within their own movement. They often found themselves moved by these other faiths. When evangelical missionaries initially encountered the followers of Islam in the Middle East, they did not see them as threats or beyond the bounds of potential salvation. A few of these evangelical missionaries to the Middle East even suggested Muslims had greater access to religious truth than Catholics or other non-Protestants. Authors of evangelical missionary literature likewise depicted Jews in positive terms. Missionaries in this vein depicted Jews as sympathetic victims because they had experienced persecution throughout their history and deserved sympathy. While the evangelical imagination initially allowed affection and even grudging admiration for Muslims and Jews, religious intolerance toward these groups increased later during the antebellum period. Followers of Islam transitioned from pious believers to murderers and tyrants in the minds of antebellum evangelicals. Evangelicals came to see Jews as stubborn, superstitious, and intolerant.[36]

Mormonism then provided antebellum evangelicals both an enemy to contend with and a useful foil to make changes about piety, education, missions, and infrastructure within their own movement. They wanted their own movement to become more like the learned, pious, and devoted Mormons. Contrasting them with their unrefined western neighbors, the editors of the *Christian Reflector* described Mormon communities in Missouri as having all the "rudiments of learning, taught under our school system at the East." Mormons were eager to acquire education, the editors of the *New York Evangelist* wrote, and had brought in a Hebrew teacher and "pursue studies until midnight and attend to nothing else." James M'Chesney believed the one true antidote to Mormonism was "not the carnal weapons of swords," but the "sword of divine truth." With the continued expansion of Mormonism, M'Chesney argued that this showed the religious ignorance and "unregenerate state" of "people in general . . . and how little we are prepared to combat such dark, designing influence." Were evangelicals better trained religiously, he said "delusions in Churches would vanish, and the pure influence of Divine Truth would shine with resplendent lustre in every heart."[37]

The missionary James Eels likewise saw the example of Mormonism at Kirtland as demonstrating the importance of having sound instruction, "along with high excitement." His experience with the converts to Mormonism demonstrated that "men may have some other evidences on which their faith rests than the *impulses* of their own unstable minds." Eels saw it as a credit to the Presbyterian denomination and educational infrastructure "that scarcely a convert has been made from Presbyterian ranks." Education had saved them from the clutches of Mormonism.[38]

The leaders of the AHMS had anxieties about their own mission efforts in the West because of the successes and spirituality of the Mormon community at Nauvoo. They worried "the Mormonites are making numerous proselytes to their faith where the Gospel is not preached." Praising the Mormons as a "people who read the Bible . . . and who could so readily quote any part of Scripture," the leaders of the AMHS claimed "they shame all other denominations" and jealously looked at how Mormon missionaries were "always on foot, with a zeal always burning, and a sanctity which excites a reverence in the minds of many." The evangelical community needed to respond to Mormonism with more active, focused, and organized mission work, the leaders of the AHMS believed, "because the preaching of the Gospel is the only antidote" at a time when "it seems as though every form of error which the devil can devise, is rolling in here like a flood."[39]

In Caswall's thinking, more missionary activity would "check the rising heresy" of Mormonism. He wanted the right kinds of missionaries, ones "thoroughly acquainted with the Mormon controversy." Caswall wanted these missionaries to be "patient, willing to endure contradiction and persecution, and able to accommodate [themselves] readily to all circumstances." The leaders of the ATS concluded similarly that the "machinery of gospel means . . . needs to be set in motion by the benevolence of American Christians." If Christians did not respond to that plea, millions could become "neglecters of religion." The leaders of the ATS concluded American society needed "large expenditures for "colporteurs, missionaries, books, and Bible" until people "can be taught the value of a pure faith."[40]

Solving the problem of Mormonism would finally come with more religious infrastructure, according to these moderate evangelicals. The Nauvoo temple provided the template of what would happen if a group of fully committed converts gave everything they had for a religious cause. Milton Badger, a prominent member of the AHMS, envied the construction of the Nauvoo temple. He wrote that Mormons had built such an impressive sanctuary because every Mormon had to give "one tenth of all the property he has as the time, and one tenth of all he may earn afterwards, and to hold the remainder subject to the prophet's order, as God shall reveal." If only evangelicals would give the same, he wondered, if they "were willing to make the sacrifices in the cause of Christ, which these poor creatures are making to a false prophet, how soon . . . might the earth be filled with his glory!" The editors of the *Weekly Messenger*, a periodical of the German Reformed Church, felt similarly about the Nauvoo temple. Telling their readers that the Mormons at Nauvoo had just completed a temple at the cost of more than $100,000, they speculated why members of the German Reformed Church could not even "raise just half as much to secure" the services of educated ministers.[41]

These specific remedies of institutionalism implicitly attacked aspects of revivalism. Many of the same people who called for this series of prescriptions had spent their theological careers critiquing the revivalism of their coreligionists. Evangelicals concerned about revivalism had concluded that two pillars of their movement—camp meetings and itinerancy—had limited effectiveness and endurance. Camp meetings and itinerancy, they thought, led to shallow belief. Without deep religious roots, converts would look elsewhere for religious fulfillment. Since both of these practices focused on individual judgment, a dominant theme within anti-Mormon criticism, evangelicals critical of revivalism encouraged converts to seek safe haven in the form of ecclesiastical structures. Horace Bushnell believed that radical evangelicals had made "conversion . . . too nearly every thing with us." Evangelicals no longer had ways to "gather in disciples, save by means of certain marked experience, developed in such scenes" according to Bushnell. With churches exhausted, Bushnell concluded "no nation can long thrive by a spirit of conquest; no more can a church." Rather than relying on a shallow faith, he wanted evangelicalism to focus on "internal growth, that is made by holy industry, in the common walks of life and duty." To oppose the barbarism of Mormonism, Bushnell called on all Christians to "not cease, till a Christian nation throws up its temples of worship on every hill and plain," and the entire continent is a "new Christian Empire."[42]

Epilogue

Evangelicals saw Mormonism in contradictory ways from their earliest encounter. They looked down on the followers of Joseph Smith as uncivilized, impotent, and destined to fail. Mormon theology, evangelicals thought, led to strange, sectarian, and militant ends. But although evangelicals viewed Mormonism as weak, they also saw it as a dangerous threat. Powerful and charismatic Mormon leaders hoodwinked converts in order to gain vast numbers of followers and to dominate American society. A fascist-like argument that their enemy was both too weak and too strong dominated evangelical perceptions of Mormonism from the start. The irony was evangelical Christians saw themselves in a similar fashion. While they worried that their movement was on the verge of collapse because of a lack of effort and organization, antebellum evangelicals fearful of the radical consequences of revivalism blamed their coreligionists for too much success. Revivalism had created thousands of converts, these evangelical critics believed, but their accomplishments had come at a cost. Critics of revivalism charged their coreligionists with aiding the growth of Mormonism, and they concluded that their own movement either needed to change or cease to exist. Critical of revivalism, they used anti-Mormonism to define heresy within their own ranks and to promote group identity.[1]

Anti-Mormonism was successful, but not in the way antebellum evangelicals hoped. Mormonism survived. The faith inaugurated by Joseph Smith grew in the face of vicious opposition. Religious intolerance worked instead by changing evangelical beliefs and practices. The use of anti-Mormonism to define evangelical identity had a lasting legacy. It altered the future relationship between evangelicalism and Mormonism by continuing to influence evangelical perspectives on themselves, fashioning evangelicalism into a more respectable faith, and making cultural revanchism and heresy-hunting markers of evangelical identity.

The early history and work of anti-Mormonism described in this book cast a long shadow on future relations between evangelicalism and Mormonism. Once the leaders of Mormonism established a theocracy in the West and publicly proclaimed the teaching of plural marriage, anti-Mormonism dominated the national discourse in new and old ways. Polygamy became the commanding impression many Americans had about Mormonism. While arguments against polygamy overwhelmed some of the anti-Mormon tradition described in this book, earlier criticisms never went away. Mormonism continued to cause evangelicals anxiety not just because of their differences, but because of their similarities.

The establishment of Mormonism's home at Nauvoo upset not just antebellum evangelicals, but people throughout the region. Local residents saw Joseph Smith and the Mormon community along the Mississippi as a threat. After a series of confrontations, Illinois officials arrested Joseph Smith on charges of civil disturbance in 1844. While awaiting a trial in Carthage, Illinois, a mob surrounded the jail and assassinated the Mormon prophet. Most of the Mormon converts followed Brigham Young westward to the Utah territory in late 1845. What began as a trickle culminated in the migration of tens of thousands of Mormons over the course of the nineteenth century. They established a community outside the bounds of the United States—one dedicated to the commitments of Mormonism.[2]

The practice of plural marriage became one of the dominant images Americans had about Mormonism during the middle of the nineteenth century. Americans of all faith traditions derided polygamy as lascivious and tyrannical. Common descriptions referred to Mormonism as "an institution founded in the lustful and unbridled passions of men, devised by Satan himself to authorize whoredom." Mormonism also became known as a "society for the seduction of young virgins" and Utah as the "biggest whorehouse in the world." Through literature and legal means, Americans depicted Mormonism as a threat to civilization because of their unorthodox political and social arrangements.[3]

Dozens of works of antipolygamy fiction appeared in the mid-to-late nineteenth century with the aim of creating sympathy for women involved in polygamous marriages and enacting legal proscriptions against the practice of plural marriage in Utah. Antipolygamist authors wanted the federal government to intervene against this practice in order to protect women and American society. They got their wish when the Republican party made the prohibition of polygamy a prominent part of their platform in the election of 1856. President James Buchanan dispatched military forces to bring Mormonism under the authority of the American government in the late 1850s. The US government later used legal means to prosecute thousands of Mormon men throughout the Utah territory for the practice of polygamy. The Supreme Court unanimously decided in 1878 that the Constitution did not protect the practice of polygamy and that Mormonism was not a religion.[4]

This well-known history of the tensions between the federal government and Mormonism in Utah diverged somewhat from the earlier anti-Mormonism described in this book. It focused on a smaller set of issues, the federal government played a much greater role, and Mormonism loomed larger in American consciousness. Similarities still mattered. As in the earlier period of anti-Mormonism, evangelicals in this later period found Mormonism threatening not just because it was so different. Evangelicals still recognized it all too well. Criticisms over a theocratic government and polygamy dominated discussions about Mormonism in the later nineteenth century, issues on which evangelicals suffered internal disagreement.

The perceived social ramifications of plural marriage—polygamous wives in mortal danger and Mormon men as tyrants—led many evangelicals to seek out the federal government as the arbiter of polygamy. Embracing the state as the judge of acceptable religious practice was a reversal for many evangelicals. They had experienced the successes of the Benevolent Empire without significant help from the state. Evangelicals had created numerous, large-scale reform societies for the purpose of transforming the world. The wide-ranging accomplishments of the Benevolent Empire convinced many evangelicals that they did not need state support, and it had convinced many evangelicals to support religious disestablishment during the antebellum period. The threat of Mormon polygamy led many evangelicals to ask the state to intervene and force Latter-day Saints to renounce tenets of their faith, a choice that more closely aligned evangelicals with the state.[5]

Evangelicals attacked plural marriage with a fierce intensity, but not just because they found it unusual. Polygamy challenged prevailing conceptions of marriage that evangelicals had helped to erect. Antebellum evangelicals played a key role in making spousal love, emotional satisfaction, and happiness the foundations of marriage. This ideal of companionate marriage came under assault by the middle of the nineteenth century. Many Americans wanted more out of their marriages. Divorce laws loosened, making it a little easier to leave an unfulfilling marriage. Feminists even portrayed marriage as a confining institution, like slavery. When Americans could not find the marriage of their dreams, some people sought alternatives to heteronormative monogamy. The challenge of polygamy, an institution threatening the institution of traditional marriage, created evangelical anxiety about their own social arrangements.[6]

Changing conceptions of masculinity likewise influenced the future relationship between evangelicalism and Mormonism by reflecting back on evangelicalism. Evangelical men saw themselves as the manly rescuers of Mormon women caught in polygamy. Authors of antipolygamy fiction sought to engender sympathy toward women trapped in polygamous marriages. Gender norms were still unsettled within evangelicalism by the middle of the nineteenth century. Victorian ideas about inherent differences between men and women had yet to be solidified. Women had come to dominate evangelical churches and societies by the middle of the nineteenth century and some elements of evangelical belief and practice had become increasingly feminine. An increasingly vocal group of male evangelicals found this state of affairs untenable. Female dominance posed a cultural, financial, and political threat to their established position. Focusing on the heroic exploits of men saving Mormon women from polygamy and the forceful denunciation of Mormonism worked to remake evangelicalism into a cult of militant masculinity.[7]

The earlier period of anti-Mormonism also persisted in familiar criticisms. The Methodist minister Daniel Dorchester, writing in 1890, continued the trope that Mormonism grew out of "popular superstitions for a time quite prevalent among the more ignorant classes." He attacked the character of Joseph Smith and charged him as involved in counterfeiting faith and money. Dorchester derivatively rehashed the Solomon Spaulding conspiracy, reprinting the testimony of Spaulding's widow that the Book of Mormon derived wholly from the imagination of Spaulding. This Methodist minister also attacked Mormons for their professions "to have power to heal diseases, to cast out devils, to impart the Holy Ghost, and also to speak in unknown tongues." Dorchester saw Mormonism's Nauvoo as the site of fanatical behavior.

Plural marriage only received a brief mention in his work, while the earlier anti-Mormon tradition received the bulk of the attention for this New England evangelical.[8]

Dorchester's solution to the Mormon problem would have been familiar to any antebellum evangelical critical of revivalism. He concluded that "political, educational, and religious solutions have all been deeply pondered" concerning Mormonism. Dorchester fell back on institutional solutions to combat Mormonism. He wanted a more aggressive and expanded religious education that was "loyal to the Bible, but without fanaticism." It should be "spiritual, but not superstitious; permeated with the true spirit of reform, but not revolutionary," he said. He ended his book with a grand call for Christian unity that he viewed as the only way to cut out the "ulcer" of Mormonism.[9]

The persistent use of anti-Mormonism in shaping evangelical beliefs and practices has continued into more contemporary religious polemics. Executives within the interfaith witness department of the Southern Baptist Convention published a book in the late 1990s that characterized Mormonism as a "fabricated and artificial form of Christianity." R. Philip Roberts and his coauthors focused mainly on what they believed were points of theological contradiction between evangelical Christianity and the Church of Jesus Christ of Latter-day Saints. These included charges that Mormonism relied too much on the heart in the discernment of truth, accepted belief in multiple gods, embraced the materiality of God, believed that God and Jesus were separate beings, had an unorthodox view of salvation, fashioned a new religious writ, read the Bible in a different fashion, structured a corporate Church, and held an unscriptural conception of the afterlife. Their focus on Mormonism's scriptural practices, the business structures of the church, and an overreliance upon feelings hearkened back to many of the earliest anti-Mormon criticisms.[10]

These leaders in the Southern Baptist Convention viewed Mormonism enviously, praising their mission work, finances, and public relations. Those factors, they believed, were most responsible for Mormonism posing a "major challenge to Christian churches." Roberts believed the Church of Jesus Christ of Latter-day Saints to have one of the "most effective and efficient programs of and religious group in the world today." Like many antebellum evangelicals, twentieth-century evangelicals saw Mormonism's active missionary efforts as responsible for much of their success. Roberts described the young men and women engaged in this mission program as diligent and pious, and willing to sacrifice money and time to take on a mission. The church was a "powerful economic machine." Roberts likewise viewed Mormonism's public relations efforts in positive terms. He argued they obscured the differences between Mormonism and evangelical Christianity by emphasizing the importance of Jesus and families in the Church of Jesus Christ of Latter-day Saints.[11]

Roberts and his coauthors concluded with a playbook for how evangelicals should respond to Mormonism. Their response would have been familiar to Jonathan Turner or other evangelicals critical of revivalism. Roberts believed evangelicals needed to embark on a more vibrant missionary effort and develop a more corporate structure. Roberts wanted to fix the ways modern evangelicals read their Bibles, practiced their faith, and worked toward unity. He wanted evangelicals to make sure they knew their faith and held fast to his conception of orthodox Christianity. Roberts warned evangelicals not to trust their feelings too much, a familiar fear among many evangelicals, like those antebellum evangelicals critical of revivalism. This Southern Baptist finally discouraged sectarianism. He wanted evangelicals to avoid arguing about minor matters of faith with their coreligionists or with members of Mormonism. Roberts, like many evangelicals described in this book, believed if evangelicals faithfully taught orthodoxy, then evangelical Christianity would inevitably succeed in winning the world to Christ.

Anti-Mormonism also succeeded by remaking evangelicalism into a more respectable and conforming faith. Evangelical religious practices became more acceptable to mainstream American society because of religious animus toward Mormonism. Evangelicals critical of revivalism used religious animus toward Mormonism to portray revivals as having a variety of negative consequences. They saw revivalism creating charismatic leaders would lead astray susceptible people. Conversions would not stick and converts would depart from religious truth. Division occurred, they believed, because revivalists taught conflicting messages. Evangelicals critical of revivalism worked to undo these excesses, and anti-Mormonism became one of their primary tools. The religious enthusiasm associated with revivalism did move out of the mainstream. Despite several large instances of revivalism in the late 1850s, revivals changed in character, declined in usage, and no longer had cultural cachet. No longer did revivals contain the most public kinds of bodily manifestations, like the jerks, speaking in tongues, and other instances of the indwelling of the Holy Spirit.[12]

Evangelicals critical of revivalism also wanted a respectable theological conformity for believers. By the time Mormonism made its way out of the United States to Utah, these more moderate evangelicals had many accomplishments. They identified Mormonism, Catholicism, Islam, their fellow evangelicals, and many other groups as acting without accordance to theological standards or authority. Where evangelicals concerned about revivalism worried about the doctrinal creativity of the Second Great Awakening, they also increasingly agreed with one another on matters of faith. They focused more on sacramentalism and sentimentality than on questions of theological complexity. Nineteenth-century evangelicals wanted to establish the fundamental reasonableness of Christianity, and they used similar techniques to advance that goal. Evangelicals of all stripes, learned and populist, increasingly acted in accordance with the principles of evidentialism. A consensus had developed that observable evidence proved the veracity of the biblical account. Anti-Mormonism, with its emphasis on questioning the evidences for the truthfulness of Mormonism, fostered this new shape to theology.[13]

Anti-Mormonism succeeded in altering the relationship between evangelicalism and Mormonism, and in influencing the rise and dominance of antebellum evangelicalism, but these successes came at a vicious cost. Antebellum evangelicals depicted the followers of Joseph Smith as lazy cheats. They saw Mormons as people who invented a new religious text out of whole cloth, modified the Bible to fit their theology, worshipped in overly emotional fashion, believed that God continued to have intercourse with them on a daily basis, and selfishly denounced all others who did not agree with them. Evangelicals likewise believed Mormonism posed an existential threat. For all their obvious heterodoxy, they thought the leaders of Mormonism had figured out the recipe to acquiring converts. Mormonism's success would come at the expense of their own movement, and this fear of loss led them to label the followers of Joseph Smith as impure deviants from orthodoxy.

Evangelicals depicted their coreligionists engaged in revivalism with a similar kind of uncleanness. It was not just that the beliefs and practices of their coreligionists differed from established religious dogma. They described their fellow believers as immoral, dishonest, unintelligent, and close-minded. Evangelicals critical of revivalism used anti-Mormonism to depict their coreligionists as heretics and sought to excommunicate them. Demonizing their coreligionists for acting and believing like the Mormons shaped the rise and progress of evangelicalism. While questions of slavery and sectionalism led to denominational schism in the middle of the nineteenth century, depicting their enemies as heretics was powerful ammunition to use against their coreligionists. The successes of anti-Mormon polemics showed evangelicals that grievance and fear were the keys to power.

Religious intolerance does not always arise out of difference. The anti-Mormon bent of antebellum American evangelicalism suggests an alternative story about the development and uses of religious hostilities. Mormonism and the internal problems it revealed within antebellum evangelicalism made evangelicals feel inadequate and powerless. They felt they needed to respond somehow. The irony was they found that answer within Mormonism, but intolerance remained too great to treat this new group like brothers or sisters in Christ. The hatred and resentment religious intolerance unleashed sowed division that would contribute to the unmaking of America itself.

Notes

Introduction

1. Ezra Booth to Ira Eddy, in Eber Howe, *Mormonism Unvailed; or, a Faithful Account of That Singular Imposition and Delusion: From Its Rise to the Present Time with Sketches of the Characters of Its Propagators, and a Full Detail of the Manner in Which the Famous Golden Bible Was Brought Before the World* (Painesville, OH: Printed and Published by the Author, 1834), 175–77; Robert C. Brown and J. E. Norris, *History of Portage County, Ohio: Containing a History of the County, Its Townships, Towns, Villages, Schools, Churches, Industries, Etc.; Portraits of Early Settlers and Prominent Men; Biographies; History of the Northwest Territory; History of Ohio; Statistical and Miscellaneous Matter, Etc., Etc. . . .* (Chicago: Warner, Beers & Company, 1885), 533; Historical Society of Geauga County O. (Ohio), *Pioneer and General History of Geauga County: With Sketches of Some of the Pioneers and Prominent Men* (N.p.: Historical Society of Geauga County, 1880), 295; *The Eddy Family in America* (Boston: Published under the Direction of the Eddy Family Association, Inc., 1930), 408–9. The Church of Jesus Christ of Latter-day Saints has historically had a number of names. When founded in 1830, Joseph Smith simply called it the Church of Christ. By the later 1830s, the church used the name Church of Jesus Christ of Latter-day Saints. That name has continued unchanged to the present, with the current president of the church, Russell Nelson, affirming in 2018 the official name as The Church of Jesus Christ of Latter-day Saints. Throughout the church's history, members and nonmembers of the church have used "Mormon" or "Mormonism" to indicate ideas, people, rituals, and structures that trace their beginnings to Joseph Smith. This book will use "Mormonism" to refer to the cultural ideas and practices of the followers of Joseph Smith in the nineteenth century, and "Mormons" as those people identifying with and as identified as members of that cultural movement. This follows the naming practices of groups like the *Journal of Mormon History* and the Mormon History Association.

2. Ezra Booth to Ira Eddy, in Howe, *Mormonism Unvailed*, 179; H. Michael Marquadt, "Ezra Booth on Early Mormonism: A Look at His 1831 Letters,"

John Whitmer Historical Association Journal 28 (2008): 65–87. For more on Booth, see Amos Sutton Hayden, *Early History of the Disciples in the Western Reserve, Ohio: With Biographical Sketches of the Principal Agents in Their Religious Movement* (Cincinnati: Chase and Hall, 1876), 250.

3. Pew Research Center, "Americans Learned Little About the Mormon Faith, But Some Attitudes Have Softened," December 14, 2012, https://www.pewforum.org/2012/12/14/attitudes-toward-mormon-faith/.

4. J. Spencer Fluhman, *A Peculiar People: Anti-Mormonism and the Making of Religion in Nineteenth-Century America* (Chapel Hill: University of North Carolina Press, 2012), 24.

5. For apologetic views of anti-Mormonism, see Milton Backman, "The Quest for a Restoration: The Birth of Mormonism in Ohio," *BYU Studies* (1972); Kenneth Winn, *Exiles in a Land of Liberty: Mormons in America, 1830–1846* (Chapel Hill: University of North Carolina Press, 1989); Marvin Hill, *Quest for Refuge: The Mormon Flight from American Pluralism* (Salt Lake City: Signature Books, 1989). For examples of how scholars have seen evangelicalism and Mormonism as opposites, see Fawn Brodie, *No Man Knows My History: The Life of Joseph Smith, the Mormon Prophet*, 2d ed., rev. enl. (New York: Alfred A. Knopf, 1971); Gordon Wood, "Evangelical America and Early Mormonism," *New York History* 61, no. 4 (October 1980): 359–86; R. Laurence Moore, *Religious Outsiders and the Making of Americans* (New York: Oxford University Press, 1986); Sarah Barringer Gordon, *The Mormon Question: Polygamy and Constitutional Conflict in Nineteenth-Century America* (Chapel Hill: University of North Carolina Press, 2002); Jon Krakauer, *Under the Banner of Heaven: A Story of Violent Faith* (New York: Doubleday, 2003); Patrick Q. Mason, *The Mormon Menace: Violence and Anti-Mormonism in the Postbellum South* (New York: Oxford University Press, 2011); Tammy Heise, "Marking Mormon Difference: How Western Perceptions of Islam Defined the 'Mormon Menace,'" *Journal of Religion and Popular Culture* 25, no. 1 (January 1, 2013): 82–97; David Brion Davis, "Some Themes of Counter-Subversion: An Analysis of Anti-Masonic, Anti-Catholic, and Anti-Mormon Literature," *Mississippi Valley Historical Review* 47, no. 2 (September 1960): 205–24.

6. Terryl Givens, *The Viper on the Hearth: Mormons, Myths, and the Construction of Heresy* (New York: Oxford University Press, 1997); Fluhman, *A Peculiar People.*

7. John Corrigan, *Emptiness: Feeling Christian in America* (Chicago: University of Chicago Press, 2015).

8. Catherine A. Brekus, "Contested Words: History, America, Religion," *William and Mary Quarterly* 75, no. 1 (January 2018): 3; John Corrigan, *Emptiness.*

Chapter 1. "The Greatest Fraud of Our Time in the Field of Religion"

1. Dan Vogel, "John Sherer to Absalom Peters, 18 October 1830," in *Early Mormon Documents*, vol. 4 (Salt Lake City: Signature Books, 2002); H. Michael Marquardt and W. P. Walters, *Inventing Mormonism: Tradition and the Historical Record* (Salt Lake City: Signature Books, 1994); Newel Knight, "Newel

Knight Journal," in *Scraps of Biography. Tenth Book of the Faith-Promoting Series* (Salt Lake City: Juvenile Instructor Office, 1883); Emily Austin, *Mormonism; or, Life among the Mormons: Being an Autobiographical Sketch Including an Experience of Fourteen Years of Mormon Life* (Madison, WI.: M. J. Cantwell, Book and Job Printer, 1882).

2. Austin, *Mormonism; or, Life among the Mormons.*

3. Absalom Peters, ed., "John Sherer to Absalom Peters," in *The Home Missionary and American Pastor's Journal*, vol. 3 (New York: Clayton and Van Norden, 1831).

4. Daniel Walker Howe, *What Hath God Wrought?: The Transformation of America, 1815–1848* (New York: Oxford University Press, 2007), 217.

5. Ronald Shaw, *Erie Water West a History of the Erie Canal, 1792–1854* (Lexington: University of Kentucky Press, 1966), 263; Brodie, *No Man Knows My History*, 10–11; Krakauer, *Under the Banner of Heaven*, 53–66; Paul Johnson, *Sam Patch, the Famous Jumper* (New York: Hill and Wang, 2003).

6. On the consequences of the market economy, see Charles Sellers, *The Market Revolution: Jacksonian America, 1815–1846* (New York: Oxford University Press, 1991); Paul Johnson, *A Shopkeeper's Millennium: Society and Revivals in Rochester, New York, 1815–1837* (New York: Hill and Wang, 1978).

7. Mark Noll, *America's God: From Jonathan Edwards to Abraham Lincoln* (New York: Oxford University Press, 2002), 160–86.

8. Charles Hambrick-Stowe, *Charles G. Finney and the Spirit of American Evangelicalism* (Grand Rapids, MI: William B. Eerdmans, 1996); Noll, *America's God*, 306–8; Whitney Cross, *The Burned-Over District: The Social and Intellectual History of Enthusiastic Religion in Western New York, 1800–1850* (Ithaca, NY: Cornell University Press, 1950).

9. Peters, "John Sherer to Absalom Peters"; Marquardt and Walters, *Inventing Mormonism*; Dan Vogel, "Diedrich Willers to Reverend Brethren," in *Early Mormon Documents*, vol. 5 (Salt Lake City: Signature Books, 2003), 271–78; Givens, *The Viper on the Hearth*; D. Michael Quinn, "The First Months of Mormonism: A Contemporary View by Rev. Diedrich Willers," *New York History* 54, no. 3 (July 1973): 317–33; Alexander Campbell, *Delusions: An Analysis of the Book of Mormon with an Examination of Its Internal and External Evidences, and a Refutation of Its Pretences to Divine Authority* (Boston: Benjamin H. Greene, 1832); RoseAnn Benson, *Alexander Campbell and Joseph Smith* (Provo, UT: Brigham Young University Press, in cooperation with Abilene Christian University Press, 2017); Susan Juster, *Doomsayers: Anglo-American Prophecy in the Age of Revolution* (Philadelphia: University of Pennsylvania Press, 2003).

10. Peter Wosh, *Spreading the Word: The Bible Business in Nineteenth-Century America* (Ithaca, NY: Cornell University Press, 1994), chap. 5; Candy Gunther Brown, *The Word in the World: Evangelical Writing, Publishing, and Reading in America, 1789–1880* (Chapel Hill: University of North Carolina Press, 2004).

11. Brown, *The Word in the World.*

12. Candy Gunther Brown, "Print Culture and the Changing Faces of Religious Communication," in *Religious Periodicals and Publishing in Transnational*

Contexts: The Press and the Pulpit, ed. Oliver Scheiding and Anja-Maria Bassimir (Newcastle upon Tyne: Cambridge Scholars Publishing, 2017).

13. "Golden Bible," *Rochester Daily Advertiser and Telegraph*, August 31, 1829.

14. "Superstition," *Palmyra Reflector*, June 12, 1830; Marquardt and Walters, *Inventing Mormonism*, 147.

15. "The Book of Mormon," *Palmyra Reflector*, September 16, 1829; "Impostors," *Palmyra Reflector*, January 2, 1830; "Diabolical," *Palmyra Reflector*, February 27, 1830; "[We Are Informed]," *Palmyra Reflector*, May 1, 1830; Richard Bushman, *Joseph Smith: Rough Stone Rolling* (New York: Alfred A. Knopf, 2005), 81.

16. "The Book of Pukei.—Chap. 1," *Palmyra Reflector*, June 12, 1830.

17. "The First Book of John," *Palmyra Reflector*, August 14, 1830; "The First Book of John," *Palmyra Reflector*, August 28, 1830; "For the Reflector," *Palmyra Reflector*, May 1, 1830; "Communications," *Palmyra Reflector*, June 30, 1830. For the evangelical relationship to freethinkers, see Lori D. Ginzberg, "'The Hearts of Your Readers Will Shudder': Fanny Wright, Infidelity, and American Freethought," *American Quarterly* 46, no. 2 (June 1994): 195–226. For evidence of evangelicals reprinting Cole, see "Unidentified Palmyra Residents to Editor," *Painesville Telegraph*, March 12, 1831; "The Gold Bible Fever . . . ," *Painesville Telegraph*, March 29, 1831; Howe, *Mormonism Unvailed.*

18. "A New Way of Raising the Wind," *Rochester Republican*, March 30, 1830; Nancy A. Hewitt, *Women's Activism and Social Change: Rochester, New York, 1822–1872* (Ithaca, NY: Cornell University Press, 1984), 30–31; Johnson, *A Shopkeeper's Millennium.*

19. "Imposition and Blasphemy!!—Money Diggers, &c.," *Rochester Gem*, May 15, 1830.

20. "Imposition and Blasphemy!!—Money Diggers, &c."

21. "Editorial Note," *Morning Courier and New-York Enquirer*, December 7, 1830.

22. "Editorial Note"; see also Campbell, *Delusions*, 15; Bushman, *Joseph Smith: Rough Stone Rolling*, 77–79; Matthew Bowman, *The Mormon People: The Making of an American Faith* (New York: Random House, 2012), 13–17. Note on terminology: To describe the restorationist movement begun by Alexander Campbell, Barton Stone, and others, this book will use the term Stone-Campbell movement.

23. "Book of Mormon," *Rochester Republican*, December 28, 1830.

24. David S. Burnet, "Something New—The Golden Bible," *Evangelical Inquirer*, March 7, 1831; "Imposition and Blasphemy!!—Money Diggers, &c.,"; "Book of Mormon," *Rochester Gem*, December 25, 1830; David Marks, *The Life of David Marks, to the 26th Year of His Age. Including the Particulars of His Conversion, Call to the Ministry, and Labours in Itinerant Preaching for Nearly Eleven Years* (Limerick, ME: Printed at the Office of the Morning Star, 1831), 341; Quinn, "The First Months of Mormonism," 327.

25. M.S.C., "Mormonism," *Evangelical Inquirer*, March 7, 1831; Campbell, *Delusions*, 6. For more on the comparisons between Islam and Mormonism, see Givens, *The Viper on the Hearth*; Fluhman, *A Peculiar People*; Timothy Marr,

The Cultural Roots of American Islamicism (New York: Cambridge University Press, 2006); Arnold Green, "Joseph Smith, an American Muhammad?: An Essay on the Perils of Historical Analogy," *Dialogue* 6, no. 1 (Spring 1971): 46–58.

26. Campbell, *Delusions*, 5; "Mormonist," *Boston Recorder*, October 10, 1832; George Bush, *The Life of Mohammed: Founder of the Religion of Islam, and of the Empire of the Saracens*, Harper's stereotype ed. (New York: Harper & Brothers, 1837); Fluhman, *A Peculiar People*, 35; Samuel Brown and Matthew Bowman, "Reverend Buck's Theological Dictionary and the Struggle to Define American Evangelicalism, 1802–1851," *Journal of the Early Republic* 29, no. 3 (Fall 2009): 441–73.

27. James Gordon Bennett, "Mormonism—Religious Fanaticism—Church and State Party," *Christian Register*, September 24, 1831. The most popular studies of Islam in antebellum America included *The Life of Mahomet; or, The History of That Imposture Which Was Begun, Carried On, and Finally Established by Him in Arabia: and Which Has Subjugated a Larger Portion of the Globe, Than the Religion of Jesus Has Yet Set at Liberty* (Worcester, [MA]: Printed by Isiah Thomas, 1802); Edward Gibbon, *The Life of Mahomet with Sketches of the Reigns of His Successors Abubeker, Omar, Othman, and Ali: From the Decline & Fall of the Roman Empire* (Leominster, [MA]: Printed by Salmon Wilder for John Whiting Lancaster, 1805); David Benedict, *A History of All Religions: As Divided into Paganism, Mahometanism, Judaism and Christianity, with an Account of Literary and Theological Institutions: And Missionary, Bible, Tract and Sunday School* (Providence, RI: John Miller printer, 1824); Charles Forster, *Mahometanism Unveiled: An Inquiry, in Which That Arch-Heresy, Its Diffusion and Continuance, Are Examined on a New Principle, Tending to Confirm the Evidences, and Aid the Propagation, of the Christian Faith* (N.p.: Printed for J. Duncan and J. Cochran, 1829); Bush, *The Life of Mohammed*. For more on non-evangelicals explicitly comparing Islam and Mormonism, see "Miscellaneous-Squibs," *Palmyra Reflector*, February 13, 1830.

28. Campbell, *Delusions*, 6.

29. Campbell, *Delusions*, 6; "MORMONISM RELIGIOUS FANATICISM CHURCH AND STATE PARTY," *Philadelphia Album and Ladies' Literary Portfolio* 5, no. 38 (September 17, 1831): 299; "Mormon Emigration," *Brattleboro Messenger*, June 11, 1831; "Article 7—No Title," *Christian Secretary* 10, no. 22 (June 18, 1831): 87; Benton Pixley, "INTELLIGENCE RESPECTING MORMONITES," *Christian Index*, November 24, 1832; "Unidentified Palmyra Residents to Editor"; "The First Book of John," August 28, 1830; "The Mormon Delusion," *St. Louis Beacon*, December 29, 1831; Catherine A. Brekus, *Strangers and Pilgrims: Female Preaching in America, 1740–1845* (Chapel Hill: University of North Carolina Press, 1998), 97–113.

30. "Imposition and Blasphemy!!—Money Diggers, &c."; Thomas Campbell, "The Mormon Challenge," *Evangelical Inquirer*, March 7, 1831; Abram Benton, "MORMONITES," *Evangelical Magazine and Gospel Advocate* 2, no. 15 (April 9, 1831): 120; Brekus, *Strangers and Pilgrims*, 80–97; Fluhman, *A Peculiar People*, 29.

31. "Imposition and Blasphemy!!—Money Diggers, &c."; "Money Diggers," *Palmyra Register*, July 24, 1822; Alan Taylor, "The Early Republic's Supernatural

Economy: Treasure Seeking in the American Northeast, 1780–1830," *American Quarterly* 38, no. 1 (1986): 6–34.

32. William Stafford affidavit, in Howe, *Mormonism Unvailed*, 237–40.

33. Benton, "MORMONITES."

34. Pomeroy Tucker, "Jesse Townsend to Phineas Stiles," in *Origin, Rise, and Progress of Mormonism* (New York: D. Appleton, 1867), 288–91; Benton, "MORMONITES."

35. Adam Jortner, "'Some Little Necromancy': Politics, Religion, and the Mormons, 1829–1838," in *Contingent Citizens: Shifting Perceptions of Latter-day Saints in American Political Culture*, ed. Spencer W. McBride, Brent M. Rogers, and Keith A. Erekson (Ithaca, NY: Cornell University Press, 2020), 17–28.

36. Editor, "Something New—The Golden Bible," *Evangelical Inquirer*, March 7, 1831.

37. Taylor, "The Early Republic's Supernatural Economy"; Richard Lloyd Anderson, "Joseph Smith's New York Reputation Reappraised," *BYU Studies* 10 (Spring 1970): 283–314.

38. "Mormonism," *Buffalo Patriot*, September 6, 1831.

39. Fluhman, *A Peculiar People*, 29; John R. Dichtl, *Frontiers of Faith: Bringing Catholicism to the West in the Early Republic* (Lexington: University Press of Kentucky, 2008), 174–81.

40. "Mormonism," *Broome County Courier*, December 29, 1831; Bennett, "Mormonism—Religious Fanaticism—Church and State Party"; Dan Vogel, "Nathaniel W. Howell, Walter Hubbell, Ansel D. Eddy, Henry Chapin, Jared Willson, and Lewis Jenkins to Ancil Beach, January 1832," in *Early Mormon Documents*, vol. 3 (Salt Lake City: Signature Books, 2000), 11–16; Tucker, "Jesse Townsend to Phineas Stiles."

41. "Imposition and Blasphemy!!—Money Diggers, &c."; "Editorial Note"; Campbell, *Delusions*, 11–12; "Book of Mormon," *Rochester Republican*, December 28, 1830.

42. "Mormonism," *Broome County Courier*, December 29, 1831; Bushman, *Joseph Smith: Rough Stone Rolling*, 123–25.

43. Tucker, "Jesse Townsend to Phineas Stiles"; Benton, "MORMONITES"; Jared Carter, "Jared Carter Journal," 1831, 19th Century Western and Mormon Manuscripts, L. Tom Perry Special Collections, Harold B. Lee Library, Brigham Young University; Marvin S. Hill, "Joseph Smith and the 1826 Trial: New Evidence and New Difficulties," *BYU Studies* 12 (Winter 1972): 223–33; Marquardt and Walters, *Inventing Mormonism*, chap. 8.

44. "Mormonism," *Salem Gazette*, December 6, 1831; "Mormonism," *Broome County Courier*, December 29, 1831; Orasmus Turner, *History of the Pioneer Settlement of Phelps and Gorham's Purchase* (Rochester, NY: William Alling, 1851); David Stafford Testimony, in Howe, *Mormonism Unvailed*. For more on Stafford, see John Brooke, *The Refiner's Fire: The Making of Mormon Cosmology, 1644–1844* (Cambridge: Cambridge University Press, 1994), 51–53, 151, 171.

45. Editor, "Something New—The Golden Bible"; "Mormon Emigration"; "Conversation," *Haverhill Gazette*, August 20, 1831; Vogel, "Diedrich Willers to Reverend Brethren," 271–78; Brooke, *The Refiner's Fire*, 144.

46. Matthew J. Grow, "The Whore of Babylon and the Abomination of Abominations: Nineteenth-Century Catholic and Mormon Mutual Perceptions and Religious Identity," *Church History* 73, no. 1 (March 2004): 139–67; Michael G. Reed, *Banishing the Cross: The Emergence of a Mormon Taboo* (Independence, MO: John Whitmer Books, 2012).

Chapter 2. "Restoration of Body and Mind"

1. Burnet, "Something New—The Golden Bible." For more on Burnet, see Douglas A. Foster et al., eds., *The Encyclopedia of the Stone-Campbell Movement* (Grand Rapids, MI: William B. Eerdmans, 2004), 102–3; Nathan Hatch, *The Democratization of American Christianity* (New Haven: Yale University Press, 1989), 71–81; Richard T. Hughes, *Reviving the Ancient Faith: The Story of Churches of Christ in America* (Grand Rapids, MI: William B. Eerdmans, 1996), chap. 4.

2. Marks, *The Life of David Marks*, 341; Burnet, "Something New—The Golden Bible"; Bushman, *Joseph Smith: Rough Stone Rolling*, 89, 149; Stephen J. Fleming, "The Religious Heritage of the British Northwest and the Rise of Mormonism," *Church History: Studies in Christianity and Culture* 77, no. 1 (March 2008): 73–104; Mario S. De Pillis, "The Social Sources of Mormonism," *Church History* 37, no. 1 (March 1968): 50–79; Davis, "Some Themes of Counter-Subversion: An Analysis of Anti-Masonic, Anti-Catholic, and Anti-Mormon Literature"; Givens, *The Viper on the Hearth*; Fluhman, *A Peculiar People*; Chris Beneke, "What Kind of Prejudice Was Anti-Mormonism?," *Mormon Studies Review* 1 (2014): 75–85.

3. David Bebbington, *Evangelicalism in Modern Britain: A History from the 1730s to the 1980s* (Boston: Unwin Hyman, 1989); Heyrman, *Southern Cross*, 3–5; Noll, *America's God*, 9–15; Foster et al., *The Encyclopedia of the Stone-Campbell Movement*, 314; James L. Gorman, *Among the Early Evangelicals: The Transatlantic Origins of the Stone-Campbell Movement* (Abilene, KS: Abilene Christian University Press, 2016); Hughes, *Reviving the Ancient Faith*, 32–37; Robert Baird, *Religion in America; or, An Account of the Origin, Progress, Relation to the State, and Present Condition of the Evangelical Churches in the United States, with Notices of the Unevangelical Denominations* (New York: Harper & Brothers, 1844), 573; Douglas A. Foster, *A Life of Alexander Campbell* (Grand Rapids, MI: William B. Eerdmans Publishing Company, 2020), 88–89, 114–34; William R. Baker, "Christian Churches (Independent): Are We Evangelical?," in *Evangelicalism and the Stone-Campbell Movement*, ed. William R. Baker (Downers Grove, IL: InterVarsity Press, 2002), 35.

4. Editor, "Something New—The Golden Bible"; "THE METHODIST OBJECTOR," *Catholic Telegraph* 1, no. 29 (May 5, 1832): 230; Warren Isham, "The Golden Bible, or Campbellism Improved," *Observer and Telegraph*, November 18, 1830; Benson, *Alexander Campbell and Joseph Smith*, 218–19; Burnet, "Something New—The Golden Bible."

5. Noll, *America's God*, 285; Paul C Gutjahr, "The Golden Bible in the Bible's Golden Age: The Book of Mormon and Antebellum Print Culture," *American Transcendentalist Quarterly* 12, no. 4 (December 1998): 275–94. For Unitar-

ian views of revivalism, see Paul J. Zwirecki, "Fighting 'a Spirit of Fanaticism': Antirevivalism in Antebellum America" (PhD diss., State University of New York at Buffalo, 2014), chap. 3.

6. Editor, "The Gospel—No. I," *Evangelical Inquirer*, August 2, 1830; Editor, "Inquiries, No. IV," *Evangelical Inquirer*, October 4, 1830; Burnet, "Something New—The Golden Bible"; Campbell, "The Mormon Challenge."

7. Marks, *The Life of David Marks*, 341; Campbell, *Delusions*, 13; "Unidentified Palmyra Residents to Editor."

8. M.S.C., "Mormonism."

9. "From the Christian Examiner," *Evangelical Inquirer*, September 6, 1830; Editor, "The Gospel—No. II," *Evangelical Inquirer*, October 4, 1830.

10. Editor, "The Gospel—No. II"; Noll, *America's God*, 231; James D. Bratt, "Religious Anti-Revivalism in Antebellum America," *Journal of the Early Republic* 24, no. 1 (Spring 2004): 72.

11. "Inquiries—No. III," *Evangelical Inquirer*, August 2, 1830; Wosh, *Spreading the Word*; Harold P. Scanlin, "Bible Translation by American Individuals," in *The Bible and Bibles in America*, ed. Ernst Frerichs (Atlanta: Scholars Press, 1988); Seth Perry, *Bible Culture and Authority in the Early United States* (Princeton, NJ: Princeton University Press, 2018).

12. For more on the religious services of early Mormonism, see Bushman, *Joseph Smith: Rough Stone Rolling*, chap. 5.

13. "Mormonism," *Broome County Courier*, December 29, 1831; "FANATICISM," *Western Luminary* 7, no. 46 (May 18, 1831): 391; "FANATICISM," *Christian Advocate and Journal and Zion's Herald* 5, no. 28 (March 11, 1831): 109; "Article 5—No Title," *Christian Intelligencer and Eastern Chronicle* 5, no. 7 (February 18, 1831): 27.

14. "Mormonism," *Broome County Courier*, December 29, 1831; M.S.C., "Mormonism"; "Fanaticism," *Christian Advocate and Journal and Zion's Herald*, March 11, 1831; "FANATICISM," May 18, 1831.

15. M.S.C., "Mormonism"; James Gordon Bennett, "Mormon Religion—Clerical Ambition—Western New York—The Mormonites Gone to Ohio," *Christian Register*, September 24, 1831; Bennett, "Mormonism—Religious Fanaticism—Church and State Party"; Brooke, *The Refiner's Fire*, 187; Bushman, *Joseph Smith: Rough Stone Rolling*, 123–24.

16. A Wesleyan Methodist, *Methodist Error; or, Friendly, Christian Advice, to Those Methodists: Who Indulge in Extravagant Emotions and Bodily Exercises* (Trenton, NJ: Published by D. & E. Fenton, 1819). For the influence and presence of Watson's critique on the Western Reserve, see Bratt, "Religious Anti-Revivalism in Antebellum America."

17. Lyman Beecher and Asahel Nettleton, *Letters of the Rev. Dr. Beecher and Rev. Mr. Nettleton, on the "New Measures" in Conducting Revivals of Religion* (New York: G. & C. Carvill, 1828), 80; see also William Buell Sprague, *Lectures on Revivals of Religion* (Glasgow: Printed for William Collins, 1832); Joseph Conforti, *Jonathan Edwards, Religious Tradition, and American Culture* (Chapel Hill: University of North Carolina Press, 1995); Bratt, "Religious Anti-Revivalism in Antebellum America," 75–76.

18. Charles Buck, *A Theological Dictionary, Containing Definitions of All*

Religious Terms (Philadelphia: J. J. Woodward, 1831); Brown and Bowman, "Reverend Buck's Theological Dictionary and the Struggle to Define American Evangelicalism, 1802–1851."

19. Buck, *A Theological Dictionary*, 163–64; Brown and Bowman, "Reverend Buck's Theological Dictionary and the Struggle to Define American Evangelicalism, 1802–1851," 452. For use of the term *charisma* to describe early nineteenth-century revivals, see Douglas Winiarski, "Seized by the Jerks: Shakers, Spirit Possession, and the Great Revival," *William & Mary Quarterly* 76, no. 1 (January 2019): 111–50.

20. Buck, *A Theological Dictionary*, 178–79.

21. Buck, 179.

22. M.S.C., "Mormonism"; Bushman, *Joseph Smith: Rough Stone Rolling*, 92.

23. M.S.C., "Mormonism."

24. M.S.C., "Mormonism"; Foster et al., *The Encyclopedia of the Stone-Campbell Movement*, 652–53.

25. M.S.C., "Mormonism."

26. M.S.C., "Mormonism."

27. M.S.C., "Mormonism."

28. Campbell, *Delusions*; Richard Hughes, *Illusions of Innocence: Protestant Primitivism in America, 1630–1875* (Chicago: University of Chicago Press, 1988); Hughes, *Reviving the Ancient Faith*; Hatch, *The Democratization of American Christianity*, 71–73.

29. Howe, *Mormonism Unvailed*; John Mason Peck, *Mormonism, One of the Delusions of Satan, Exposed* (Galena, IL, 1835); Truman Coe, "Mormonism," *The Religious Intelligencer . . . Containing the Principal Transactions of the Various Bible and Missionary Societies, with Particular Accounts of Revivals of Religion*, July 2, 1836; Truman Coe, "Mormonism," *Ohio Observer*, August 11, 1836; James M'Chesney, *An Antidote to Mormonism: A Warning to the Church and Nation the Purity of Christian Principles Defended and Truth Disentangled from Error and Delusion* (New York: Published by the Author at the Book Store of Burnett and Pollard, 1838); David Meredith Reese, *Humbugs of New-York: Being a Remonstrance against Popular Delusion; Whether in Science, Philosophy, or Religion* (New York: John S. Taylor, 1838); Joshua V. Himes, *Mormon Delusions and Monstrosities: a Review of the Book of Mormon, and an Illustration of Mormon Principles and Practices* (Boston: Joshua V. Himes, 1842).

30. Campbell, *Delusions*, 5–6.

31. Campbell, 6.

32. Campbell, *Delusions*, 7–8; E. Brooks Holifield, *Theology in America: Christian Thought from the Age of the Puritans to the Civil War* (New Haven: Yale University Press, 2003), 187–90.

33. Campbell, *Delusions*, 12.

34. Campbell, *Delusions*, 13; see also "MORMONISM RELIGIOUS FANATICISM CHURCH AND STATE PARTY."

35. Campbell, *Delusions*, 15.

36. Campbell, 6, 15–16.

37. Foster, *A Life of Alexander Campbell*, 177.

38. Campbell, *Delusions*, 6, 15–16; "HINDOO SHOPKEEPING," *New England Farmer, and Horticultural Register* 10, no. 45 (May 23, 1832): 360; Pixley, "INTELLIGENCE RESPECTING MORMONITES"; Hughes, *Reviving the Ancient Faith*.

39. Paul Conkin, *Cane Ridge: America's Pentecost* (Madison: University of Wisconsin Press, 1990); Foster, *A Life of Alexander Campbell*, 231; Matt McCook, "Aliens in the World: Sectarians, Secularism, and the Second Great Awakening" (PhD diss., Florida State University, 2005), 24.

40. Foster, *A Life of Alexander Campbell*, 236–37.

41. Foster, 241–47.

42. Foster, 247–48.

43. Thomas H. Olbricht, "The Holy Spirit in the Early Restoration Movement," *Stone-Campbell Journal* 7, no. 1 (2004): 3–26; Lane Scruggs, "Alexander Campbell and the Holy Spirit: A Reconsideration," *Restoration Quarterly* 60, no. 2 (2018).

44. James M. Mathes, *Works of Elder B. W. Stone, to Which Is Added a Few Discourses and Sermons* (Cincinnati: Moore, Wilsatch, Keys & Co., 1859), 15; Barton W. Stone, "The Gift of the Holy Spirit," *Christian Messenger* 6, no. 4 (April 1832): 111; Hughes, *Reviving the Ancient Faith*, 99–101; *Christian Messenger*, no. 5 (1831): 167; Olbricht, "The Holy Spirit in the Early Restoration Movement."

45. Hughes, *Reviving the Ancient Faith*, 115.

46. "Our Name—No. 3," *The Evangelist*, November 1, 1839, Americana Collection, L. Tom Perry Special Collections, Harold B. Lee Library, Brigham Young University.

Chapter 3. "Peddling the Holy Scriptures"

1. Stephen Mihm, *A Nation of Counterfeiters: Capitalists, Con Men, and the Making of the United States* (Cambridge, MA: Harvard University Press, 2007), 181–82.

2. Lane, quoted in *A Nation of Counterfeiters*, 181.

3. E. G. Lee, *The Mormons, or Knavery Exposed* (Frankford, PA: Published by E. G. Lee; Philadelphia: E. G. Lee; Frankford, PA: George Weber and William Fenimore, 1841), 16–18.

4. Seth Rockman, "What Makes the History of Capitalism Newsworthy?" *Journal of the Early Republic* 34, no. 3 (Fall 2014): 439–66; Stewart Davenport, *Friends of the Unrighteous Mammon: Northern Christians and Market Capitalism, 1815–1860* (Chicago: University of Chicago Press, 2008); Naomi R. Lamoreaux, "Rethinking the Transition to Capitalism in the Early American Northeast," *Journal of American History* 90 (September 2003): 437–61; Paul A. Gilje, "The Rise of Capitalism in the Early Republic," *Journal of the Early Republic* 16 (Summer 1996): 159–81.

5. Sven Beckert et al., "Interchange: The History of Capitalism," *Journal of American History* 101 (2014): 503–36.

6. Testimony of Roswell Nichols, in Howe, *Mormonism Unvailed*, 257–58.

7. "Editorial Note"; "Mormonism," *Christian Register*, December 20, 1834; "MORMONISM," *Western Christian Advocate* 1, no. 33 (December 12, 1834): 131; Vogel, "Early Mormon Documents."

8. Burnet, "Something New—The Golden Bible"; Testimony of Joseph Capron, in Howe, *Mormonism Unvailed*, 260, 237; Vogel, "Early Mormon Documents." For more evangelical attacks on Smith's inability to secure a job, see "Mormonism," *Zion's Herald*, September 16, 1835; John Hayward, *The Religious Creeds and Statistics of Every Christian Denomination in the United States and British Provinces. with Some Account of the Religious Sentiments of the Jews, American Indians, Deists, Mahometans, &c., Alphabetically Arranged* (Boston: Published by Jonathan Howe, 1836), 130.

9. Daniel Vickers, "Competency and Competition: Economic Culture in Early America," *William and Mary Quarterly* 47, no. 1 (January 1990): 3–29; Clare A. Lyons, *Sex among the Rabble: An Intimate History of Gender and Power in the Age of Revolution, Philadelphia, 1730–1830* (Chapel Hill: Published for the Omohundro Institute of Early American History and Culture, Williamsburg, Virginia, by the University of North Carolina Press, 2006); Christine Stansell, *City of Women: Sex and Class in New York, 1789–1860* (New York: Alfred A. Knopf, 1986); Larry Whiteaker, *Seduction, Prostitution, and Moral Reform in New York, 1830–1860* (New York: Garland Publishing, 1997); Richard W. Pointer, "Philadelphia Presbyterians, Capitalism, and the Morality of Economic Success," in *God and Mammon: Protestants, Money, and the Market, 1790–1860*, ed. Mark A. Noll (New York: Oxford University Press, 2002), 171–91. Pointer argues Philadelphia's Old School and New School Presbyterians both shared middle-class work values; see also Ruth Wallis Herndon, *Unwelcome Americans: Living on the Margin in Early New England*, Early American Studies (Philadelphia: University of Pennsylvania Press, 2001); Bruce H. Mann, *Republic of Debtors: Bankruptcy in the Age of American Independence* (Cambridge, MA: Harvard University Press, 2002), 82–85.

10. JAC, "MISCELLANEOUS," *Christian Observer*, November 12, 1840; "Mormonism," *Western Christian Advocate*, September 4, 1835; Nancy F. Cott, *The Bonds of Womanhood: "Woman's Sphere" in New England, 1780–1835* (New Haven: Yale University Press, 1977); Toby L. Ditz, "The New Men's History and the Peculiar Absence of Gendered Power: Some Remedies from Early American Gender History," *Gender & History* 16 (April 2004): 1–35.

11. Johnson, *A Shopkeeper's Millennium*, 34–42; Howe, *What Hath God Wrought?: The Transformation of America, 1815–1848*, 544–45.

12. Scott A. Sandage, *Born Losers: A History of Failure in America* (Cambridge, MA: Harvard University Press, 2005).

13. Taylor, "The Early Republic's Supernatural Economy."

14. Howe, *Mormonism Unvailed*, 11.

15. Origen Bacheler, *Mormonism Exposed, Internally and Externally* (New York: [s.n.], 1838), 39; Richard Livesey, *An Exposure of Mormonism Being a Statement of Facts Relating to the Self-Styled "Latter Day Saints," and the Origin of the Book of Mormon* (Manchester: William Shackleton and Son, 1840), 3.

16. Vogel, "Early Mormon Documents."

17. Vogel, "Early Mormon Documents."

18. "THE MORMON DELUSION," *Western Luminary* 8, no. 9 (August 31, 1831): 4.

19. Juster, *Doomsayers*; Taylor, "The Early Republic's Supernatural Economy," 6–34; Mihm, *A Nation of Counterfeiters*; Jane Kamensky, *The Exchange Artist: A Tale of High-Flying Speculation and America's First Banking Collapse* (New York: Penguin Books, 2008); Lukas Rieppel, "Hoaxes, Humbugs, and Frauds: Distinguishing Truth from Untruth in Early America," *Journal of the Early Republic* 38 (Fall 2018): 501–29.

20. La Roy Sunderland, *Mormonism Exposed: In Which Is Shown the Monstrous Imposture, the Blasphemy, and the Wicked Tendency, of That Enormous Delusion, Advocated by a Professedly Religious Sect, Calling Themselves "Latter Day Saints"* (New York: Printed and Published at the Office of the N.Y. Watchman, 1842), 21–26; Himes, *Mormon Delusions and Monstrosities*, 58.

21. James M'Chesney, *Supplement to an Antidote to Mormonism* (Brooklyn, NY, 1839), 1.

22. "MORMONS IN ENGLAND," *Christian Observer*, November 19, 1840.

23. Bacheler, *Mormonism Exposed, Internally and Externally*, 4; Himes, *Mormon Delusions and Monstrosities*, 58.

24. Howe, *Mormonism Unvailed*, 200. For reception of Ezra Booth, see Wesley Perkins, "Wesley Perkins Letters," February 11, 1832, MSS SC 637: Wesley Perkins Letters; 19th Century Western and Mormon Manuscripts, L. Tom Perry Special Collections, Harold B. Lee Library, Brigham Young University.

25. Brian P. Luskey, "Jumping Counters in White Collars: Manliness, Respectability, and Work in the Antebellum City," *Journal of the Early Republic* (2006): 206.

26. Himes, *Mormon Delusions and Monstrosities*, 47–48; Marks, *The Life of David Marks*, 341; Howe, *Mormonism Unvailed*, 13–14.

27. Benson, *Alexander Campbell and Joseph Smith*, 280–81.

28. Howe, *Mormonism Unvailed*, 196–97.

29. James Briggs, "Origin of the Mormons," *Christian Watchman*, January 31, 1834. For more on Briggs, see David Grua, "Joseph Smith and the 1834 D. P. Hurlbut Case," *BYU Studies* 44, no. 1 (2005): 33–54; Coe, "Mormonism." For more on Coe, see Milton Backman, "Truman Coe's 1836 Description of Mormonism," *BYU Studies* 17 (Spring 1977): 347–55.

30. Campbell, "The Mormon Challenge"; "Mormonism, Again," *Connecticut Mirror*, May 7, 1831; Howe, *Mormonism Unvailed*, 125.

31. Fluhman, *A Peculiar People*, 83–84; Bob Scribner, "Practical Utopias: Pre-Modern Communism and the Reformation," *Comparative Studies in Society and History* 36 (1994): 743–74. For more on the feminization of American Protestantism, see Cott, *The Bonds of Womanhood*; Curtis D. Johnson, *Islands of Holiness: Rural Religion in Upstate New York, 1790–1860* (Ithaca, NY: Cornell University Press, 1989); David W. Kling, *A Field of Divine Wonders: The New Divinity and Village Revivals in Northwestern Connecticut, 1792–1822* (University Park: Pennsylvania State University Press, 1993).

32. Campbell, "The Mormon Challenge"; Campbell, *Delusions*, 6; Fluhman, *A Peculiar People*, 129.

33. "Mormonist."

34. "Mormonist"; Nancy Towle, *Vicissitudes Illustrated, in the Experience of Nancy Towle, in Europe and America* (Charleston, SC: Printed for the authoress, by James L. Burges, 1832), 140; Brodie, *No Man Knows My History*, 103–4.

35. "REVIVALS," *Zion's Herald* 8, no. 9 (March 1, 1837): 35; Coe, "Mormonism"; Bushman, *Joseph Smith: Rough Stone Rolling*, 329–30; Bowman, *The Mormon People*, 58–59; Dean A. Dudley, "Bank Born of Revelation: The Kirtland Safety Society Anti-Banking Company," *Journal of Economic History* 30 (December 1970): 848–53; Dale W. Adams, "Chartering the Kirtland Bank," *BYU Studies* 23 (Fall 1983): 467–82.

36. "Constitution of the Kirtland Safety Society Bank, 2 November 1836, Joseph Smith Papers," accessed February 7, 2019, https://www.josephsmithpapers.org/paper-summary/constitution-of-the-kirtland-safety-society-bank-2-november-1836/1; Mihm, *A Nation of Counterfeiters*, 152–54; Joshua R. Greenberg, "The Era of Shinplasters," in *Capitalism by Gaslight: Illuminating the Economy of Nineteenth-Century America*, ed. Brian P. Luskey and Wendy A. Woloson (Philadelphia: University of Pennsylvania Press, 2015), 53–75.

37. Bushman, *Joseph Smith: Rough Stone Rolling*, 330; Mihm, *A Nation of Counterfeiters*, 11; Adams, "Chartering the Kirtland Bank"; Bowman, *The Mormon People*, 59–60.

38. Himes, *Mormon Delusions and Monstrosities*, 79–80.

39. M'Chesney, *An Antidote to Mormonism*, 22–25; Reese, *Humbugs of New York*.

40. Lee, *The Mormons, or Knavery Exposed*, 14.

41. Taylor, "The Early Republic's Supernatural Economy," 25. For the accusations of Smith as a con artist as evidence that Mormonism did not share the political values of most Americans, see Grow, "The Whore of Babylon and the Abomination of Abominations," 160. The economic charges against Mormonism provided additional evidence of Smith's fraudulence. On the ways his money digging, communitarianism, and cheating pressed against cultural boundaries, leading Protestant Christians to define themselves against Mormonism, see Fluhman, *A Peculiar People*, 39.

42. R. Laurence Moore, *Selling God: American Religion in the Marketplace of Culture* (New York: Oxford University Press, 1994); Hatch, *The Democratization of American Christianity*, 195, 200; Debby Applegate, *The Most Famous Man in America: The Biography of Henry Ward Beecher* (New York: Three Leaves Press, 2006), 4.

43. David Paul Nord, "Benevolent Capital: Financing Evangelical Book Publishing in Early Nineteenth-Century America," in *God and Mammon: Protestants, Money, and the Market, 1790–1860*, ed. Mark A. Noll (New York: Oxford University Press, 2002), 149.

44. Charles Foster, *An Errand of Mercy the Evangelical United Front, 1790–1837* (Chapel Hill: University of North Carolina Press, 1960); Anne M. Boylan, *Sunday School: The Formation of an American Institution, 1790–1880* (New Haven: Yale University Press, 1988); Wosh, *Spreading the Word*; Mark S. Schantz, "Religious Tracts, Evangelical Reform, and the Market Revolution in Antebellum America," *Journal of the Early Republic* 17, no. 3 (Autumn 1997): 425–66;

Brown, *The Word in the World*; Emily Conroy-Krutz, *Christian Imperialism: Converting the World in the Early American Republic* (Ithaca, NY: Cornell University Press, 2015).

45. Hatch, *The Democratization of American Christianity*, 170–76.

46. Elias Smith, *The Clergyman's Looking-Glass*, vol. 3 (Portsmouth [NH]: Printed by N. S. & W. Peirce, 1803), 3; Freeborn Garrettson, *A Letter to the Rev. Lyman Beecher Containing Strictures and Animadversions on a Pamphlet Entitled an Address of the Charitable Society for the Education of Indigent Pious Young Men for the Ministry of the Gospel* (Boston: Re-printed by Thomas Rowe, 1817), 11–12; L. F Greene, *The Writings of the Late Elder John Leland Including Some Events in His Life* (New York: Printed by G. W. Wood, 1845), 193–95; Hatch, *The Democratization of American Christianity*, 170–76.

47. Henry A. Boardman, *The Bible in the Counting-House: A Course of Lectures to Merchants* (Philadelphia: Lippincott, Grambo & Co., 1853), 174–76. See also Francis Wayland, *The Moral Law of Accumulation: The Substance of Two Discourses* (Providence, RI: John E. Brown, 1837); Davenport, *Friends of the Unrighteous Mammon*, 173–75; Pointer, "Philadelphia Presbyterians, Capitalism, and the Morality of Economic Success," 181. For more on the discomfort between legitimate and illegitimate forms of commerce, see Katie M. Hemphill, "Selling Sex and Intimacy in the City: The Changing Business of Prostitution," in *Capitalism by Gaslight: Illuminating the Economy of Nineteenth-Century America*, ed. Brian P. Luskey and Wendy A. Woloson (Philadelphia: University of Pennsylvania Press, 2015), 168–89.

48. Boardman, *The Bible in the Counting-House*, 174–76.

49. Taylor, "The Early Republic's Supernatural Economy," 8; Leonard Bacon, *The Duties Connected with the Present Commercial Distress: A Sermon Preached in the Center Church, New Haven, May 21, 1837, and Repeated May 23* (New Haven, CT, 1837), 8; Boardman, *The Bible in the Counting-House*, 138–39; Davenport, *Friends of the Unrighteous Mammon*, 3, 195; Will B. Mackintosh, "The Loomis Gang's Market Revolution," in *Capitalism by Gaslight: Illuminating the Economy of Nineteenth-Century America*, ed. Brian P. Luskey and Wendy A. Woloson (Philadelphia: University of Pennsylvania Press, 2015), 10–30.

50. Albert Barnes, "Vindication of Revivals," cited in Pointer, "Philadelphia Presbyterians, Capitalism, and the Morality of Economic Success," 181–82.

51. James M'Chesney, *A Brief Review of the Proceedings of the Annual Conference of the Methodist Episcopal Church, Her Discipline, and Administration of Government Embracing a Historical Sketch of the Difficulties Existing between Washington Street Church, Brooklyn and Some of the Higher Powers of This Connection* (New York: The Author, 1839), 9, 17.

52. "Of the True Gospel," *The Evangelist*, October 1, 1838, Americana Collection, L. Tom Perry Special Collections, Harold B. Lee Library, Brigham Young University.

53. "Preaching for Fame," *Western Recorder*, April 21, 1841, L. Tom Perry Special Collections, Harold B. Lee Library, Brigham Young University; "A Preacher to Please the People," *Western Recorder*, July 18, 1839, L. Tom Perry Special Collections, Harold B. Lee Library, Brigham Young University.

54. John Fea, *Bible Cause: A History of the American Bible Society* (New

York: Oxford University Press, 2016), 27; Brown, *The Word in the World*, 51; John L. Brooke, "Cultures of Nationalism, Movements of Reform, and the Composite-Federal Polity: From Revolutionary Settlement to Antebellum Crisis," *Journal of the Early Republic* 29, no. 1 (April 2009): 1–33; Peter J. Wosh and Lorraine A. Coons, "A 'Special Collection' in Nineteenth-Century New York: The American Bible Society and Its Library," *Libraries & Culture* 32, no. 3 (July 1997): 324–36.

55. A Member, *An Exposé of the Rise and Proceedings of the American Bible Society: During the Thirteen Years of Its Existence* (New York: [s.n.], 1830). For more on the ABS, see Brown, *The Word in the World*, chap. 2; Nord, "Benevolent Capital: Financing Evangelical Book Publishing in Early Nineteenth-Century America"; Richard Carwardine, "Trauma in Methodism: Property, Chuch Schism, and Sectional Polarization in Antebellum America," in *God and Mammon: Protestants, Money, and the Market, 1790–1860*, ed. Mark A. Noll (New York: Oxford University Press, 2002), 195–216.

56. A Member, *An Exposé of the Rise and Proceedings of the American Bible Society*, 9, 17.

57. A Member, 19–24.

58. A Member, 9–12.

59. A Member, 9–12.

60. A Member, *An Exposé of the Rise and Proceedings of the American Bible Society*, 9–12; Nord, "Benevolent Capital: Financing Evangelical Book Publishing in Early Nineteenth-Century America," 158, 162; Robert J. Gamble, "The Promiscuous Economy: Cultural and Commercial Geographies of Secondhand in the Antebellum City," in *Capitalism by Gaslight: Illuminating the Economy of Nineteenth-Century America*, ed. Brian P. Laskey and Wendy A. Woloson (Philadelphia: University of Pennsylvania Press, 2015), 39; Brian P. Luskey, "Jumping Counters in White Collars," 209–10; Anne G. Myles, "Queering the Study of Early American Sexuality," *William & Mary Quarterly: A Magazine of Early American History and Culture* 60 (January 2003): 199–202.

61. A Member, *An Exposé of the Rise and Proceedings of the American Bible Society*, 13–14.

62. Herman Hooker, *An Appeal to the Christian Public on the Evil and Impolicy of the Church Engaging in Merchandise and Setting Forth the Wrong Done to Booksellers and the Extravagance, Inutility and Evil-Working of Charity Publication Societies* (Philadelphia: King & Baird, printers, 1849), 10–14. For more on Hooker's evangelicals sensibilities, see Herman Hooker, *The Portion of the Soul; or, Thoughts on Its Attributes and Tendencies as Indicating Its Destiny* (Philadelphia: H. Perkins, 1835); Herman Hooker, *The Family Book of Devotion: Containing Daily Morning and Evening Prayers for Four Weeks, a Sermon or Contemplation and an Evening Prayer for Every Sunday in the Year, an Appendix of Prayers for Particular Occasions, with an Introduction on the Importance of Family Religion* (Philadelphia: Desilver, Thomas, 1836).

63. "Black Rock Address," quoted in Bratt, "Religious Anti-Revivalism in Antebellum America"; see also Bertram Wyatt-Brown, "The Antimission Movement in the Jacksonian South: A Study in Regional Folk Culture," *Journal of Southern History* 36 (November 1970): 501–29.

64. M'Chesney, *An Antidote to Mormonism*, 16, 26–28; Charles Cohen, "The Construction of the Mormon People," *Journal of Mormon History* 32, no. 1 (2006): 25–64.

65. M'Chesney, *An Antidote to Mormonism*, 28.

66. M'Chesney, 28.

67. M'Chesney, 43, 30–31.

68. M'Chesney, 30.

69. Democritus, "Excerpts: 'Original and Second-Hand,'" *Western Monthly Magazine, and Literary Journal*, June 1835.

70. "AMERICAN BIBLE SOCIETY," *Episcopal Recorder* 12, no. 17 (July 26, 1834): 65.

71. M'Chesney, *An Antidote to Mormonism*, 24–27.

72. Democritus, "Excerpts," 35–39.

Chapter 4. "God Has Been Pleased to Give a Revelation to Mankind"

1. John Storrs, "Mormonism," *Boston Recorder*, April 19, 1839; Matilda Davidson, *Folly and Falsehood of the Golden Book of Mormon* (Hexham, UK: F. Pruddah, 1839); Alexander Campbell, "The Mormon Bible," *Millennial Harbinger*, June 1839. See also "DOMESTIC INTELLIGENCE," *The Presbyterian*, June 8, 1839, American Historical Periodicals from the American Antiquarian Society; John Storrs, "ORIGIN OF MORMONISM. HOLLISTON, APRIL 8, 1839," *Southern Christian Sentinel*, May 11, 1839.

2. Storrs, "Mormonism."

3. Storrs, "Mormonism."

4. Storrs, "Mormonism." For more on Hurlburt, see Dale W. Adams, "Doctor Philastus Hurlbut: Originator of Derogatory Statements about Joseph Smith, Jr.," *John Whitmer Historical Association Journal* 20 (2000): 76–93.

5. Howe, *Mormonism Unvailed*, 287–88; Jonathan Turner, *Mormonism in All Ages; or, The Rise, Progress, and Causes of Mormonism; with the Biography of Its Author and Founder, Joseph Smith, Junior* (New York: Printed by Platt & Peters, 1842), 213; Adam Jortner, "Solomon Spaulding's Indians: Or, What the 'Manuscript Found' Really Tells Us," *Journal of Mormon History* 38, no. 4 (Fall 2012): 226–47.

6. H. Stevenson, *A Lecture on Mormonism* (Newcastle: J. Blackweel and Co., 1839), 12–13; Marks, *The Life of David Marks*, 342.

7. Marks, *The Life of David Marks*, 340; Campbell, *Delusions*, 15; Oliver Barr, "Mormonism No. III," *Christian Palladium*, January 16, 1837; Seth Perry, "The Many Bibles of Joseph Smith: Textual, Prophetic, and Scholarly Authority in Early-National Bible Culture," *Journal of the American Academy of Religion* 84 (September 2016): 758.

8. Alexander Evans, "Mormonites," *Christian Secretary* 12, no. 11 (March 30, 1833): 41.

9. Turner, *Mormonism in All Ages*, 193.

10. Gutjahr, "The Golden Bible in the Bible's Golden Age," 278.

11. Benjamin Winchester, *An Examination of a Lecture Delivered by the Rev. H. Perkins on the Religious Opinions and Faith of the Latter-Day Saints, and*

Some of His Most Prominent Errors and Misstatements Corrected (N.p., 1840), 4, 11. For more on Perkins's evangelical leanings, see American Tract Society, *First Annual Report of the American Tract Society* (New York: Printed at the Society's House, No. 87 Nassau Street, 1826).

12. Eli Gilbert, "Communication from Eli Gilbert," *Latter Day Saints' Messenger and Advocate*, October 1834, 9–10. See also Janiece Johnson, "Becoming a People of the Books: Toward an Understanding of Early Mormon Converts and the New Word of the Lord," *Journal of Book of Mormon Studies* 27 (2018): 14–15.

13. Philip L. Barlow, *Mormons and the Bible: The Place of the Latter-day Saints in American Religion*, Religion in America Series (New York: Oxford University Press, 1991), 16, 26; Janiece Johnson, "Becoming a People of the Books," 23.

14. Perry, "The Many Bibles of Joseph Smith."

15. Perry, "The Many Bibles of Joseph Smith."

16. Terryl Givens, *By the Hand of Mormon: The American Scripture That Launched a New World Religion* (New York: Oxford University Press, 2002), 39–40.

17. Campbell, *Delusions*, 15; Howe, *Mormonism Unvailed*, 94–99.

18. Campbell, *Delusions*, 15; John Clark, *Gleanings by the Way* (Philadelphia: W. J. & J. K. Simon, 1842), 229; La Roy Sunderland, "Mormonism," *Zion's Watchman*, March 3, 1838.

19. Testimony of Willard Chase, in Howe, *Mormonism Unvailed*, 240–48; Anderson, "Joseph Smith's New York Reputation Reappraised"; Taylor, "The Early Republic's Supernatural Economy," 23–24.

20. "The Mormonites," *Baptist Chronicle and Literary Register* 2, no. 12 (December 1831): 272; Coe, "Mormonism"; "The New Heresy!! An Exposure of Mormonism, Shewing Its Origin, Absurdity, & Impiety. A Conversation between James Anxious, and His Cousin Henry" (N.p.: Printed and Sold by Harper Twelvetrees, 1839); Towle, *Vicissitudes Illustrated, in the Experience of Nancy Towle, in Europe and America*, 139; David Marks, "[Untitled Remarks on Mormonism]," *Morning Star*, March 7, 1833.

21. Peck, *Mormonism, One of the Delusions of Satan, Exposed*, 1; Marks, "[Untitled Remarks on Mormonism]"; Howe, *Mormonism Unvailed*, 19; Bacheler, *Mormonism Exposed, Internally and Externally*, 1.

22. Howe, *Mormonism Unvailed*, 17; Clark, *Gleanings by the Way*, 229. For more on Clark's evangelical orientation, see John Alonzo Clark, *The Christian Keepsake and Missionary Annual* (N.p.: W. Marshall and Company, 1838); Givens, *The Viper on the Hearth*, chap. 3.

23. Bacheler, *Mormonism Exposed, Internally and Externally*, 27–28; Bowman, *The Mormon People*, 19–20; Paul C. Gutjahr, *The Book of Mormon: A Biography* (Princeton, NJ: Princeton University Press, 2012), 19.

24. Rieppel, "Hoaxes, Humbugs, and Frauds," 511.

25. "The Gold Bible Fever . . . "

26. *A Little Talk, Between John Robinson and His Master About Mormonism, Shewing Its Origin, Absurdity, and Impiety* (Bedford, MA: Printed and Sold by W. White, 1840), 3–4.

27. "History of Mormonism," *Ohio Repository*, September 1, 1836; see also

Peck, *Mormonism, One of the Delusions of Satan, Exposed*; Alexander Campbell, "Mormonism Unveiled," *Millennial Harbinger* 6, no. 1 (January 1835): 44–45; Bacheler, *Mormonism Exposed, Internally and Externally*; Livesey, *An Exposure of Mormonism Being a Statement of Facts Relating to the Self-Styled "Latter Day Saints," and the Origin of the Book of Mormon*; M'Chesney, *An Antidote to Mormonism*; Clark, *Gleanings by the Way*; Tyler Parsons, *Mormon Fanaticism Exposed: A Compendium of the Book of Mormon, or Joseph Smith's Golden Bible: Also, the Examination of Its Internal and External Evidences with the Argument to Refute Its Pretences to a Revelation from God, Argued . . . between Freeman Nickerson, a Mormon, and the Author, Tyler Parsons* (N.p.: Printed for the author, 1841); Daniel Parish Kidder, *Mormonism and the Mormons: A Historical View of the Rise and Progress of the Sect Self-Styled Latter-Day Saints* (New York: G. Lane & P. P. Sandford, 1842).

28. Samuel Haining, *Mormonism Weighed in the Balances, of the Sanctuary and Found Wanting: The Substance of Four Lectures* (Douglas [Isle of Man]: Printed for the author by Robert Fargher, 1840); Peck, *Mormonism, One of the Delusions of Satan, Exposed*; "Mormonism," *New York Weekly Messenger and Young Men's Advocate*, April 29, 1835; Gutjahr, "The Golden Bible in the Bible's Golden Age," 287; Holifield, *Theology in America*, 188. See also Robert Heys, *A Third Address to the Members of the Wesleyan Societies and Congregations in Douglas and Its Vicintiy* [*sic*] *on the Romantic Character of the Book of Mormon* (Douglas, UK: Printed by W. Walls and Co., 1840); Cassandra L. Yacovazzi, "'Are You Allowed to Read the Bible in a Convent?': Protestant Perspectives on the Catholic Approach to Scripture in Convent Narratives, 1830–1860," *U.S. Catholic Historian* 31 (2013): 23–46.

29. Perry, *Bible Culture and Authority in the Early United States*; Paul Gutjahr, *An American Bible: A History of the Good Book in the United States, 1777–1880* (Stanford, CA: Stanford University Press, 1999), 182.

30. Susan Warner, *The Wide, Wide World* (New York: G. P. Putnam, 1852), 34–35; Ann Douglas, *The Feminization of American Culture* (New York: Alfred A. Knopf, 1977), 64; Sara E. Quay, "Homesickness in Susan Warner's *The Wide, Wide World*," *Tulsa Studies in Women's Literature* 18 (Spring 1999): 39–58.

31. Jonathan Sheehan, *The Enlightenment Bible: Translation, Scholarship, Culture* (Princeton, NJ: Princeton University Press, 2005).

32. Christopher Grasso, *Skepticism and American Faith: From the Revolution to the Civil War* (New York: Oxford University Press, 2018), 256–58; Milette Shamir, "On the Uselessness of Knowledge: William F. Lynch's 'Interesting' Expedition to the Dead Sea," *Journal of the Early Republic* 38 (Fall 2018): 485; Barlow, *Mormons and the Bible*, 9.

33. Charles Hodge, *Biblical Repertory*, vol. 1 (New York: Princeton Press, 1825), 1–2; David F. Holland, *Sacred Borders: Continuing Revelation and Canonical Restraint in Early America* (New York: Oxford University Press, 2011), 109–11.

34. James Henry Thornwell, "The Office of Reason in Regard to Revelation," *Southern Presbyterian Review* (June 1847); Grasso, *Skepticism and American Faith*, 418–19.

35. "Antiquities of the Jews, Carefully Compiled from Authentic Sources, and Their Customs Illustrated from Modern Travels," *Christian Advocate*, July 1, 1823. On Hodge's criticisms of the more outwardly forms of revivalism, see Paul C. Gutjahr, *Charles Hodge: Guardian of American Orthodoxy* (New York: Oxford University Press, 2011), 190.

36. *The Panoplist, and Missionary Magazine United* (N.p.: Farrand, Mallory, and Company, 1811); Holland, *Sacred Borders*, 106–7; Gutjahr, *An American Bible: A History of the Good Book in the United States, 1777–1880*, 129, 135. On the scientific discoveries challenging evangelicalism, see Herbert Hovenkamp, *Science and Religion in America, 1800–1860* (Philadelphia: University of Pennsylvania Press, 1978).

37. Hovenkamp, *Science and Religion in America, 1800–1860*, 121–28; Cameron Strang, *Frontiers of Science: Slavery and Geology in the Antebellum Era* (Chapel Hill: Published by the Institute of Early American History and Culture and the University of North Carolina Press, 2018), 266.

38. Perry, *Bible Culture and Authority in the Early United States*, 26–27, 49–50.

39. Gutjahr, "The Golden Bible in the Bible's Golden Age," 288.

40. Alexander Campbell, *The Sacred Writings of the Apostles and Evangelists of Jesus Christ, Commonly Styled the New Testament* (Bethany, VA: M'Vay & Ewing, 1835), 27; Gutjahr, "The Golden Bible in the Bible's Golden Age," 284.

41. Campbell, quoted in Gutjahr, "The Golden Bible in the Bible's Golden Age," 281–84; Holland, *Sacred Borders*, 128, 143.

42. Perry, "The Many Bibles of Joseph Smith," 171. For more on how Campbell read scripture, see Hatch, *The Democratization of American Christianity*; Hughes, *Illusions of Innocence*; Hughes, *Reviving the Ancient Faith*.

43. Eran Shalev, "'Written in the Style of Antiquity': Pseudo-Biblicism and the Early American Republic, 1770–1830," *Church History* 79 (December 2010): 800–26; Eran Shalev, *American Zion: The Old Testament as a Political Text from the Revolution to the Civil War* (New Haven: Yale University Press, 2013), chap. 3.

44. Jenny Franchot, *Roads to Rome: The Antebellum Protestant Encounter with Catholicism* (Berkeley: University of California Press, 1993); Marr, *The Cultural Roots of American Islamicism*; Stephen A. Marini, *Radical Sects of Revolutionary New England* (Cambridge, MA: Harvard University Press, 1982); Stephen J. Stein, "Inspiration, Revelation, and Scripture: The Story of a Shaker Bible," in *Proceedings of the American Antiquarian Society*, vol. 105 (Worcester: American Antiquarian Society, 1996), 347–76; Steven J. Stein, "America's Bibles: Canon, Commentary, and Community," *Church History* 64 (June 1995): 169–84; Holland, *Sacred Borders*, chap. 5; Stephen J. Stein, *The Shaker Experience in America: A History of the United Society of Believers* (New Haven: Yale University Press, 1992), 180–82; Erik R. Seeman, *Speaking with the Dead in Early America* (Philadelphia: University of Pennsylvania Press, 2019), 160.

45. Stein, *The Shaker Experience in America*, 180–82.

46. Stein, *The Shaker Experience in America*, 112; Holland, *Sacred Borders*, 136–37; Winiarski, "Seized by the Jerks."

47. Holifield, *Theology in America*, 174–78.

48. Holifield, 187–90; Yacovazzi, ""Are You Allowed to Read the Bible in a Convent?," 29–30.

49. Noll, *America's God*, 379–92.

50. Grasso, *Skepticism and American Faith*, 329–31.

51. *Eyes and No Eyes, or Eyes That See Not How to Read the Bible Aright* (Philadelphia: American Sunday-School Union, 1827), 5–9.

52. Gutjahr, *An American Bible: A History of the Good Book in the United States, 1777–1880*; Brown, *The Word in the World*; Shamir, "On the Uselessness of Knowledge," 493.

53. *Eyes and No Eyes, or Eyes That See Not How to Read the Bible Aright*, 12–14; Brown, *The Word in the World*, 97.

54. Brown and Bowman, "Reverend Buck's Theological Dictionary and the Struggle to Define American Evangelicalism, 1802–1851," 445; Holifield, *Theology in America*, 8–10; Buck, *A Theological Dictionary*, 138, 152–53.

55. Turner, *Mormonism in All Ages*, 275, 181, 234.

56. Turner, 99, 274, 281.

57. Turner, 286–87.

58. Turner, 4, 278.

59. Turner, 279–80.

60. Reese, *Humbugs of New York*, 246.

61. M'Chesney, *An Antidote to Mormonism*, 19–20.

62. M'Chesney, 12–14.

63. Stevenson, *A Lecture on Mormonism*, 18, 30–31; Turner, *Mormonism in All Ages*, 278.

64. Turner, *Mormonism in All Ages*, 285; Reese, *Humbugs of New York*, 248–49.

65. Turner, 276.

66. Turner, 277.

67. Reese, *Humbugs of New York*, 233–45, 265–66.

68. Franchot, *Roads to Rome: The Antebellum Protestant Encounter with Catholicism*; Ryan K. Smith, *Gothic Arches, Latin Crosses: Anti-Catholicism and American Church Designs in the Nineteenth Century* (Chapel Hill: University of North Carolina Press, 2006).

69. Archibald Alexander, *The Canon of the Old and New Testaments Ascertained; or, The Bible Complete, without the Apocrypha & Unwritten Traditions* (New York: Princeton Press, 1826), 45, 302–14. For more on the presence of the apocrypha in antebellum America, see Mark A. Noll, *In the Beginning Was the Word: The Bible in American Public Life, 1492–1783* (Oxford: Oxford University Press, 2016), 347.

70. Alexander, *The Canon of the Old and New Testaments Ascertained*, 14; Holland, *Sacred Borders*, 115, 119.

71. Turner, *Mormonism in All Ages*, 235.

72. Turner, *Mormonism in All Ages*, 284, 278, 290; Stevenson, *A Lecture on Mormonism*, 18.

73. Turner, *Mormonism in All Ages*, 284.

74. Stevenson, *A Lecture on Mormonism*, 30–31.

75. M'Chesney, *An Antidote to Mormonism*, 9–10, 13.

76. Reese, *Humbugs of New York*, 251–64.

Chapter 5. "Mormonism, Whether Found . . . in Kentucky, or at Nauvoo"

1. Henry Caswall, *The City of the Mormons, or; Three Days at Nauvoo, in 1842* (London: Printed for J.G.F. & J. Rivington, 1842), 1–3, 56. For the most recent and sustained scholarship on Mormonism's Nauvoo, see Benjamin E. Park, *Kingdom of Nauvoo: The Rise and Fall of a Religious Empire on the American Frontier*, 1st ed. (New York: Liveright Publishing Corporation, 2020).

2. Henry Caswall, *The Prophet of the Nineteenth Century; or, The Rise, Progress, and Present State of the Mormons, or Latter-Day Saints: To Which Is Appended, an Analysis of the Book of Mormon* (London: Printed for J.G.F. & J. Rivington, 1843).

3. M.S.C., "Mormonism"; "FANATICISM," March 11, 1831; Ann Taves, *Fits, Trances, and Visions: Experiencing Religion and Explaining Experience from Wesley to James* (Princeton, NJ: Princeton University Press, 1999), 16–18; Brooke, *The Refiner's Fire*; Taylor, "The Early Republic's Supernatural Economy"; Marini, *Radical Sects of Revolutionary New England*; Sunderland, *Mormonism Exposed*, 13–14.

4. "TRAGICAL EVENT!" *Liberator* 4, no. 8 (February 22, 1834): 32; "TRAGICAL EVENT," *Christian Secretary* 13, no. 7 (March 1, 1834): 28; Stanley J. Thayne, "Walking on Water: Nineteenth-Century Prophets and a Legend of Religious Imposture," *Journal of Mormon History* 36, no. 2 (2010): 160–204.

5. Coe, "Mormonism."

6. Parley P. Pratt, *A Dialogue between Joseph Smith and the Devil*, 1845; Adam Jortner, *Blood from the Sky: Miracles and Politics in the Early American Republic* (Charlottesville: University of Virginia Press, 2017).

7. "MORMONISM," *Evangelical Magazine and Gospel Advocate* 4, no. 28 (July 13, 1833): 224; "Article 9—No Title," *Christian Secretary* 12, no. 29 (August 3, 1833): 115; Pratt, *A Dialogue between Joseph Smith and the Devil*. For the ways both evangelicals and Mormonism used evidential Christianity to make religious arguments, see Jortner, *Blood from the Sky*.

8. "Strange Fanaticism," *Christian Secretary* 13, no. 5 (February 15, 1834): 19; Coe, "Mormonism"; Pixley, "INTELLIGENCE RESPECTING MORMONITES."

9. "Anecdote of Mormonism," *Zion's Herald*, July 10, 1839.

10. "The Mormons," *Religious Monitor and Evangelical Repository*, January 1842; William Ivins Appleby, *Mormonism Consistent! Truth Vindicated, and Falsehood Exposed and Refuted: Being a Reply to A. H. Wickersham, by W. I. Appleby, Elder in the Church of "Latter-Day Saints"* (Wilmington, DE: Porter and Naff, 1843); "[Letter on Mormonism, July 29, 1841]," *Christian Advocate and Journal*, August 11, 1841; Fluhman, *A Peculiar People*, 96.

11. "The Mormons," *Western Christian Advocate*, August 6, 1841; "[Letter on Mormonism, July 29, 1841]"; Parsons, *Mormon Fanaticism Exposed*, 82.

12. "Celebration of the Anniversary of the Church-Military Parade—Prest. Rigdon's Address—Laying the Corner Stones of the Temple," *Times and Seasons*, April 15, 1841; John E. Hallwas and Roger D. Launius, "Celebrating the Power of Mormon Nauvoo," in *Cultures in Conflict: A Documentary History of the Mormon War in Illinois* (Logan: Utah State University Press, 1995), 55–58.

13. "Extracts," *Times and Seasons*, January 15, 1842; Sunderland, *Mormonism Exposed*, 31; A Disciple, "[Reply to John E. Page]," *Morning Chronicle*, July 7, 1842. See also La Roy Sunderland, "Mormonism," *Zion's Watchman*, February 3, 1838; "BATTLE WITH THE MORMONS," *Christian Reflector*, November 30, 1838; M'Chesney, *A Brief Review of the Proceedings of the Annual Conference of the Methodist Episcopal Church, Her Discipline, and Administration of Government Embracing a Historical Sketch of the Difficulties Existing between Washington Street Church, Brooklyn and Some of the Higher Powers of This Connection.*

14. Kidder, *Mormonism and the Mormons*, 183; Sunderland, *Mormonism Exposed*, 32; Turner, *Mormonism in All Ages*, 105, 99.

15. Ezra Booth letters, in Howe, *Mormonism Unvailed*, chap. 15. For more on fears of Mormon-Indian conspiracies, see W. Paul Reeve, *Religion of a Different Color: Race and the Mormon Struggle for Whiteness* (Oxford: Oxford University Press, 2015), 103.

16. Howe, *Mormonism Unvailed*, 1834; Reeve, *Religion of a Different Color: Race and the Mormon Struggle for Whiteness*, 60–64.

17. Baird, *Religion in America*, v–vii; "Western Correspondence," *New York Evangelist*, September 25, 1841.

18. Howe, *Mormonism Unvailed*, 196–97, 220, 213; A Disciple, "[Reply to John E. Page.]"; Sunderland, *Mormonism Exposed*, 35–37; Bowman, *The Mormon People*, 86.

19. Sunderland, *Mormonism Exposed*, 14; Turner, *Mormonism in All Ages*, 102; Walter Scott, "Mormon Bible.—No. IV," *The Evangelist*, May 1, 1841; Stevenson, *A Lecture on Mormonism*, 30–31.

20. "Religious Miscellany," *Christian Watchman*, August 23, 1833; Jesse Townsend, *Salem Landmark*, December 3, 1834; Coe, "Mormonism."

21. Turner, *Mormonism in All Ages*, 258; M'Chesney, *An Antidote to Mormonism*, 22.

22. Coe, "Mormonism"; "James H. Eels to Joshua Leavitt," *New York Evangelist*, April 1, 1836.

23. Caswall, *The City of the Mormons; or, Three Days at Nauvoo, in 1842*; Kidder, *Mormonism and the Mormons*, 227.

24. Hill, *Quest for Refuge*; Bushman, *Joseph Smith: Rough Stone Rolling*; Fluhman, *A Peculiar People.*

25. Beecher and Nettleton, *Letters of the Rev. Dr. Beecher and Rev. Mr. Nettleton, on the "New Measures" in Conducting Revivals of Religion*; Grant Powers, *Essay Upon the Influence of the Imagination on the Nervous System: Contributing to a False Hope in Religion* (Andover, MA: Flagg and Gould, 1828); Methodist, *Methodist Error; or, Friendly, Christian Advice, to Those Methodists.*

26. Jortner, *Blood from the Sky*, ix, xi.

27. Heyrman, *Southern Cross*, 62–66, 72–73; Lorraine Daston and Katharine Park, "The Enlightenment and the Anti-Marvelous," in *Wonders and the Order of Nature, 1150–1750* (Cambridge, MA: MIT Press, 1998); Michael Saler, "Modernity and Enchantment: A Historiographic Review," *American Historical Review* 111, no. 3 (2006): 692–716; Holifield, *Theology in America*, 174–96.

28. Jortner, *Blood from the Sky*, 35–36; Horace Bushnell, *Nature and the Su-*

pernatural: As Together Constituting the One System of God (New York: Charles Scribner's Sons, 1895); Juster, *Doomsayers*, 57–60; David D. Hall, *Worlds of Wonder, Days of Judgment* (Cambridge, MA: Harvard University Press, 1989), 75.

29. Turner, *Mormonism in All Ages*, 101–3.

30. Turner, 250, 102–7.

31. Hatch, *The Democratization of American Christianity*, 206–9; John H. Wigger, *Taking Heaven by Storm: Methodism and the Rise of Popular Christianity in America* (New York: Oxford University Press, 1998), 80–103; Paul E. Johnson, "Democracy, Patriarchy, and American Revivals, 1780–1830," *Journal of Social History* 24, no. 4 (Summer 1991): 843–50.

32. John E. Hallwas and Roger D. Launius, "A Minister Criticizes Warsaw and Nauvoo," in *Cultures in Conflict: A Documentary History of the Mormon War in Illinois* (Logan: Utah State University Press, 1995), 32–35; Reese, *Humbugs of New York*.

33. Caswall, *The Prophet of the Nineteenth Century*, 5–8; Sara Lynn Crosby, *Poisonous Muse: The Female Prisoner and the Framing of Popular Authorship in Jacksonian America* (Iowa City: University of Iowa Press, 2016), 114–15.

34. Henry Caswall, *America and the American Church* (London: Printed for J. G. & F. Rivington, 1838), 323–26; George Peck, "Mormonism and the Mormons," *Methodist Quarterly Review*, January 1843, 111–27. For evangelicals quoting Caswall, see "Notices of Recent Publications," *Christian Examiner and Religious Miscellany*, March 1855.

35. Caswall, *The Prophet of the Nineteenth Century*, 1, 4–5, 102–3.

36. Turner, *Mormonism in All Ages*, 253–58, 272–74, 278–81.

37. Turner, 278.

38. Bertram Wyatt-Brown, "Andrew Jackson's Honor," *Journal of the Early Republic* 17, no. 1 (Spring 1997): 1–36; Seth Rockman, "Jacksonian America," in *American History Now*, ed. Eric Foner and Lisa McGirr (Philadelphia: Temple University Press, 2011), 52–74; Kirsten E. Wood, "'One Woman so Dangerous to Public Morals': Gender and Power in the Eaton Affair," *Journal of the Early Republic* 17, no. 2 (Summer 1997): 266–68; Amy Greenberg, *Manifest Manhood and the Antebellum American Empire* (Cambridge: Cambridge University Press, 2005); Amy S. Greenberg, "'The Way of the Transgressor Is Hard': The Black Hawk and Mormon Wars in the Construction of Illinois Political Culture, 1832–1846," in *Contingent Citizens: Shifting Perceptions of Latter-day Saints in American Political Culture*, ed. Spencer W. McBride, Brent M. Rogers, and Keith A. Erekson (Ithaca, NY: Cornell University Press, 2020), 75–91.

39. Sarah Barringer Gordon and Jan Shipps, "Fatal Convergence in the Kingdom of God: The Mountain Meadows Massacre in American History," *Journal of the Early Republic* 37, no. 2 (2017): 307–48.

40. Heyrman, *Southern Cross*, 234–49; Dee Andrews, *The Methodists and Revolutionary America, 1760–1800: The Shaping of an Evangelical Culture* (Princeton, NJ: Princeton University Press, 2000), chap. 8; Janet Lindman, "Acting the Manly Christian: White Evangelical Masculinity in Revolutionary Virginia," *William and Mary Quarterly* 57, no. 2 (April 2000): 393–416.

41. Caswall, *America and the American Church*, 316–17, 324; Heyrman,

Southern Cross, 234–36; Andrews, *The Methodists and Revolutionary America*, 229; Neil Meyer, "Falling for the Lord: Shame, Revivalism, and the Origins of the Second Great Awakening," *Early American Studies: An Interdisciplinary Journal* 9, no. 1 (Winter 2011): 142–66.

42. Andrew Reed, *A Narrative of the Visit to the American Churches, by the Deputation from the Congregational Union of England and Wales by Andrew Reed, D.d. and James Matheson, D.d.* (New York: Harper & Brothers, 1835), 203–5; Heyrman, *Southern Cross*; Andrews, *The Methodists and Revolutionary America*, 227–28.

43. Observer [George Elley], "Methodistic Enthusiasm," *Millennial Harbinger*, March 1845; James D Bratt, ed., *Antirevivalism in Antebellum America: A Collection of Religious Voices* (New Brunswick, NJ: Rutgers University Press, 2005), 3–4.

44. Heyrman, *Southern Cross*, 208–13; Wood, "'One Woman so Dangerous to Public Morals': Gender and Power in the Eaton Affair"; Carroll Smith-Rosenberg, "Beauty, the Beast, and the Militant Woman: A Case Study in Sex Roles and Social Stress in Jacksonian America," *American Quarterly* 23, no. 4 (October 1971): 562–84.

45. Observer [George Elley], "Methodistic Enthusiasm," *Millennial Harbinger*, January 1845; Albert Baldwin Dod, "Finney's Lectures," *Biblical Reperatory and Theological Review* 7 (October 1835): 662–67; Bratt, "Religious Anti-Revivalism in Antebellum America." Unitarians made many of the same arguments about the combative tone of revivalists. See Zwirecki, "Fighting 'A Spirit of Fanaticism,'" 128.

46. Horace Bushnell, in Bratt, *Antirevivalism in Antebellum America*; Calvin Colton, *Thoughts on the Religious State of the Country: With Reasons for Preferring the Episcopacy* (New York: Harper & Brothers, 1836), 173–80.

47. Turner, *Mormonism in All Ages*, 101, 113, 97.

48. Sam Haselby, *The Origins of American Religious Nationalism* (New York: Oxford University Press, 2015), 22.

49. "REGULATING 'THE MORMONITES,'" *New York Observer and Chronicle*, August 24, 1833; "The Mormonites," *Religious Intelligencer* 18, no. 15 (September 7, 1833): 233; "Death Blow to Mormonism," *Western Luminary* 10, no. 9 (September 11, 1833): 34. For the conflict between eastern and western evangelicals, see Haselby, *The Origins of American Religious Nationalism*; April E. Holm, *A Kingdom Divided: Evangelicals, Loyalty, and Sectionalism in the Civil War Era* (Baton Rouge: Louisiana State University Press, 2017); Richard Maxwell Brown, *Strain of Violence: Historical Studies of American Violence and Vigilantism* (New York: Oxford University Press, 1975), vii; Patrick Q. Mason, *Mormonism and Violence: The Battles of Zion* (Cambridge: Cambridge University Press, 2019).

50. Isaac McCoy, "Disturbances in Jackson County," *Missouri Republican*, December 20, 1833; Richard L. Bushman, "Mormon Persecutions in Missouri, 1833," *Brigham Young University Studies* 3, no. 1 (January 1961): 11–20; Warren Jennings, "Isaac McCoy and the Mormons," *Missouri Historical Review* 61, no. 1 (October 1966): 62–82.

51. Bowman, *The Mormon People*, 61–62.

52. "HORRIBLE REVELATIONS!" *Christian Advocate and Journal*, January 11, 1839.

53. H. L. Dodds, "MISCELLANEOUS," *Christian Advocate and Journal*, February 1, 1839; W. S. Woodard, *Annals of Methodism in Missouri: Containing an Outline of the Ministerial Life of More than One Thousand Preachers, and Sketches of More than Three Hundred; Also Sketches of Charges, Churches and Laymen from the Beginning in 1806 to the Centennial Year, 1884, Containing Seventy-Eight Years of History* (Columbia, MO: E. W. Stephens, 1893).

54. "Article 8—No Title," *Christian Secretary*, September 7, 1838; "Article 1—No Title," *Zion's Herald*, September 26, 1838; "Article 1—No Title," *New York Evangelist*, September 29, 1838; "The Mormons," *Zion's Herald*, October 17, 1838; "The Mormons: Mormon Troubles," *Zion's Herald*, October 17, 1838; "Secular Intelligence: Items from Foreign Papers," *New York Evangelist*, October 27, 1838; "THE MORMONS: Extract from a Letter to the Editors of the Missouri Daily Argus, Dated Elk Horn, Oct. 30. 1838," *Christian Secretary*, November 23, 1838; "BATTLE WITH THE MORMONS."

55. Hatch, *The Democratization of American Christianity*, 64–66; Noll, *America's God*, 310–11; Curtis D. Johnson, "'Sectarian Nation': Religious Diversity in Antebellum America," *OAH Magazine of History* 22, no. 1 (January 1, 2008): 14–18. Unitarians made many of the same criticisms of the sectarian fanaticism of revivalism. See Zwirecki, "Fighting 'A Spirit of Fanaticism,'" 128–32.

56. Joseph Smith, "History, 1838," in *The Personal Writings of Joseph Smith*, ed. Dean C. Jessee (Salt Lake City: Deseret Book Company, 1984), 197–206.

57. Reese, *Humbugs of New York*, 246–49.

58. Reese, *Humbugs of New York*, 264; Caswall, *The Prophet of the Nineteenth Century*, 103–4.

59. Caswall, *The Prophet of the Nineteenth Century*, 9.

60. Reese, *Humbugs of New York*, 13–14; Fluhman, *A Peculiar People*, 179–80; M'Chesney, *An Antidote to Mormonism*, 40–41; Baird, *Religion in America*, 219–20, 273–74; Turner, *Mormonism in All Ages*. For more on the evangelical leanings of Reese, see Edwin Warriner, *Old Sands Street Methodist Episcopal Church, of Brooklyn, N.Y.: An Illustrated Centennial Record, Historical and Biographical* (New York: Published for the author by Phillips & Hunt, 1885); Lawrence B. Goodheart, *Mad Yankees: The Hartford Retreat for the Insane and Nineteenth-Century Psychiatry* (Amherst: University of Massachusetts Press, 2003).

61. Reese, *Humbugs of New York*, 180, 210, 245; Turner, *Mormonism in All Ages*, 284–86.

62. Reese, *Humbugs of New York*, 14–15.

63. Turner, *Mormonism in All Ages*.

64. Grow, "The Whore of Babylon and the Abomination of Abominations"; "THE METHODIST OBJECTOR"; A, "The Mormons," *Free Enquirer*, January 5, 1834.

65. "Western Correspondence"; "Anti-Mormon Almanac," *New York Evangelist*, July 31, 1841; Anti-Mormon, *An Account of the Origin of the Mormonites*,

Or Latter-Day Saints (Tunstall, UK: Printed at the Office of Henry Adams, 1846); "DOMESTIC INTELLIGENCE," *The Presbyterian*, September 4, 1841; Fluhman, *A Peculiar People*, 96, 101–2.

66. Maartje Janse, "'Anti Societies Are Now All the Rage': Jokes, Criticism, and Violence in Response to the Transformation of American Reform, 1825–1835," *Journal of the Early Republic* 36, no. 2 (2016): 247–82. For the lumping together of temperance, abolition, and anti-Mormonism, see Reese, *Humbugs of New York*.

67. "Article 6—No Title," *Christian Secretary*, November 23, 1838; "MISSOURI AND THE MORMONS," *Christian Reflector*, May 3, 1839; see also "DOMESTIC INTELLIGENCE," *The Presbyterian*, September 19, 1846; "THE MORMONS," *The Liberator*, April 12, 1839.

68. "MISSOURI AND THE MORMONS."

69. James H. Perkins and John Mason Peck, *Annals of the West* (Cincinnati: Published by James R. Albach, 1847).

70. Caswall, *The City of the Mormons; or, Three Days at Nauvoo, in 1842*, 1–2, 57–58.

Chapter 6. "Apprehension for the Future"

1. "James H. Eels to Joshua Leavitt"; Coe, "Mormonism."

2. "Mormonism," *Western Christian Advocate*, June 17, 1836; Coe, "Mormonism"; "Mormons and Mormonism," *Christian Register and Boston Observer*, December 25, 1841.

3. Coe, "Mormonism"; Kidder, *Mormonism and the Mormons*, 13; "Mormonism and Mormon Tenets," *Home Missionary*, June 1840, Church History Library, Church of Jesus Christ of Latter-day Saints, Salt Lake City, UT.

4. Coe, "Mormonism"; "The Mormons," *Christian Watchman*, April 22, 1836; "Mormonism," June 17, 1836; "Mormonism and Mormon Tenets."

5. "James H. Eels to Joshua Leavitt"; "Mormonism," June 17, 1836; "Religious Miscellany."

6. "Editorial Note."

7. "Religious Miscellany."

8. Bowman, *The Mormon People*, 49–52; Bushman, *Joseph Smith: Rough Stone Rolling*, 316.

9. Coe, "Mormonism"; "The Mormons in Ohio," *Christian Secretary*, January 16, 1836; James H. Eels, "Article 1—No Title," *New York Evangelist*, April 9, 1836.

10. "The Mormons in Ohio"; Eels, "Article 1—No Title."

11. Eels, "Article 1—No Title."

12. William West, *A Few Interesting Facts Respecting the Rise, Progress, and Pretensions of the Mormons* (Warren, OH: [s.n.], 1837), 4–5.

13. West, 5–6.

14. Coe, "Mormonism"; "REVIVALS"; Campbell, *Delusions*.

15. Bowman, *The Mormon People*, 75–79.

16. "Selected Summary," *Christian Secretary*, July 14, 1843; "The Mormon City," *Christian Advocate and Journal*, February 12, 1845. For a discussion

of the language used to describe museums in antebellum America, see Rachel Stephens, "Curious Men and Their Curiosities: Ralph E. W. Earl's Nashville Museum and the Precedent of Charles Willson Peale," *Early American Studies* 16, no. 3 (Summer 2018): 545–77.

17. Caswall, *The City of the Mormons; or, Three Days at Nauvoo, in 1842*, 16; Parsons, *Mormon Fanaticism Exposed*; Turner, *Mormonism in All Ages.*

18. Milton Badger, "Joe Smith at Home," *New York Observer and Chronicle*, August 6, 1842.

19. Walter Scott, "The Mormon Bible," *The Evangelist*, July 1, 1839.

20. American Tract Society, *Home Evangelization a View of the Wants and Prospects of Our Country, Based on Facts and Relations of Colportage* (New York: American Tract Society, 1849).

21. Holm, *A Kingdom Divided*, 26–27.

22. Holm, 24–25.

23. Hallwas and Launius, "A Minister Criticizes Warsaw and Nauvoo," 32–35; American Tract Society, *Home Evangelization a View of the Wants and Prospects of Our Country, Based on Facts and Relations of Colportage*, 24, 27.

24. Colton, *Thoughts on the Religious State of the Country*, 180; La Roy Sunderland, "Essay on a Theological Education. Written by Request of the 'Junior Preachers' Society of the New-England Conference,'" *Methodist Magazine and Quarterly* 16, no. 4 (October 1834): 423–27.

25. "Extract from the Fourteenth Annual Report of the Portage County Bible Society," *Monthly Extracts from the Correspondence of the American Bible Society*, October 30, 1836.

26. "MORMONS," *Home Missionary and American Pastor's Journal*, July 1, 1841.

27. American Home Missionary Society, *Our Country, Its Capabilities, Its Perils, and Its Hope: Being a Plea for the Early Establishment of Gospel Institutions in the Destitute Portions of the United States* (New York: Executive Committee of the American Home Missionary Society, 1842), 3, 16, 24–28, 33, 37.

28. American Home Missionary Society, 22–44.

29. American Home Missionary Society, *The Sixteenth Report of the American Home Missionary Society* (New York: Printed by William Osborn, 1842), 95.

30. Smith, *Gothic Arches, Latin Crosses*, 53–54, 80; Robert S. Levine, "'Antebellum Rome' in *The Marble Faun*," *American Literary History* 2, no. 1 (1990): 19–38; Peter Williams, *Religion, Art, and Money: Episcopalians and American Culture from the Civil War to the Great Depression* (Chapel Hill: University of North Carolina Press, 2016).

31. Smith, *Gothic Arches, Latin Crosses*, 98–102. For a representative description of Mormonism's temples as mummery, see Coe, "Mormonism."

32. Smith, *Gothic Arches, Latin Crosses*, 34–43.

33. Horace Bushnell, *Barbarism the First Danger: A Discourse for Home Missions* (New York: Printed for the American Home Missionary Society by William Osborn, 1847), 4–5, 16, 24; American Tract Society, *Home Evangelization a View of the Wants and Prospects of Our Country, Based on Facts and Relations of Colportage*, 24; Sunderland, *Mormonism Exposed*, iii–iv; Turner,

Mormonism in All Ages, 254; Alexander Campbell, "Remarks on the Mormon Expose," *Millennial Harbinger*, August 1843; Caswall, *The City of the Mormons; or, Three Days at Nauvoo, in 1842*, 3, 56–57.

34. Caswall, *The City of the Mormons; or, Three Days at Nauvoo, in 1842*, 56–57; Kidder, *Mormonism and the Mormons*, 7–8.

35. Caswall, *The City of the Mormons; or, Three Days at Nauvoo, in 1842*, 55–57.

36. Christine Leigh Heyrman, *American Apostles: When Evangelicals Entered the World of Islam* (New York: Hill and Wang, 2015), 164–88, 231–35; Lawrence A. Peskin, "From Shylocks to Unbelievers: Early National Views of 'Oriental' Jews," *Journal of the Early Republic* 39, no. 2 (Summer 2019): 267–98.

37. "MISSOURI AND THE MORMONS"; M'Chesney, *An Antidote to Mormonism*, 55–56.

38. "James H. Eels to Joshua Leavitt."

39. American Home Missionary Society, *Our Country, Its Capabilities, Its Perils, and Its Hope*, 44–45, 48.

40. Caswall, *The City of the Mormons; or, Three Days at Nauvoo, in 1842*, 58; American Tract Society, *Home Evangelization a View of the Wants and Prospects of Our Country, Based on Facts and Relations of Colportage.*

41. Badger, "Joe Smith at Home"; "Original: THE GERMAN PROFESSORSHIP," *Weekly Messenger*, March 8, 1843.

42. Bushnell, *Barbarism the First Danger*, 68; James D. Bratt, "The Reorientation of American Protestantism, 1835–1845," *Church History* 67, no. 1 (1998): 52–82; Bratt, "Religious Anti-Revivalism in Antebellum America."

Epilogue

1. Kathryn Gin Lum, *Heathen: Religion and Race in American History* (Cambridge, MA: Harvard University Press, 2022).

2. Bowman, *The Mormon People*, 89–95; Stephen Eliot Smith, "Political Perceptions of Mormon Polygamy and the Struggle for Utah Statehood, 1847–1896," in *Contingent Citizens: Shifting Perceptions of Latter-day Saints in American Political Culture*, ed. Spencer W. McBride, Brent M. Rogers, and Keith A. Erekson (Ithaca, NY: Cornell University Press, 2020), 131–32; Sara Patterson, *Pioneers in the Attic: Place and Memory Along the Mormon Trail* (New York: Oxford University Press, 2020).

3. Quote by Methodist minister C. P. Lyford, in Sarah Barringer Gordon, "'Our National Hearthstone': Anti- Polygamy Fiction and the Sentimental Campaign against Moral Diversity in Antebellum America," *Yale Journal of Law and the Humanities* 8, no. 2 (Summer 1996): 302; Gregory Pingree, "'The Biggest Whorehouse in the World': Representations of Plural Marriage in Nineteenth-Century America," *Western Humanities Review* 50, no. 3 (1996): 213.

4. Gordon, *The Mormon Question*; Sarah Barringer Gordon, "A War of Words: Revelation and Storytelling in the Campaign against Mormon Polygamy," *Chicago-Kent Law Review* 78, no. 2 (June 2003): 739–72; Gordon, "'Our National Hearthstone': Anti- Polygamy Fiction and the Sentimental Campaign against Moral Diversity in Antebellum America." The most famous of these

novels include Orvilla S. Belisle, *The Prophets; or, Mormonism Unveiled* (Philadelphia: W. W. Smith, 1855); Alfreda Eva Bell, *Boadicea: The Mormon Wife* (New York: Arthur R. Orton, 1855); Maria Ward, *Female Life among the Mormons: A Narrative of Many Years' Personal Experience* (New York: J. C. Derby, 1855); Metta Victoria Fuller Victor, *Mormon Wives: A Narrative of Facts Stranger Than Fiction* (New York: Derby & Jackson, 1856).

5. Sarah Pearsall, *Polygamy: An Early American History* (New Haven: Yale University Press, 2019), 284–85; Fluhman, *A Peculiar People*.

6. Christine Leigh Heyrman, *Doomed Romance: Broken Hearts, Lost Souls, and Sexual Tumult in Nineteenth-Century America* (New York: Alfred A. Knopf, 2021), 27–28; Anya Jabour, *Marriage in the Early Republic: Elizabeth and William Wirt and the Companionate Ideal* (Baltimore: John Hopkins University Press, 2012); Christine Talbot, *A Foreign Kingdom: Mormons and Polygamy in American Political Culture, 1852–1890* (Urbana: University of Illinois Press, 2013); Fluhman, *A Peculiar People*; Pearsall, *Polygamy*; Laurel Thatcher Ulrich, *A House Full of Females: Family and Faith in 19th-Century Mormon Diaries* (New York: Alfred A. Knopf, 2017).

7. Gordon, *The Mormon Question*; Gordon, "A War of Words: Revelation and Storytelling in the Campaign against Mormon Polygamy"; Gordon, "'Our National Hearthstone': Anti- Polygamy Fiction and the Sentimental Campaign against Moral Diversity in Antebellum America." The most famous of these novels include Belisle, *The Prophets*; Bell, *Boadicea: The Mormon Wife*; Ward, *Female Life among the Mormons*; Victor, *Mormon Wives*.

8. Daniel Dorchester, *Christianity in the United States from the First Settlement Down to the Present Time* (New York: Hunt & Eaton, 1890), 538–42. For more on Dorchester, see Benjamin L. Hartley, *Evangelicals at a Crossroads: Revivalism and Social Reform in Boston, 1860–1910* (Lebanon, NH: University Press of New England, 2011).

9. Dorchester, *Christianity in the United States from the First Settlement Down to the Present Time*, 647–48, 780. For similar calls to respond to Mormonism with a unified religious effort, see Leonard Bacon, *A History of American Christianity* (New York: Christian Literature Company, 1897), 335.

10. R. Philip Roberts, *Mormonism Unmasked: Confronting the Contradictions between Mormon Beliefs and True Christianity* (Nashville, TN: Broadman & Holman, 1998), 155.

11. Roberts, *Mormonism Unmasked*, 16–20.

12. Bratt, "Religious Anti-Revivalism in Antebellum America"; Bratt, "The Reorientation of American Protestantism, 1835–1845"; Winiarski, "Seized by the Jerks"; Heyrman, *Southern Cross*; Wigger, *Taking Heaven by Storm*.

13. Holifield, *Theology in America*; Heyrman, *American Apostles*, 236–37.

Index

NATHANIEL WIEWORA is an associate professor of history at Harding University.

The University of Illinois Press
is a founding member of the
Association of University Presses.

Composed in 10.5/13 Sabon
with Optima display
by Jim Proefrock
at the University of Illinois Press

University of Illinois Press
1325 South Oak Street
Champaign, IL 61820-6903
www.press.uillinois.edu